# The Anteater's Guide to Writing & Rhetoric

General Editor: Jackie Way
Consulting Editors: Bradley Queen, Elizabeth Allen

Contributors: Elizabeth Allen, Alice Berghof, Emily Brauer Rogers, Stacy Brinkman, Rachael Collins, Sue Cross, Keith Danner, Kat Eason, Loren Eason, Tagert Ellis, Brian Fonken, Leah Kaminski, Lance Langdon, Scott Lerner, Kat Lewin, Ali Meghdadi, Bradley Queen, Rebecca Schultz, Brendan Shapiro, Jackie Way

## Composition Program
## University of California Irvine

FOUNTAINHEAD
PRESS

*Fountainhead Press's green initiatives include:*

**Electronic Products and Samples.** Products are delivered in non-paper form whenever possible via Xample, an electronic sampling system. Instructor samples are sent via a personalized web page that links to PDF downloads.

**FSC-Certified Printers and Recycled Paper**. All of our printers are certified by the Forest Service Council, which promotes environmentally and socially responsible management of the world's forests. This program allows consumer groups, individual consumers, and businesses to work together hand in hand to promote responsible use of the world's forests as a renewable and sustainable resource. Most of our products are printed on a minimum of 30 percent post-consumer waste recycled paper.

Cover and text design: Lori Bryan, Fountainhead Press
Cover image from Shutterstock.com

Books may be purchased for educational purposes.

For more information, please visit our website at www.fountainheadpress.com.

Email: customerservice@fountainheadpress.com

ISBN 978-1-68036-986-1

Printed in the United States of America

# Acknowledgments

*The Anteater's Guide to Writing & Rhetoric* is the homegrown textbook for UCI's Composition Program, a collaborative work that reflects our shared pedagogical mission and dedication to the craft of writing. Much of the work has been performed on a volunteer basis and no one here at UC Irvine profits from the proceeds, which go to fund professional development for the Composition Program faculty.

This current edition of *The Anteater's Guide* could not exist without the grand vision and tireless efforts of my predecessors on previous editions of *The Anteater's Guide* (formerly *The Student Guide to Writing*). Many thanks to Lynda Haas, Kat Eason, Tira Palmquist, and Loren Eason—quite simply, you rock. Thanks also to Brad Queen and Elizabeth Allen for their invaluable feedback during this most recent revision.

A tremendous thank you to all the current chapter writers, who graciously donated their time and pedagogical expertise to this project: Rebecca Schultz, Kat Eason and Leah Kaminski, Stacy Brinkman, Emily Brauer Rogers, Loren Eason, Kat Lewin, Tagert Ellis, Elizabeth Allen, Brad Queen, Rachael Collins, Scott Lerner, and Brian Fonken.

And thanks to all the previous contributors: Jonathan Alexander, Daniel Gross, Bobbie Allen, Chieh Cheng, Jeff Clapp, Collier Nogues, Libby Catchings, Cathy Palmer, Sue Cross, Keith Danner, Jaya Dubey, Lynda Haas, Lance Langdon, Joy Palmer, Tira Palmquist, Ali Meghdadi, Brendan Shapiro, Alice Berghof, Keith Danner, and anyone else whose earlier writing and ideas survive in this book.

Thanks to all faculty, lecturers, and TAs who teach in the Composition Program and whose classroom practices inspire all that is practical in our textbook. Thanks as well to the Composition Program administrative staff, who ensure *The Anteater's Guide* shows up at the bookstore each quarter.

And thanks to everyone at Fountainhead Press for helping us put together this book and make it look great.

# Table of Contents

# Chapter 4

## Discovering Sources                                                    61

*By Stacy Brinkman*

# Chapter 5

## Drafting and Crafting                                                  81

*By Emily Brauer Rogers*

## Chapter 6

## Chapter 7

## Chapter 8

WR39B: Critical Reading and Rhetoric       157
*By Kat Lewin and Tagert Ellis with Elizabeth Allen and Jackie Way*

## Chapter 9

*By Brad Queen with Rachael Collins, Brian Fonken, Scott Lerner, and Ali Meghdadi,*
*Brendan Shapiro, Alice Berghof, and Keith Danner*

# PREFACE

By Brad Queen

Oftentimes, during polite conversation with people I have just met, I'm asked what I do for a living, how I spend my working hours. When I say that I'm an English teacher at a university, I've come to expect a certain response. It's almost never one about a great book someone remembers reading in one of their classes or a poem, a short story, or an enlightening discussion about literature's imaginative designs and moral complexity. It's almost always a story driven by an anxious memory about poor grammar and a mystified sense of nostalgia about not being a good writer: "My teacher told me my writing was awkward, and said I should work harder, even though I thought I was."

I usually respond sympathetically, hoping I might offer a comforting thought by saying, *We teach the art of communicating persuasively, we teach rhetoric, and we believe we can motivate our students to write well, communicate clearly and with style, and feel confident about their abilities and choices.* At this attempt to show just how thoughtfully we instruct, I'm usually given something of a scolding about how college students today need to learn how to write by using proper grammar because they spend all their time on their phones texting and emailing and posting on social media. This is where the conversation usually ends.

On a lighthearted note I laugh a little, knowing this is not the right moment to talk teaching and learning, to explain how we focus on grammar and sentence-level dynamics through instruction in rhetoric, style, and situated communication. As I leave, I'm thinking how ironic it is that this person implied our students are less literate than students have been in the past by inadvertently documenting three different and extensively used compositional practices that ask for clear, creative, flexible, and situationally sensitive writing.

As teachers of rhetoric and composition today, we know our students at UCI bring high levels of communicative know-how to our composition classrooms. Many are multilingual—highly skilled in more than one language, aware of several grammatical systems, and capable of negotiating communication situations in different languages, both orally and in writing. They even sometimes interweave distinctive languages in highly creative ways. These linguistic capabilities, like the use of new technological affordances, speak to resources of rhetorical flexibility.

As you will see, the pedagogical emphases and techniques found throughout this book make use of such resources while instructing in rhetoric and style, critical reading and argumentation, and research writing and information literacy. This book is written by your teachers, people whose deep commitment to their craft and their love of learning will guide you successfully through more complicated reading, writing, and communication assignments than you have experienced in the past. We see our classrooms as safe spaces for the exploration of ideas and the cultivation of minds. We invite all of you to learn with us.

# INTRODUCTION

## Introduction to *The Anteater's Guide*

By Loren Eason

*The Anteater's Guide to Writing & Rhetoric* is not your typical writing text-book. Most writing textbooks are written by composition scholars with the idea that the book will be used by many different writing programs both as a reference for students and as a guide for instructors. These textbooks are thought of as being a single volume with a unified design and a consistent voice and presentation, meant to replicate a single voice and a single point of view (albeit, an objective, abstracted point of view).

For the last four editions of *The Anteater's Guide,* we have treated this book not as a singular document like a textbook but, rather, as an anthology—a collection of separate but related works with varying tones, approaches, and points of view. Some chapters are written formally, with precise academic diction and an objective tone; others are more conversational and playful in their presentation. This is done by design in order to provide you with a range of rhetorical approaches and to provide examples of the diverse ways in which writers can approach similar topics. We've allowed the different chapters to reflect the writers' own approaches to teaching and how they interact with students in their classrooms, and we encourage our instructors, likewise, to find multiple ways to engage in the classroom and to present ideas. Rhetoric is a living, dynamic art. It shifts with time and with audience, and we hope that by exhibiting this diversity of approach in pursuit of a unified purpose, we can give you a concrete example of this range and dynamism.

Likewise, we have tried to treat this guide as a document designed to help you engage more effectively with the challenges presented by our courses. *The Anteater's Guide* is not a collection of content we are trying to deliver to our readers for them to memorize and replay on command. We have done our best to make this guide directly relevant to the context of what happens in our classrooms. It's intended to provide you with different ways of ap-proaching the challenges we are asking you to face when you are learning to read, analyze, interrogate, and respond to the different viewpoints you are introduced to in the Writing Program here at UCI. *The Anteater's Guide* is, by conception and design, meant to support you as you learn the skills, practices, and habits of mind that will allow you to communicate effectively across a wide range of circumstances, audiences, and genres. But this guide is not your most important text for the class—your own writing, and the process that produces it, is the main object of study. *The Anteater's Guide* is merely a guide meant to help you navigate the challenges we have arranged for you to face in your assignments. It's there to draw your attention to the features of your writing landscape and to help you find ways to understand and navigate that landscape and to approach new opportunities for communication with a more tactical frame of mind.

We'd love it if, rather than treating this book as a collection of information to be absorbed and reproduced on command for as long as is necessary to secure a good grade, you instead treated each chapter as an extension of the discussions you have in your classrooms when you ask questions about how to negotiate the challenges you face when writing. These chapters are nothing more than other writers discussing the ways that they approach these particular challenges. (Granted, these particular writers are more experienced with these challenges and have had a lot more practice both with addressing these challenges and with explaining their methods to others, but they are still, just like you, people who are learning how to write better.) I'm not asking you to think of these writers in this way in order to make them appear humble or to humanize them. I'm asking you to do this because it is important for you to learn to examine all writing—all communication—not just for what it is trying to communicate, but also for how it was constructed in order to make that communication happen.

Allow me to peel back the curtain and show you some of what goes on behind the scenes as we write a book like this. Each chapter in the guide has been read by and commented on in the same way that the papers you write for your courses will be. We discussed things like how early in the guide we should define what rhetoric is and which definitions we should use. We debated when and how many examples we should use when we introduce key terms and whether that is something that is better done in *The Anteater's Guide* . . . or if it is best to keep these paragraphs brief and leave space for your instructors to provide you with examples appropriate to your individual classes. We went back and forth on how many labels each of the figures we used should have and what exactly those labels should be. Should the people who are reading a particular text be called the "audience" or the "receivers" or something else? We wrote far more words discussing these matters than there are words in the sections that gave rise to these questions.

> **AGWR review comment:**
>
> *"I'm fairly averse to using this term [audience] in a writing class, as it seems to connote passivity, as in people assembled to watch a movie or a play or a commercial."*

One of the hardest tasks we ask you to do in all lower-division writing courses is to write a document that gives an account of the most significant choices you made over the various assignments of the quarter and provide evidence that demonstrates the effect of those choices within your writing process. It's intimidating to look at all the things you have written on topics about which you have thought deeply and critically and try to select only the handful of words most appropriate for showing someone else the journey you have taken as a writer. It's not enough to merely discuss the subject in its generalities; at some point you have to provide evidence and select examples that you think illustrate your point in enough depth to show the importance of what you are saying.

But no single example is ever sufficient to cover all eventualities—some examples speak more to one group of readers than another—and it doesn't take too many examples before the reader becomes impatient or loses the thread of your argument in all the individual details of the examples.

Which brings me to the last point I want to make in the introduction before we move on to talk about the rest of the book: This guide is in no way a thorough discussion of the subjects of writing and rhetoric. Both of those topics are subtle and complex. Just as we debated (and sometimes disagreed over) what the *The Anteater's Guide* should cover, so did we spend days negotiating how the individual courses and the program as a whole wanted to approach the questions of what rhetoric is and how it functions. Entire books are dedicated to these questions alone—you can find many of them mentioned in the bibliographies that follow many of the chapters in this guide—so the short discussions you find here are not meant to be *definitive*, so much as they are *tactical*. We attempt to give you as much of an explanation as you will need to appreciate the complexity of the task and to start building an understanding of the larger issues involved, but we realize that a fuller understanding of the topic will only come with wider experience and experimentation as you try to put the principles we discuss into use in your own writing. Think of our explanations here as the start of a very long conversation that you will have to continue on your own as you move on from our writing classes into your upper-division work and the rest of your lives.

## A Quick Guide to *The Anteater's Guide*

By Jackie Way

*The Anteater's Guide to Writing & Rhetoric* is intended to be as practical and hands-on a guide as we can make it. Throughout the book, our authors:

- define key terms and explain core concepts;
- ask guiding questions to strengthen your rhetorical awareness and prepare you to succeed in your assignments;
- provide examples of the kind of strategies that will help you improve your communication skills;
- offer step-by-step guidance, tips, and suggestions on a wide range of reading and writing tasks; and
- invite you to practice specific reading and writing techniques in brief exercises.

The first part of the book, comprising Chapters 1–6, is written to be broadly applicable in Writing 39A/AP, 39B/37, and 39C, although you can expect that your instructors will emphasize these topics differently depending on the course you're currently taking.

Chapter 1, "Introducing Rhetoric and Genre," defines the two key concepts that underpin all of our lower-level writing courses and explores the relationship between them.

Chapter 2, "Practicing Critical Reading," offers concrete steps and guiding questions to help you strengthen your reading comprehension and develop an eye for rhetorical detail.

Chapter 3, "Citing and Integrating Sources," and Chapter 4, "Discovering Sources," discuss complementary aspects of conducting research and managing sources in your writing.

Chapter 5, "Drafting and Crafting," takes up the nuts and bolts of the writing process, including techniques for invention, soliciting feedback, and revision.

Chapter 6, "I Came Here for an Argument," tackles the finer points of argumentation, especially how effective arguments work and how to put them together.

The second part of the book, comprising Chapters 7–9, concentrates on the particular learning objectives and writing processes of our three lower-division writing courses.

Chapter 7 addresses Writing 39A/AP Introduction to Writing and Rhetoric, where students focus on style, organization, and analysis.

Chapter 8 addresses Writing 39B/37 Critical Reading and Rhetoric, where students further develop their critical reading skills and awareness of genre and rhetorical situation.

Chapter 9 addresses Writing 39C Argument and Research, where students pursue their own quarter-long research projects and situate their arguments within a larger conversation about their chosen topics.

We hope that this book serves you well on your journey through lower-division writing, and we encourage you to revisit these chapters as needed whenever you need a quick refresher.

## CHAPTER 1

# Introducing Rhetoric and Genre

*By Rebecca Schultz*

I'm Rebecca Schultz, a Lecturer in UCI's Composition Program. I've taught Writing 39B and C, in classes themed around fairy tales, dystopia, coming-of-age stories, and more. I started teaching composition courses at UCI five years ago, when I was graduate student working toward an MFA in Fiction. I still think teaching and learning go hand in hand. The best days as an instructor are when my students and I make discoveries together as we discuss our readings.

## What Is Rhetoric?

Rhetoric is a crucial concept in the Writing 39 series at UCI. It's also a big part of our lives, whether we know it or not. On the highway, we pass billboards; on quiet nights, we watch TV and we're interrupted, maybe, by ads. Our politicians make speeches. We read—for school, and perhaps also on our own—fiction and poetry and magazine profiles and opinion pieces. We write text messages and emails. When you applied to college, you wrote a personal statement. **In short: _any_ text, or piece of music, or image, or video, or social media post, that is created by someone, in order to communicate something to someone else, can be considered a piece of rhetoric.**

Extremely vague, I know. Let's continue.

The art of **rhetoric** goes back to ancient Greece, when it referred to persuasive speech-making. Students of rhetoric would practice composing, arranging, memorizing, and delivering their speeches: a useful skill, in an ancient democracy, where bills were voted into law based on speeches made in the assembly and military leaders spoke in the wake of battles and at other civic ceremonies. A strong speech, naturally, was one that successfully persuaded the listener of whatever the speaker wanted to persuade them of.

But what are the components of a successfully persuasive speech, whether in ancient Greece or today? You need to make your listener trust you. Maybe you need to make them laugh or cry, maybe you need to use incontrovertible evidence to make them see things as you do. Maybe you need to successfully engage with a counterargument, carefully striking down all the points that the *other* guy made.

In our classes, the emphasis is more on reading and writing than on speech-making, but the concept of **persuasion** remains crucial: when we write, in the WR39 series, we are *writing rhetorically*, meaning we are writing with the conscious knowledge that we are making choices in order to persuade our audience of something, and that the choices we make are conditioned, in part, by an understanding of whom we are trying to persuade and in what context.

Similarly, when we read, in the WR39 series, we are *reading rhetorically*, meaning we are reading with an eye toward figuring out *what* the author is trying to persuade us of and *how* they are persuading us. What choices are they making, and how do those choices work on us, the reader—in ways that may be obvious or subtle—to make us believe whatever the writer wants us to believe? To make us trust the writer, make us like them, make us feel something, make us understand something? And by the way, who is the "us" supposed to be—who is the writer talking to, and how does that shape what they say and how?

The point of all this is twofold.

We want, on the one hand, to use *rhetorical reading* in order to become thoughtful critics instead of helpless consumers of the various texts around us. It's easy to move through the world without thinking that the pieces of rhetoric around us have any particular intentions toward us, beyond what's immediately apparent. How is a politician, say, in a speech or campaign ad, subtly evoking centuries-old racist myths in order to stoke the fears of a certain subset of voters—and thereby get their vote? How is your favorite childhood movie altering a four-hundred-year-old fairy tale in order to better reflect the American filmmakers' capitalist values? **Rhetorical analysis** will help you find out.

We are also, on the other hand, using *rhetorical writing* as a way to become effective writers. We want to become aware of the choices available to us in our writing and of the situations that might make some choices more relevant and powerful than others. Anyone who's taken high school English has no doubt learned certain essay-writing "rules": the thesis comes at the end of the introduction paragraph, the conclusion summarizes the argument, etc. The Writing 39 series is here to tell you that those rules are flexible and that what you do in any given piece of writing depends on why and for whom you're doing it. Certain kinds of essays don't need a thesis at all, while others will have a paragraph-long thesis that comes at the end of the final paragraph. Some will use the first-person "I," whereas others will not, etc. The point isn't to memorize all the rules, it's to develop a subtle sensitivity to rhetorical situation and a flexible "writing mind": an internalized understanding of when and how the rules change and when we don't necessarily need to follow them.

Whether we're reading or writing, if we're thinking rhetorically, we're going to want to answer certain questions:

1. *What* is the writer trying to persuade us of? In other words, what is their **rhetorical purpose**?

2. *How* is the writer trying to persuade us? In other words, what **rhetorical choices or strategies** are they making within the text in order to get us on their side?

3. *Who* is the "us," or in other words, the **audience**? Whom is the writer talking to? Whom are they trying to persuade?

Let's begin with number one, rhetorical purpose. But as I explain it, I need to introduce a second concept, almost as important to the WR39 series as rhetoric: **genre**. The kinds of rhetorical purposes any given text might have are going to depend on what genre they're working in.

## Rhetorical Purpose and Genre

Many of you have likely already heard the term "genre" before. You know that horror and fantasy are genres and that hip-hop and country music are genres. Your 39B class is likely focused on one particular genre. You know that a genre is a "category" within which pieces of writing fall and that each such category has themes, or unwritten rules, in common. We refer to these rules as **conventions**, as in the word "conventional," which means "expected," verging on "required." It is "conventional" for comedies to end with weddings and tragedies to end with deaths. It is "conventional" for the teen-soaps of my youth to contain characters whose love for one another is doomed because they "come from two different worlds." It is "conventional" for academic essays, at least academic essays written by students, to have a one-sentence thesis statement that comes at the end of the introduction. It is "conventional" for academic essays written by anyone to end with a Works Cited page or bibliography.

Genre affects rhetorical purpose simply because writers necessarily express themselves differently in different genres.

## Narrative Genres

Some genres are **narrative**, or _implicitly persuasive_. We can include in this category fiction, narrative nonfiction, poetry, TV, and film—the kinds of texts you will most likely encounter in Writing 39B. On the surface, these texts are just telling a story—not making an argument. They don't have a thesis, or any one "main point." But they do have ideas about the world around them: they might be taking a stance on current social, cultural, and political debates; they might be endorsing or critiquing the cultural values of their time; they might be responding to historical events or situations; they might be posing moral and existential questions and, perhaps, suggesting answers to them. They are, one way or another, holding a mirror to the world: representing a fictional world on the page in order to show the reader something about the actual world they live in.

Because they are multiple and multifaceted, and because they aren't stated explicitly, the rhetorical purpose(s) of narrative texts can be mysterious, difficult to locate and define—they might be, in fact, the kind of thing that critics and scholars debate for centuries and that you could write a nuanced rhetorical analysis essay about for your Writing 39B class.

Note that I keep saying narrative works are responding to "the world." But that's awfully general.

I don't mean the entire world. I mean the _specific_ world—time, place, culture—in which the writer lives and to which they are responding. We can refer to that time/place/culture as the writer's **cultural context**. Every cultural context comes with its own value system: what that culture thinks is right and wrong, important and unimportant. A culture is never one hundred percent aware of or in agreement about what its "value system" is. Often, too, we assume that our own value system is universal, rather than situational: something that changes depending on your time, place, and culture. Secondary source readings by scholars can often help illuminate elements of the value system of any given writer's time, place, and culture—and therefore, what questions or notions our writers might be responding to.

## GUIDING QUESTIONS: CONNECTING A WRITER'S RHETORICAL PURPOSE TO CULTURAL CONTEXT

1. *From my secondary sources, what do I already know about the cultural moment that the author lives in?* *It's likely that your instructor has supplied readings to help illuminate this for you. For example: if you're in Writing 39B, and your class is themed around fairy tales, and you're reading some of Perrault's tales, then you were likely assigned folktale scholar Maria Tatar's introduction, where she talks through*

*some of the seventeenth-century French ideas about gender roles and marriage that Perrault is responding to. Ask yourself where in the text the writer seems to be responding to these ideas, directly or indirectly.*

2. **From reading the main text, what issues does it seem like the writer might be responding to? What then do I need to know about the cultural values of his time?** *For example, maybe you're in Writing 39B, and your class is themed around coming-of-age stories. You haven't read any secondary sources yet, but you know from reading Junot Diaz's short story "Fiesta, 1980" that Yunior, the young boy who narrates the story, is afraid of his father and knows that his father is cheating on his mother. This father is, of course, an individual character, but is it possible that Diaz is also using him to show us something larger about how fathers feel entitled to behave within...what? American culture? Yunior's particular Dominican-American culture? And the complex way that these fathers can affect their children? Are there secondary sources I can read that might tell me more about masculinity and patriarchy within this culture?*

---

**PRO TIP: BE AWARE OF OVER-SIMPLIFYING CONTEXT**

Don't assume an author's relationship to their cultural context is straightforward or moralistic, that our authors are ever giving a simple "yes" or "no" to the big questions of their time. Rhetorical analysis gets much more interesting when we can see the ways in which stories are complex, even contradictory.

Here's an example of the kind of conversations scholars have about rhetorical purpose in narrative works. This is a paragraph from an introduction by scholar Kathryn Sutherland to Jane Austen's 1814 novel *Mansfield Park*, whose heroine is named Fanny Price:

> Fanny Price continues to puzzle critics and readers. Her portrayal contributes to the lively late-eighteenth-and early-nineteenth-century debate on...the acceptable range of female behavior in terms of self-expression and self-control. But if, in the intensity and even violence of her feelings, Fanny can seem the heir of a Romantic-revolutionary feminine tradition...it is important to notice how deeply her extravagant emotional responses are internalized and kept from view.

Note how this introduction frames a question about Austen's rhetorical purpose. During the time when Austen wrote the novel, there was, according to the paragraph above, a debate about how women should behave. Should they speak their minds ("self-expression") or hold back ("self-control")?

This is, in other words, a conversation about *cultural values*. According to this paragraph, Austen portrays Fanny as a character who feels deeply and intensely, which seems to show that Austen is on the "self-expression" side of the debate. But Sutherland points out that Austen *also* portrays Fanny as a character who *hides* her intense emotions, thus implying that Austen may be on the "self-control" side of that debate. In short, according to this scholar, Austen isn't coming down clearly on any one side of this question about cultural values—instead, through its portrayal of Fanny, the novel expresses a complex, multifaceted idea about the role of women in Austen's rigid, patriarchal society, which had strict rules about how women could and couldn't behave. Austen was critical of that society, but she did also live in it, and absorb some of its values. Perhaps, therefore, the novel wants more for its character Fanny than it can allow Fanny herself to want.

This is an example of the way scholars might look for rhetorical purpose in narrative works: by examining rhetorical choices Austen made in her portrayal of her character (making Fanny emotional; making her restrained), and seeing what those add up to, in terms of a statement about early nineteenth-century English values about what and how women should be.

Now, to throw a wrench in it: sometimes, when we are dealing with narrative genres, we are going to work from the assumption that the author is fully in control of their rhetorical purpose and choices and that that purpose is complex and multifaceted. When choices seem to contradict each other (i.e., Fanny is emotional, but also restrained), we figure out instead that they're really adding onto and complicating one another. That's what we do when we're rhetorically analyzing works of literary art.

But not all narrative genres rise to the level of art.

Other times, when we're analyzing narrative genres, we assume instead that the author might be responding to a number of different competing interests and that the rhetorical purpose might be contradictory and vague. For example, check out this moment from Carina Chocano's essay "Let It Go," about Disney's *Frozen*:

> Elsa still makes no sense to me as a character. What does she actually want? What exactly is she "letting go" of, her perfectionism? Her desire for approval? Her internalized self-loathing? Her rightful claim to the throne? Her concern for what other people think of her? Her superpowers? It really could be anything. Is she submitting or rebelling?

In other words, the creators of *Frozen* made choices in the song "Let It Go" that, to this critic, don't seem to add up to a clear rhetorical purpose. Is the song advocating for the values of submission or rebellion, in young viewers who look up to Elsa? Note that, rather than trying to find some complex way in which the seemingly contradictory choices that the filmmakers made actually add up to an interesting, nuanced message about the values our society has about how women should behave, Chocano decides that, no, the creators of *Frozen* were confused. That's because, for her, *Frozen* doesn't rise to the level of being art. It's more like entertainment. But the method is the same: we examine the choices that the creator has made, and we see how they add up to a critique or endorsement of the values of the time in which the film was made.

## PRO TIP: COMPLEX, RHETORICALLY-FOCUSED CLAIMS

An interesting, nuanced rhetorical analysis thesis statement will never come down completely on any one side, because the works we're dealing with are always more complex than that. It'll acknowledge the nuance and layers of the text and of the question at hand. As in:

> *Many scholars see* Mansfield Park's *heroine Fanny Price as the most submissive and least empowered of all of Austen's heroines. But the strength of Fanny's emotions, and the way she suffers in concealing them, indicate that Austen was struggling with, and perhaps even making a statement about, the cultural value that women were supposed to be submissive.*

Or:

> *Although* Frozen *seems to be all about girl power, in fact it actually undermines that message when Elsa and Anna conform to the gender norms endorsed by previous Disney princess movies.*

Note what these thesis statements do:

→ They use the writer's rhetorical choices to make a statement about how they are responding to some element of their cultural context ("the cultural value that women were supposed to be submissive" and "previous Disney princess movies.")

→ But they also acknowledge the complexity of the work they're discussing and therefore create thesis statements that are surprising.

### Argumentative Genres

Other genres are **argumentative**, or *explicitly persuasive*. These are the genres you will read in Writing 39C. We can include in this category any example of argument-based writing, of which there are many sub-genres: the academic essay (including the rhetorical analysis essay that you'll write in Writing 39B), the newspaper opinion piece, the book review, and more.

At some point, in each of these genres, the writer is going to clearly and directly "get to the point"—tell us the thing they are trying to persuade us of. Whenever I assign a text like this to my students, I ask them to come to class making sure they have a paragraph or sentence that they've underlined, and have written next to it, in the margins, the point of the whole essay. I tell them that it's not easy to find this sentence or paragraph on a first read: often, we have to already have worked through the essay once in order to find it. But once we have found it, the rest of the essay, or article, or whatever it is, becomes easier to understand, because we can see how everything else exists to support that main point in one way or another.

## Sample Annotation: Identifying the Main Point

Here are two examples of "point of the whole essay" sentences my Writing 39C students have underlined in recent weeks:

1. "The owner-renter divide is as salient as any other in this nation, and this divide is a historical result of statecraft designed to protect and promote inequality."

*This is from a* New York Times *article by Matthew Desmond. The rest of the article supports this "main point" by using various kinds of evidence to show us what makes the lives of homeowners so much easier than the lives of renters, and shows how and why American laws and policies (that's what "statecraft" means) have deliberately made homeowners richer and renters poorer.*

2. "Perhaps no statistic better illustrates the enduring legacy of our country's shameful history of treating black people as sub-citizens, sub-Americans, and sub-humans than the wealth gap. Reparations would seek to close this chasm. But as surely as the creation of the wealth gap required the cooperation of every aspect of the society, bridging it will require the same."

*This is from an article in the* Atlantic *by Ta-Nehisi Coates. The rest of the article supports this "main point" by explaining how the history of American racism has led to the current wealth gap between white and black people, and also by explaining how and why reparations—the idea that the nation could discuss and calculate what we owe to black Americans, and then pay what we owe—would be an ambitious policy, perhaps unfeasible to implement (i.e., would require "the cooperation of every aspect of society"), and also why it's a deeply necessary one.*

Notice that both these statements make *interpretive, arguable claims*. Both writers are making claims, in particular, about the effect of specific American social policies on the gap between the rich and the poor. What makes these claims *interpretive* and *arguable*? The fact that other people, whether ordinary people or fellow scholars, could look at the same policies and the same wealth gap and *not* think of the causal connection. The causal relationships that Coates and Desmond both point to are connections that *they* saw and are trying to prove to their readers are real and important.

We're not always writing about government policies, of course, but in argument-based writing we *are* always making claims that other people might disagree with. Here is the main point of a book review by Anand Giridharadas, published in the *New York Times Book Review*, that I was reading the other day:

> At the end of each chapter, each mini-history, Diamond pauses to ask some variant of: "How does Indonesia's crisis fit into our framework?" And this is a tell. The Framework is driving the inquiry here, and everything stands at its service. The people we encounter are seldom richly portrayed, because only The Framework matters. The stories we learn about each country are often partial and slanted, because only The Framework matters. Countries where racism and tolerance, sexism and equality have long been in tension are portrayed as being entirely one thing before magically becoming the opposite thing, because The Framework can only process monoliths.

The "main point," in other words, is that Jared Diamond's new book has this major flaw where it misconstrues facts because it's trying to make all its examples fit into a big idea. Again, the writer is making an interpretive, arguable statement, this time about the quality of a book. Still though, if you were reading the book review, on your second read or so you could pick this paragraph out as expressing the main thing that the writer wants to say.

## PRO TIP: FIGURING OUT RHETORICAL PURPOSE

Generally speaking, when you are looking for the rhetorical purpose of an argumentative text, first read it through once. Then ask yourself what the topic is of the text. Giridharadas's topic is Jared Diamond's new book; Coates's topic is the racial wealth gap. Then read the text a second time, asking yourself where the writer makes their biggest, most comprehensive claim about the nature of the thing they are writing about.

## Rhetorical Choices in Narrative Texts

In order to do any of this, of course, we need to understand where and how to locate an author's **rhetorical choices**. Rhetorical choices are the elements of a story that you interpret in order to decide what the rhetorical purpose might be. For instance, in one of the examples above, we are interpreting Jane Austen's choice to portray her heroine a certain way and deciding that that choice speaks to the text's larger purpose regarding the question of how women should behave.

Let's look, too, at a second moment from Chocano's essay on *Frozen*, which we also discussed earlier:

> Let it go, let it go," [Elsa] belts out, "that perfect girl is gone!" as she transforms into an even icier and more perfect girl than before, a sexy version of her uptight self in a skintight dress slit up to here and high heels made of jagged shards of ice.

How many *choices* in the film is Chocano referencing?

*   The lyrics "Let it go," and "That perfect girl is gone."
*   Elsa's costume change into a sexy dress.

For Chocano, these two choices that the creators of the film made add up to a contradictory rhetorical purpose. Is the song about letting go of the idea that girls need to be "perfect," as the lyrics seem to tell us, or is it advocating for a vision of female "perfection," in the form of the sexy, hyper-feminine costume? Both the lyrics and the costume represent a choice that the creators of the film made. They could have written different lyrics; they could have designed a different costume.

Of course, every plot point, every scene, every image, every character, every single word in *Mansfield Park* is a choice that Austen has made. In a movie, you have not only characters and plot points and dialogue but also costume, soundtrack, and camera angles to examine. But some choices are more significant than others. So how do you do what Chocano has done here? How do you isolate which of the *many* choices that the creators of any given text made are important, and make a statement about the text's purpose and values?

### LOCATING KEY RHETORICAL CHOICES

1.  Ask yourself what surprised you in the text—what struck you as being weird, or interesting? Maybe you're surprised by a plot point, by a line of dialogue, by just how much time the writer spends on a single scene, or how little time they spend on another scene, or of where they chose to begin, or how they chose to end. More often than not,

you have an intuitive sense of what's expected, of what's *normal* in a story. When an author does something that surprises you or moves you or that you think is weird, that's a good sign that that something is worth further thought. Ask yourself how you reacted to that part. Were you entranced by the beauty of Elsa's ice palace? If you were, then the filmmakers' choice to make the ice palace so beautiful is something you could then unpack. Perhaps they wanted to show us just how beautiful a young woman realizing her powers can be. Were you less happy for Fanny Price than you felt you should have been at the end of *Mansfield Park*, when (spoiler alert) she marries Edmund, since she and Edmund are both so moral and upright, and other, less-moral characters have all the fun? Austen's choice to make the "bad" characters so appealing is worth unpacking, then.

2.  Ask yourself, "If X was different, would the text's meaning or purpose be significantly altered?" For example, if Elsa put on pants instead of a sexy dress during "Let It Go," would the song be more clearly empowering? If the answer is yes, then that means the dress is an important rhetorical choice. If the answer is no, then forget it.

3.  Genre conventions often offer an interesting place to start. Since, as discussed above, genre conventions are the set of usually unwritten "rules" that we follow in a certain genre, it's always going to be interesting—and always represents a powerful choice—when an author chooses to *break* with convention. Two examples of this:

    *   Back to *Frozen*: Although "Let It Go," is obviously confusing, other parts of the film are extremely clear. One "genre convention" of Disney movies, as many of you know, is "true love's first kiss." That's what saves Snow White and Sleeping Beauty. In *Frozen*, though, the princess, Anna, is saved not by a prince's kiss but by an "act of true love" from her sister. The movie is purposefully messing with the genre convention, to make a statement that there are more kinds of "true love" that save us, besides just romantic love between a man and a woman.

    *   There's a convention that exists across any genre of written English, that if you are using a phrase from a foreign language, you put it in italics to distinguish it from the rest of the text. The fiction writer Junot Diaz breaks that convention, weaving fluidly between English and Spanish in his writing. Why? To make a statement about the limiting assumptions that most works of fiction make about their reader: that the reader isn't an immigrant, nor are their parents; that the reader speaks only English; and that we need to cater to that reader's needs. What would it mean, Diaz is asking, to cater instead to a different kind of reader? Note that this is a statement criticizing some of the *cultural values* of his time.

## Rhetorical Choices in Argument-Based Texts

In argument-based texts, as in narrative texts, authors are making choices all the time in order to persuade their reader. Because the persuasion is happening explicitly, it's easier to identify these choices. Authors may choose to bring in a counterargument, in order to show their reader how carefully they've considered alternatives. They may choose to carefully work through **evidence** for each of their claims. They may share a poignant anecdote that illustrates their point. They may remind their reader of their own expertise in the field. Aristotle referred to three major modes of persuasion, which you may have learned about in high school: *pathos*, *logos*, and *ethos*. Any given choice—to bring in a counterargument, to use the first person—might contribute to the writer's persuading us via one or more of these modes.

**Pathos** is all about using emotion, making the reader feel something. I just saw an advertisement, for example, for a migraine medication, that was mostly about a mother playing with her daughter—the idea being that because of the medication, she feels well enough to play. The creators of the ad are hoping, presumably, that the mother-daughter scenes move us emotionally and make us want to buy the medication, though whether that works may depend on who "we" are: whether we have children, whether we're nostalgic for our own childhood, etc. In the context of argumentative writing, an author might use pathos by telling a story of someone whose life is affected by the social policy that the writer is trying to argue is harmful.

An ad that uses **logos**, by contrast, would be one that uses logic to persuade us as to the greatness of this migraine medication: explain the science behind it, comparing it to other, similar medications on the market, etc. When you're writing an essay, you likely traffic mostly in *logos*, too: you back up your claims with carefully analyzed evidence and create logical connections.

**Ethos** may be the trickiest of these three concepts to grasp. It's Greek for character. It's about how the writer creates a trustworthy character or **persona** for themselves in the text. They might do this literally using the first person, "I," or they might not. They might do it by showing they know where the reader is coming from, that they've thought through all of the reader's possible objections to their argument. In the context of our migraine ad, we might say that the ad builds trust by implicitly showing that it gets us, knows our sorrows, and sees how migraines have disrupted our life.

In the context of argumentative writing, engaging with **counterarguments** can be a powerful way of building ethos—getting the reader to trust the writer—because that's where you show the reader that you are knowledgeable about the many sides of this argument, and it's through careful consideration that you chose the one that you did. In certain genres, referring to oneself, one's credentials, beliefs, and experiences, can also build *ethos*.

It's a way of making the reader trust you, either by saying, *I know a lot, so I'm obviously qualified to talk about this*, or the opposite, *I'm just like you, really. I didn't used to think this way, either, which is why I'm qualified to persuade you.* For example, Michelle Alexander in *The New Jim Crow*, one of our Writing 39C texts, introduces her main point—the idea that mass incarceration is a system of social control created on purpose by the government in order to suppress black Americans—by saying that when she was a young lawyer, this idea seemed crazy to her, too, but after much research and work in the field, she's come around. That way, she builds ethos: if you're a reader for whom this idea sounds crazy, too, you now trust her more.

## THE SMALL STUFF: STYLE, TONE, AND LITERARY DEVICES

When I meet students on the first day of class, they often talk about close reading in English class, how it seems to involve decoding small "details" in a book and figuring out how those details operate as symbols to access some secret "deeper meaning." But that's a hoax! There is no secret code. What I dislike about this way of thinking is that it takes you far away from your own best instincts and observations about which moments in the story are affecting you and how.

That isn't to say that "details" aren't important or that we don't want to make sentence-level observations about both argument-based and narrative works. We do! We ask questions all the time, like:

- Why does Carina Chocano use such a casual tone, in her essay on *Frozen*, in phrases like, "Elsa still makes no sense to me as a character," compared to Kathryn Sutherland, in her introduction to *Mansfield Park*, who says instead, "Fanny Price continues to puzzle scholars and critics"? How do the different contexts and purposes of both essays cause the writers to make different choices about tone? How do the different choices in terms of tone make you engage differently, as a reader, with each of these essays, and build a different kind of ethos, or persona, for the writer?

- Why does Junot Diaz use the following simile in his short story "Fiesta, 1980," after Yunior tells his aunt that his father is "at work too much":

    Work, Tía said, like it was somebody's name she didn't like.

What does that simile reveal about where Tía really thinks Yunior's father goes? And why does Diaz present it in a simile, instead of using this much lamer sentence I just wrote:

    Work, Tía said, like she didn't think Papi was really at work at all.

We might note that Diaz's simile, unlike the bad sentence I just wrote, leaves room for the idea that Yunior doesn't understand the meaning of his aunt's expression. Maybe he thinks his father is at work, even though we and his aunt know better.

Notice that these questions aren't about unpacking a "hidden meaning," nor are they about assuming any one-size-fits-all ideas about what a certain tonal or stylistic choice amounts to. In the case of the essays, they're about asking ourselves why in different contexts, different choices are appropriate and effective. In the case of the short story, they're about what the use of a certain phrase in a particular moment in the story tells us about the narrator who uses it in that moment—what he knows, what he doesn't know. Later in our process, we could try to relate that particular rhetorical choice to our ideas about Diaz's purpose and context. For instance, we could say that, perhaps by making the reader, as well as Tía, more knowledgeable than Yunior is in that moment, Diaz makes us feel for his innocent character and for what his father is doing to him.

## Audience and Context

We said at the beginning of this chapter that pieces of rhetoric are trying to persuade some particular "us"—an audience on whom the author's rhetorical choices are meant to work.

Defining that audience is slippery and interesting. Demographics don't often get us very far. Is the audience of *Frozen* children? Sure, plus their parents, and plus movie critics like Chocano, but that's too obvious to get us anywhere interesting. Is the audience of *Hamlet* young, wealthy men from Denmark who have lost their father? No, definitely not—that's too literal and narrow. Is the audience of Ta-Nehisi Coates's "The Case for Reparations" (referenced earlier in this chapter) "all Americans," or "Americans who care about race," or "Americans who have experienced racism," as my Writing 39C students said the other day? Sure, but where do I go from there?

If I really wanted to work toward an interesting, generative answer to the question of who the "us" is—who Coates was writing to in that piece—I would look for the moments where it feels like Coates is making rhetorical choices as a writer, based on his idea of what "we" might be thinking. As a reminder, the main point of Coates's essay is about systemic racism in America. Coates makes the argument that we need a national conversation about what we as a country might owe to African Americans. Check out this moment from that essay:

> One cannot escape the question by hand-waving at the past, disavowing the acts of one's ancestors, nor by citing a recent date of ancestral immigration.

This is a great passage to think about audience, because it includes a reference to what "one" might be thinking, i.e., what "we," the audience, might be thinking. "One" might respond to the concept of reparations by "citing a recent date of ancestral immigration." Meaning: Coates imagines that his readership might respond to his ideas by saying, *hey, I don't "owe" anything to anybody, my ancestors weren't even here during slavery.* Coates also anticipates readers "hand-waving at the past," and "disavowing the acts of [their] ancestors," meaning that he imagines them saying, *Of course, slavery and Jim Crow were terrible, and my ancestors did unspeakable things then. Thank God that's all over now.* Meaning: he is writing, at least in this moment, to a reader who yes, may "care about racism," but who also resists the idea of reparations, who sees American racism as something in which they are not personally implicated and from which the country has moved on.

Now, isn't that a more interesting answer than "Americans who care about racism"?

## GUIDING QUESTIONS FOR UNDERSTANDING AUDIENCE

1. *What would someone need to think, or know about, or care about, in order for this piece of rhetoric to work on them?*

2. *Where in the text can we see the author make a rhetorical move that would only work on you if you had a certain experience or a certain value system?*

Cultural context is an important aspect of the "us," too. Shared experiences, knowledge, and values are, as discussed earlier in this chapter, determined by time, place, and culture. "The Case for Reparations" was written in 2014, which my Writing 39C students would point out, is during Barack Obama's presidency, and also during what legal scholar Michelle Alexander would call "the age of colorblindness," a period where it was popular to look at figures like President Obama and conclude that one's race no longer limited one's opportunities in America. That context might then explain a readership that wants to "hand-wave at the past," i.e., to say that the past is in the past and the present is something different, when it comes to race. So I'd add the following questions to the list above:

## GUIDING QUESTIONS FOR UNDERSTANDING CONTEXT

1. *When and where was this piece published?*

2. *What do I already know about the historical events, social values and customs, and systems of belief from that particular historical moment? What do I need to look up or ask about?*

3. *How might these historical events, social values and customs, and systems of belief have shaped the audience's assumptions?*

4. *Where in the piece can I see the author trying to address these assumptions?*

These questions apply to narrative genres as well.

Going back to *Frozen* for a second, of course the audience is children, but the more interesting question is: What experiences or sets of beliefs might have shaped those children, and how does *Frozen* seem to be responding to that? *Frozen* came out in 2013, meaning we're dealing with children whose parents grew up with a previous generation of Disney movies that ended with "true love's first kiss," etc. So perhaps the film is speaking to an audience who has a certain set of assumptions about what a princess is and what counts as a "happy ending."

Similarly, in *Mansfield Park*, an important part of the audience will certainly be young women of the landed gentry—women like Austen and her heroine. But the more interesting question, again, is about the experiences and value systems that those young women have been inculcated in, and how Austen is responding to that. What have these young women been raised to think of their role in society, and how is Austen responding to that?

## PRO TIP: DOS AND DON'TS WHEN THINKING ABOUT AUDIENCE AND CONTEXT

**Don't:**

- Assume that the demographic groups that the writer is discussing are automatically the same as the demographic audience or that the conversation ends there. This doesn't lead anywhere interesting! Instead, ask what beliefs and value systems unite those readers.

- Assume that the audience is just "people who are interested in" the topic. Sure, that's probably true, but it's also too general. Oftentimes, an author is trying to make people who have a very specific set of assumptions or beliefs about the topic change their minds.

**Do:**

- In argumentative works, examine closely the passages where the author is addressing a counterargument that they seem to think a reader might have in mind—that tells you a lot about the assumptions the writer is making about the readers' beliefs.

- In both argumentative and narrative works, pay attention to how the author is framing historical events and cultural values and customs—are they assuming the audience already knows what these events are and holds those values, too? Or are they giving information so that "outside readers" can participate? That tells you a lot about who they imagine they're writing to.

- Think through any outside information that you may have about the piece. For example, maybe you know from reading a secondary source that Perrault wrote his fairy tales for wealthy girls and young women in seventeenth-century France—and then when you can look for moments in the text where Perrault seems to be working from an assumption about what those girls and women believe and value, or what he wants to *persuade* them to believe and value.

## Putting It All Together

We've already talked about the value and power of **rhetorical analysis**—of thinking through the choices an author is making, why they might be making those choices, what they might be trying to communicate, and to whom. Rhetorical analysis helps us see past the surface of the many texts that we encounter and to think through how the people who created them are responding to the world in which they lived.

The processes of thinking through our own choices, purpose, audience, and context is what we call rhetorical writing, and it, too, is a valuable tool. For example: Who is the audience for any given paper you write at UCI? On the one hand, yes, it's your instructor, but on the other hand, one of the "conventions" of the academic essay genre is that we write imagining that we are speaking to a larger community of interested scholars, knowing this might affect many of your rhetorical choices in the paper. For example, I often tell my students that although your instructor has to read your paper, that larger community of interested scholars does not have to. Write with an awareness that you're writing to people whom you want to keep interested and who have read many, many essays on *Mansfield Park*, only some of which are relevant to an ongoing scholarly conversation. Build your ethos by making those readers trust that you're aware of what's being said in that ongoing scholarly conversation and that you know where you fall in that conversation, whom you agree and disagree with, and what you're adding.

## Works Cited

Alexander, Michelle. *The New Jim Crow: Mass Incarceration in the Age of Colorblindness*. The New Press, 2010.

Chocano, Carina. "Let It Go." *You Play the Girl: On Playboy Bunnies, Stepford Wives, Train Wrecks, and Other Mixed Messages*, Mariner, 2017, 201-217.

Coates, Ta-Nehisi. "The Case for Reparations." *The Atlantic*, June 2014, www.theatlantic.com/magazine/archive/2014/06/the-case-for-reparations/361631/.

Desmond, Matthew. "How Homeownership Became the Engine of American Inequality." *The New York Times Magazine*, May 9, 2017, www.nytimes.com/2017/05/09/magazine/how-homeownership-became-the-engine-of-american-inequality.html.

Diaz, Junot. "Fiesta, 1980." *Drown*, Riverhead, 1996.

*Frozen*. Directed by Jennifer Lee and Chris Buck, Disney, 2013.

Giridharadas, Anand. "What To Do When You're a Country in Crisis." *New York Times Book Review*, May 17, 2019, www.nytimes.com/2019/05/17/books/review/upheaval-jared-diamond.html.

Sutherland, Kathryn. Introduction. *Mansfield Park*, by Jane Austen, 1814, Penguin, 2003.

## CHAPTER 2

# Practicing Critical Reading

*By Kat Eason and Leah Kaminski*

A small note about the personal pronouns: this chapter was not written by a disembodied and distant authority. It was, in fact, written by a we who have used, currently use, and will use the techniques listed herein when we read. The techniques detailed in this chapter have been tested, re-tested, refined, and, dare we say, perfected over time and a lot of practice. Which is to say, we—authors Leah (speaking to you in the red) and Kat (speaking in blue)—have tested all this material ourselves, and survived. So will you.

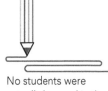

No students were actually harmed in the writing of this chapter.

I'm Kat Eason, and I and the marvelous Leah Kaminski are your guides to the tricks and techniques of critical reading, the primary ingredient of successful reading comprehension (which translates into successful writing and rhetoric!). I've been a teacher for fifteen years, the last thirteen of which have been here, in the Composition Program at UCI, where we've read critically about zombies, cyborgs, and Beowulf (although not all at once).

I teach 39A often and know from experience that even the bio majors among us can be persuaded to get animated about reading. Most of the time I assign autobiographical writing like memoirs, personal essays, and poetry. I'm a poet, too, and creative writers are really nerdy about reading: in my favorite seminar when I was here at UCI as a graduate student, we'd often spend the whole class talking (and arguing) about some of the basic questions (like, Who's speaking? Who are they speaking to?) that we include in our chapter.

## Critical Reading: What Is It?

The kind of reading we're talking about in this chapter doesn't come naturally. It requires practice. And time. And effort. And not leaving your twenty pages of Beowulf until 3 a.m. Critical reading—also sometimes called close reading—isn't something you can do quickly (if you want to do it well). Learn to treat your reading assignments like your homework from math, bio, or chem. Bring a writing utensil and some paper (or their electronic equivalents).

This sounds like a lot of work, yes, and not a bit like the quick-glance-at-the-page-reading you can use on an Instagram post. But the kind of reading we describe here is something you'll need, and use, for the rest of your career, both as a student in the university (textbooks, articles, essays), and in your later professional life as well, when you encounter specialized, difficult, formal writing (articles in scholarly journals, books, white papers, lab reports, legal briefs, scientific proposals, etc.).

You may have heard the phrase "critical reading" before (after all, it's in the title of our course "Critical Reading and Rhetoric"). The word *critical* has a somewhat negative connotation, and it sounds like to read critically is to criticize. Well, no. You aren't looking for what's wrong in a text. You are, however, looking to make judgments about the text: what it means. How it means. For whom it is intended. Why it was created. So when we use the phrase "critical reading," we mean to read something carefully, judiciously, thoughtfully. Sometimes you'll see an instructor use the phrase "close reading"—and that phrase also works for what we're talking about here.

No matter *what* you read, if you read critically (and closely), you will be reading *actively*.

What does it mean to read actively? It means paying attention. Our brains like to slide over words, filling in what we *think* the words mean, or should mean, rather than focusing on what they *do* mean. Our task, as critical readers, is to keep focused.

We need to be detectives, of a sort, learning to use context and clues from both within the text and from its rhetorical situation, to figure out what it's saying. You can totally dash past a Facebook update and get it. Probably not *Hamlet*, though. Or that chapter in your biochemistry book.

But while it requires close attention and even analysis, here's something important to know about reading literature: there are no secret codes to break. There are no exact formulas to solve. There are certain facts about texts that we can't ignore (see the sections on **What a Text Means** and **How a Text Means** for more about that), but there's also a lot of soft science involved in active reading. There's a lot of learning to respect your own impressions and responses (and then being precise and determined to explain how you got those impressions), trusting yourself as a reader, and being open to whatever you're reading.

Robots don't write books (yet?). So throw out the oversimplified, one-to-one correlations (Symbols? Boo! Foreshadowing? Grr!) that made your paper-writing experience so stale and your reading experience so tortured in high school.

So really, to read critically (or closely) means to read attentively and deliberately. Which is to say: with focus and concentration, looking at both *what* a text means and *how* a text works.

## Critical Reading: What a Text Means

One way to understand a text is to pay attention to small pieces at a time and to ask questions about what you see there. These questions are all related to context *within* the text, details inside a larger story, poem, essay, article, whatever. The answers are more or less concrete, verifiable "facts" about the text. (Either Hamlet is talking to Gertrude, or he isn't. There's not much room for interpretation.)

### Round One: Meeting Your Text for the First Time

So you just got your first reading assignment for your writing class, and you're a little freaked out. The instructor seemed to think you'd have no problem, you know, just getting it. And you didn't either, until you read the first paragraph and realized you have no idea what the author just said. And then you realized exactly how many pages of text were waiting after that paragraph . . .

Oh, sure, maybe you can go Google up a synopsis somewhere; but that's not going to help you *at all* when your instructor expects you to write an essay using specific details. Okay. So let's look at this monstrous text.

What follows are some of the most important steps you can take toward reading more actively.

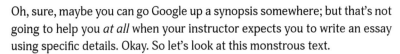

**THE SIMPLE STEPS TO ACTIVE READING**

1. *Read aloud.*

2. *Mark the words you do not understand and look them up.*

3. *Make notes on your copy of the text.*

4. *Make a note of the main idea of a paragraph or passage, either on a hard copy of your text or in a notebook or separate file.*

So, that all looks pretty basic, right? Maybe even...*too* basic? Here are some thoughts on why these steps are important and how you can make even the simplest of them powerful. Your teacher might have some other tips for you, too. Tweak these (and the other lists in the chapter, too) until they work for *your* reading and learning style, and make habitual any new strategies you discover along the way.

In this chapter I will be annotating a section from Aristotle's *Nicomachean Ethics*, in which Aristotle concludes that happiness is the final good to which all humans aspire and attempts to define what happiness must mean. The individual words are not difficult, but Aristotle's ideas are complex and sometimes hard to follow, even nailed as they are to the frame of his logic. That example appears in its entirety at the end of this section to better illustrate both my method and Aristotle's whole argument.

*Hamlet*, a play by William Shakespeare (you've probably heard of it, maybe even read it), will help me show what it looks like to ask and answer these questions as you're reading. In the following section I'll use one of the central scenes of the play, act 3, scene 4 in which Prince Hamlet talks to his mother Queen Gertrude about her betrayal of his father, kills the nosy advisor to the court, Polonius, and sees his father's ghost (who causes a lot of trouble because Gertrude can't see him and is naturally worried about her son's sanity). We get a lot of action in this scene and a lot of really emotional dialogue.

### Step One: Read aloud.

Often our minds will skip words when we read silently, especially if we're tired, distracted, or the word itself is unfamiliar. Reading aloud forces you to concentrate on the text and to face each word at it comes. It's also a very good way to discover new, unfamiliar words. And when you find such an alien. . .

Read more slowly than you think you should. Read like a real person, not like your computer's speech function. Have your pencil in hand as you read. Reading out loud will help the text come alive for you; it will force you to slow down and notice words that your brain might slide over on paper—and it will also make the text seem more human. Reading aloud will help you respond and react to the vital, fun communication the author's sending you.

### Step Two: Mark any words you do not understand and look them up.

Write down, circle, highlight, or otherwise mark any unfamiliar words. Look them up and make a note of what they mean in the margins of your reading or in your notebook. Learn them. You'll probably need them later on.

Definitely. I'll also add that it's a good idea to mark words that seem out of place, that are being used more than once, or that are used in a different way than you're used to. This can help you with figuring out *how* a text means, a question we'll talk about a little later in this chapter.

### Step Three: Make notes about what you read.

In addition to unfamiliar words, make note of thoughts you have as you are reading. I like to treat my notes as a conversation (admittedly one-sided) with the writer. *Yo, Aristotle, I don't even get this. Final product...? What?* Or *oooooh, right, the good is that thing that we're all seeking. Gotcha.* This helps me find places I don't understand and keep track of the Eureka! moments.

See this bit from when I marked up a passage from *Hamlet.* Along with marking words I don't know, I note moments that create tone, moments of characterization, important plot points, and patterns.

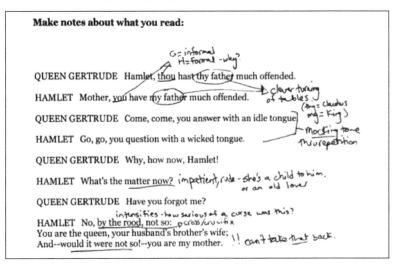

I'm less personal than Kat, but I do note moments of my own reaction. Feel free to use whatever method, marks, or madness make sense to you. Annotations and reading notes are for *your* purposes, to help you read and later write, not to check off an assignment. The only rule, as far as I'm concerned, is that you do it with care. And that you can read your own handwriting later.

### Step Four: Make a note of the main idea of a paragraph or passage.

Finally, jot down any main ideas or key words in the text, or write a quick summary in your notebook or the margins. If you find yourself staring blankly at the page, or realize you've forgotten everything you just read ... do it again.

This is especially useful for difficult-to-read texts. If you make a note of a passage's main idea and other big-picture things (like connections between one passage and another, for example) you'll have a quick reference when you go back to the text. Past-you will tell present-you whether it's import-ant, without present-you having to read it the whole way through again.

This is a full-page example of my annotation of a brief passage from *Nicomachean Ethics*. In it, I attempt to follow Aristotle's argument, point by point, by underlining and making marginal notes. I also remind myself about key terms and arguments from earlier parts of the reading—what Aristotle is referencing when he says "thing" in the first line, for instance.

> Thing = Final Good
> You never choose Happiness to get sthg else
>
> Now such a thing happiness, above all else, is held to be; for this we choose always for self and never for the sake of something else, but honour, pleasure, reason, and every virtue we choose indeed for themselves (for if nothing resulted from them we should still choose each of them), but we choose them also for the sake of happiness, judging that by means of them we shall be happy. Happiness, on the other hand, no one chooses for the sake of these, nor, in general, for anything other than itself.
>
> what? ...right. We're virtuous b/c it's good. Circular logic, A.
> Virtue/virtuous pursuits make us happy
> many little goods make a happy. Good → Good + → Happiness
> Happiness is Final Good
> Final Good: that Good sought for its own sake
>
> From the point of view of self-sufficiency the same result seems to follow; for the final good is thought to be self-sufficient. Now by self-sufficient we do not mean that which is sufficient for a man by himself, for one who lives a solitary life, but also for parents, children, wife, and in general for his friends and fellow citizens, since man is born for citizenship. But some limit must be set to this; for if we extend our requirement to ancestors and descendants and friends' friends we are in for an infinite series. Let us examine this question, however, on another occasion; the self-sufficient we now define as that which when isolated makes life desirable and lacking in nothing; and such we think happiness to be; and further we think it most desirable of all things, without being counted as one good thing among others -- if it were so counted it would clearly be made more desirable by the addition of even the least of goods; for that which is added becomes an excess of goods, and of goods the greater is always more desirable. Happiness, then, is something final and self-sufficient, and is the end of action.
>
> key word
> Wait. What? Are we still on self-sufficiency?
> So..to be happy requires some consideration of other people (but w/in reason)
> aha. So. Back to Happiness
> Happiness = goods
> more goods are better but you can't have more happiness (es)
> Virtue + action good → good → good → Happiness
>
> - Aristotle, *Nicomachean Ethics*, trans. W. D. Ross
> Book 1, Ch. 7
> Source: http://www.constitution.org/ari/ethic_01.htm

Whatever your method, engage with the text. Talk to it. (Worry if it talks back.) Talk to *yourself*. (It's okay if *you* talk back.) Think of annotating a text as a conversation with your future self.

This might seem like a lot of work, and it is. Critical reading is a messy, diffi-cult business. The process gets easier and faster as you practice. And while critical reading does take time, it also saves you work when you return to a text to write an essay or study for a test.

# Critical Reading for Creative Works: What's Happening?

Nonfiction, by definition, presents itself as itself. The writer and her words are one and the same, and those words are transparently "what's happening" in the text. Annotating or writing about that in the margins would often mean simply repeating what the writer said. You're not a time-waster, so unless what the writer said is difficult to understand on a literal level (in which case you might write a paraphrase in the margin) you're going to go straight to *responding* to their message.

The "facts" of fiction, drama, poetry, and other creative texts are less straightforward: there's a distance between the writer and her words, and her primary objective is not to speak directly to you, as herself. She speaks instead through characters and action in a play; through narration of fictional events by a fictional character in a novel; or even as a seemingly possessed, hyperreal version of herself, as in much poetry—ask your teacher for some Emily Dickinson if you want to know what I mean. Understanding the situation in this kind of literature will sometimes require a bit of detective work.

You may not record all of this on the annotated page, but you might jot it down in a reading journal or your class notebook. Whatever you do, *ask these questions, always*! They are simple, but they matter a lot. These questions, in fact, should never leave your mind, because the *what* affects meaning, message, and import just as much as the *how* and *why* we'll talk about in a bit.

Here are some questions to start with. Some may be more relevant than others, text-by-text, and there are many possible combinations of these parts.

---

## HOW TO FIGURE OUT WHAT'S HAPPENING

1. *Who is speaking? To whom?*

2. *What is the situation within the passage?*

3. *What's happening in the passage?*

4. *What happened immediately before this part of the text? What do you think will happen right after?*

---

As with our first list, these might seem See-Spot-Run obvious at first, but the more you read critically, the more complex and subtle the answers will become. They can open up a whole lot of new things to think—and then write—about.

### 1. Who is speaking? To whom?

Consider the basics: is it dialogue, monologue, internal monologue, narration, poetic speech? Are there even characters, or is it pure description? If there are characters, do we know them? Who are they? If it's not dialogue, still ask, who is being spoken to? It could be the reader, or an imagined other person, or the narrator/speaker herself. For example, let's look again at the passage from *Hamlet*:

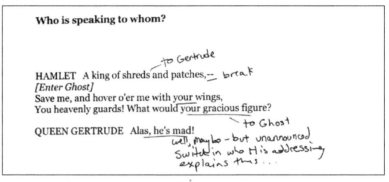

**Who is speaking to whom?**

HAMLET  A king of shreds and patches,-- *break*
*to Gertrude*
[*Enter Ghost*]
Save me, and hover o'er me with your wings,
You heavenly guards! What would your gracious figure?

QUEEN GERTRUDE  Alas, he's mad!
*to Ghost*
*well, maybe – but unannounced*
*switch in who H is addressing*
*explains this . . .*

The idea here is to remember that you are not reading words in a vacuum. Hamlet's "To be, or not to be" soliloquy in act 3, scene 1 might mean something different to the play if you establish that the evil Claudius and wily Polonius are listening in.

### 2. What is the situation within the passage?

In what physical location is this passage set? At what time (within the text)? What are the speaker's physical surroundings?

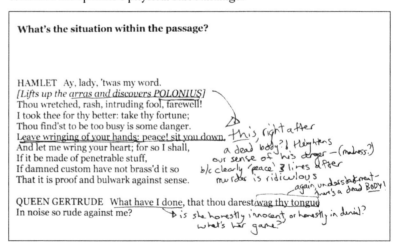

**What's the situation within the passage?**

HAMLET  Ay, lady, 'twas my word.
[*Lifts up the arras and discovers POLONIUS*]
Thou wretched, rash, intruding fool, farewell!
I took thee for thy better: take thy fortune;
Thou find'st to be too busy is some danger.
Leave wringing of your hands: peace! sit you down. *this, right after*
And let me wring your heart; for so I shall, *a dead body?! Heightens*
If it be made of penetrable stuff, *our sense of his danger – (madness?)*
If damned custom have not brass'd it so *b/c clearly 'peace' 3 lines after*
That it is proof and bulwark against sense. *murder is ridiculous*
*again, understatement – there's a dead BODY!*

QUEEN GERTRUDE  What have I done, that thou darest wag thy tongue
In noise so rude against me? *is she honestly innocent or honestly in denial?*
*what's her game?*

The fact that Polonius's body is in the room with Gertrude and Hamlet is probably important and might change the way we read the rest of the scene. Instead of a charged, intimate conversation between mother and son, we are unable to forget the larger implications of his actions, which are greatly intensified: he's not just an angry, betrayed son; he's a vengeful and unhinged prince.

Why are the character/s speaking? That is, what was the literal catalyst for this speech or conversation? The reason for speaking, the situation, can alter and shade the meaning.

## 3. What's happening, and/or what's being said?

Okay. When you're lucky, you should be able to answer this simply. We can complicate it by thinking about surrounding circumstances, catalysts for the action, and so on, but at its root it's fairly straightforward. For example, when Polonius says "I am slain," he dies.

But even when you're reading highly experimental work you can boil it down and answer this most crucial of questions. What's happening on a literal level if it's a realist work, or on the level of the reading experience or the writer's experiments if it's not? What's this text *trying to do*?

So when the immeasurably awesome James Joyce begins the immeasurably crazy *Finnegan's Wake* with this:

> **Finnegan's Wake:**
>
> *comes hard after "fall"...*
>
> The fall of (bababadalgharaghtakamminarronnkonnbronntonner-    *?!?*
> ronntuonnthunntrovarrhounawnskawntoohoohoordenenthurnuk) of a    *experimental style... ??*
> once wallstrait oldparr is retaled early in bed and later on life down
> through all Christian minstrelsy!

You will of course first look up "bababadalgharaghtakamminarronnkonn-bronntonnerronntuonnthunntrovarrhounawnskawntoohoohoordenen-thurnuk" as a word you don't know. Google will tell you that Joyce made it up and you'll be discouraged—*now* how are you supposed to know what it means? Well, after much help from your teacher, and reading about what others think about the book, you will eventually be able to say that it's (probably) Joyce's approximation of the sound of God's voice dictating the Fall of Adam and Eve.

Reading and writing skills are progressive. You won't always know the entire answers to the questions that arise as you read, no matter how carefully you follow our advice in this chapter. So just like in some of your nicer math classes, allow yourself to take partial credit even for unfinished work. *Engage*, even if you can't completely understand at first. You can't progress without taking the first step into the work, even if your first footprint is a question mark.

### 4. What happened immediately before this part of the text? What do you think will happen right after?

As with "what's happening?" these questions are always answerable in some fashion. And you should always, *always* ask them. Knowing that Polonius and Claudius planned to listen to Hamlet in Gertrude's bedroom makes a difference to how we read the scene I've been using as an example here.

Thinking about how the actions of a text are connected to each other might bring up the term "foreshadowing" for you, and if so, it's great that your synapses are firing. But let's shift the language a bit. "Foreshadowing" is not part of an algorithm that only Kat and I and your teachers know. It's straightforward: what's happening now needs to make sense based on what happened before, otherwise it's going to be a frustrating read (of course, that can sometimes be part of the point—*ahem, Finnegan's Wake*). So *of course* current events are affected ("foreshadowed") by what came before. This happens in real life too: if your friend slams the door after her boyfriend was rude to her on the phone, the phone call isn't "foreshadowing." It's an action that caused another action. The connection is still important, though, even if you have to take off your fortune-telling hat. So look back from what's *happening* to what *happened*, not the other way around.

If you can't tell what's happening and what has happened in a text and make a reasonable guess about what will happen, one of two things are going on: you're having trouble understanding the text, or there's something about it that is actively resisting the question.

Try two things then: read more carefully and talk to your teacher and peers, or think about why and how the text is trying to make understanding difficult for you. Is there a purpose to the difficulty?

## Reading and Rhetoric: How a Text Means

So now that we've established the facts of a text, it's time to explore *how* the text communicates. The answer, no surprise, lies in the words: their style, their arrangement. The words are all the writer has, after all, to communicate her message, so she's going to be very careful about how she chooses to deploy them. As you read, you should begin to pay attention to these choices and note them in your text.

Leah will use some more lines from *Hamlet* to show possible annotations based on *how* questions.

You should be able to address the following questions for every—no, really—*every* text you read.

## HOW IS THE TEXT CREATING MEANING?

1. *What is the tone? How can you tell?*

2. *What kind of language is the author using? Complicated? Formal? Casual?*

3. *Can you identify markers of style? Note any specific strategies or figures of speech that are appropriate to the genre.*

4. *What do tone, language, and style tell us about the intended audience of the piece?*

We'll use Aristotle and Shakespeare to show how each question can apply equally interesting pressure to any genre.

You'll learn a little later to think about *why* a writer chose one thing over another—what effect they meant to have. But since (as we keep repeating) this isn't an exact science, it could be that in the experience of critically reading you address the *why* questions before the *how* questions. So if you want to identify important rhetorical (*how*) choices, you can sometimes work backward from effect (*why*). What is your immediate response to this passage? What does it make you think about? What does it make you feel? Now, where are those feelings coming from—what detail is making you feel it? Our questions that follow prompt you to work both ways—starting from choice and starting from effect.

### 1. What is the tone? How can you tell?

Tone is the attitude a writer (or character) takes to her subject matter and, at least by implication, to her audience.

You can describe *tone* with adjectives: sarcastic, condescending, compassionate, snarky, pedantic (look that word up!), patient, sad, and so on. Aristotle's tone in the passage on page 24, for instance, is logical, serious, and objective.

Yes to adjectives! Of course, once you describe Hamlet's tone as prickly, spiteful, and hyperbolic, then you have to describe where you're getting your impressions (for example, from his building rhythm in this litany of a line: "Such an act / That blurs the grace and blush of modesty"). And the next few questions will help you collect that evidence.

### 2. What kind of language is the author using?

Language is another indicator of the author's attitudes toward the subject and a clue to both the audience's identity and the context of the piece itself.

Look for both the grammatical structure (how complex are the sentences?) and at the diction (word choice) an author uses. Aristotle's sentences are not particularly complex, taken individually, and his words are simple. But the way in which he strings the sentences together is extremely complex. His language also enacts his thinking patterns: in other words, his writing models his thought processes, which are methodical and logical, and, if you read slowly and carefully, make fine sense.

Shakespeare uses language to enact meaning, too. He often switches between everyday prose and blank verse, and noticing this can add to our understanding. For example, Hamlet speaks in high-flown blank verse in most of his monologues; the unrhythmical, "common," cruelly pun-filled prose he uses in dialogue with Polonius stands out from his usual polished metrical language. The difference in language imparts a different sound and texture to the scene and the characters.

If you're having trouble identifying which language choices matter and what effects they have, try thinking about what *hasn't* been chosen. So, for example, are you seeing an abundance of short sentences? Okay, what would have been different if the writer chose long, rambling sentences? Or a jumble of sentence fragments?

### 3. Can you identify markers of style?

Now is a good time to use a few remnants of high school English class **literary terms**.

Where are the metaphors? Similes? Alliteration? Even fancy-shmancy ones like synecdoche and antithesis? Are there any patterns or repetitions of these strategies within the passage or the entire text? You need to learn the arsenal of choices for whatever genre you're reading, though: the same literary terms won't apply to every kind of text.

As we foreshadowed with our "foreshadowing" chat, it's also time to shed some of the terms that oversimplify meaning in creative arts. Symbols have been known to occur (though they're less common than AP English might have had you think), but when they do they're not unchanging, thing-equals-other-thing, rule-bound, press-this-button creatures; they're a lot moodier, more shifty, and more interesting than that.

So don't oversimplify meaning by grasping for "symbol" the second something reminds you of something else. Consider softer verbs like "suggest" and "evoke" over "represents" or "symbolizes." You'll like your books more, and your teachers will probably like your papers more.

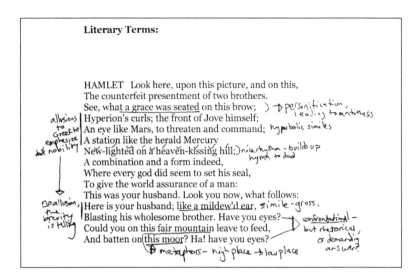

**Literary Terms:**

HAMLET   Look here, upon this picture, and on this,
The counterfeit presentment of two brothers.
See, what a grace was seated on this brow;
Hyperion's curls; the front of Jove himself;
An eye like Mars, to threaten and command;
A station like the herald Mercury
New-lighted on a heaven-kissing hill;
A combination and a form indeed,
Where every god did seem to set his seal,
To give the world assurance of a man:
This was your husband. Look you now, what follows:
Here is your husband; like a mildew'd ear,
Blasting his wholesome brother. Have you eyes?
Could you on this fair mountain leave to feed,
And batten on this moor? Ha! have you eyes?

## 4. What do tone, language, and style tell us about the intended audience of the piece?

**Tone** and **language** are major clues about a text's intended **audience**.

Just because we can all understand a text eventually doesn't mean we're the audience for it. Aristotle wasn't writing to twenty-first-century university students. The thoroughness with which he delivers his arguments, and the seriousness and objectivity of his tone, indicate that he is trying to reach an audience who will be receptive to that kind of address. He's appealing to *logos*, or reason, rather than any sort of *pathos*, and his *ethos* rests on his objectivity and thoroughness. So whomever his audience is, they must value those things.

Kat, that was so clear you've left me with nothing to say. Except: there are practical issues that help us think about audience too—and we'll get to that a little later when we discuss *context* in the section **No Text Is an Island**.

## Addressing the Audience: Why a Text Means

Contrary to popular belief, Aristotle, Shakespeare, and the authors of your chemistry book did not set out to make you miserable. They had an actual purpose in mind with their writing and a message to communicate to their readers. The key to uncovering that purpose and message lies in figuring out the ways in which the *how* connects with its particular, intended audience.

You've now learned to identify the specific details of how the text is creating meaning, and you can take the next step now, thinking about the function of those details: what the *how* actually does. Rhetorical choices have partic-ular effects (otherwise, they wouldn't exist; metaphors, for example, don't just exist for fun decoration—writers use them on purpose to create certain effects for certain readers). The choices transmit meaning, elicit emotion, create patterns, resonate with other parts of the text...

So this is getting complicated, right? We're not just *inside* the text anymore; we're also trying to see *out* of it. Here are questions to help you explore purpose, effect, and audience.

## WHY IS THE AUTHOR MAKING THESE CHOICES?

These questions will yield very different answers depending on the type of essay you read—academic, popular, personal, etc. And it can be even more varied when you're dealing with a piece of fiction.

1. *What does the author want the reader to understand, believe, or feel by the end? How can you tell? This is the text's primary message.*

2. *What kind of evidence does the author use to support his or her position? Anecdotes? Scientific data? Imaginary examples?*

3. *What does the kind of evidence tell us about the intended audience? What does the author assume the audience already knows (what information does she leave out)? What does she assume they still need to understand (what information does she deliver)?*

4. *How does the writer construct his or her ethos for the audience?*

## 1. What is the text's primary message?

The answer to the question of **primary message** depends on the types of rhetorical appeals the author is using.

Think back to tone and language. Aristotle wants his audience to *think*, yes, but he wants them to follow his reasoning and agree with his logic and, by extension, his conclusions. So Aristotle wants to persuade his audience, through an appeal to their *logos*, to agree with his arguments. This suggests an audience who will be convinced by reason and objectivity.

While the concept of "message" may not be as straightforward in **fiction, poetry,** and **drama** as it is in nonfiction writing, poets, novelists, and playwrights write because they *have something to say.* For simplicity's sake, let's call that something the text's "message." This is a tricky balance. Novels don't have thesis statements, but every writer is trying to reach her reader and effect some change. Consider the message of the whole text, **and** if you're reading a text in parts, you might also ask yourself, how does **one** passage's message resonate with the message of the whole? Does this passage add to, change, or complicate the overall message? Always imagine someone asking, *how can you tell*? A writer's every choice creates immediate effects, and those effects combine to create the text's or passage's message.

## 2. What kind of evidence does the author use?

The **types of evidence** an author uses tell us a lot about the audience as well.

Subjective evidence appeals to *pathos*. A personal anecdote or narrative can create an emotional connection to the audience. While no author *wants* his readers to be bored, obviously there are times and places where a subjective appeal would be inappropriate. The TA grading your lab report probably doesn't care what you did over the weekend. She wants to see your data. Objective evidence appeals to *logos*. And by objective, we mean not only evidence like scientific data (like your lab report), but also references to other texts. An academic essay about *Hamlet* will rely on the writer's reason and objectivity, sure, but it needs specific excerpts from the play to have any credibility with its potential readership.

For creative works, evidence usually means something different. A novel's message requires less overt "support" than does your lab report: the writer isn't *proving* anything, per se. She's cajoling the reader into buying her perspective or point of view—or even just coaxing the reader into continuing to read, responding appropriately, feeling involved. So replace "evidence" with "means of seducing/persuading/convincing the reader." Then think of those *how* questions. What's the tone? What kind of images are being used? What level of diction? And how do those things work to evoke a response in you or keep you on board with the text?

## 3. What does the evidence tell us about the intended audience?

A writer chooses the evidence to support her arguments based on what she knows about her **audience.**

You're writing about *Hamlet* for your English class*?* Better use quotes from the play, maybe a secondary article or two, to demonstrate your understanding and support your particular reading…and probably, you know, leave out the account of the time you played Gertrude in a high school production. An astrophysicist writing about stellar life cycles and planetary formation for the *Journal of Geophysical Research* will not waste time talking about what stars are made of; she'll assume that her audience knows that already. But that same astrophysicist giving a planetarium presentation to elementary school children *will* cover the basics.

Again considering "evidence" a little differently, it's still true for fiction, poetry, and drama that different writing choices help us picture the intended audience. Keep thinking about what kind of choices would appeal to certain readers. Shakespeare uses bawdy jokes because the peanut gallery of his time would get and appreciate them. Style—evidence—is the bouncer of literature. If you don't look right for the room, you're not coming in. And, of course, you have some say in it too—you wouldn't go to a club in Costa Mesa if you liked dressing for museum benefits.

### 4. How does the writer construct *ethos*?

You already know what ***ethos*** means from Chapter 1. In the same way that evidence, language, structure, and tone tell us about a text's audience, they *also* construct the author's *ethos*.

Notice that *ethos*, from our *why* questions, and tone, from our *how* questions, are quite similar. Tone is a really useful way for authors to build *ethos*.

So, Aristotle's serious, logical, objective arguments establish him as a credible thinker and, whether or not we agree with his conclusions, we have to respect the chain of logic that gets him from beginning to end. We might not much *like* his style, but his authority resonates off the page.

## No Text Is an Island: Putting Everything into Context

And finally, a word about *context*. We've looked at how words, evidence, tone, and ideas work within the context of a text; now let's think about how the text itself relates to *its* context.

The text's context affected the choices the writer made (*how*) and the effects she tried to create (*why* and for whom). So thinking about context can give you a lot of insight into what went into the author's choices.

One more list! This time, we want you to consider the historical and cultural situation in which a text was produced.

### QUESTIONS TO ASK ABOUT CONTEXT

1. *When and where was the work published?*

2. *How was it originally delivered? Was it written down? A speech? A performance?*

3. *What is the cultural background of the writer and audience? Consider geographic location, gender, ethnicity, shared beliefs, and discourse communities.*

Some of these questions may require research, especially on texts for which you, O college students, are not the primary audience.

### 1. When and where was the work published?

Considering **publishing context** is pretty self-explanatory, in most cases: all you have to do is check the copyright information at the front of the text (or the website from which it was taken).

But sometimes you might encounter a really *old* text from before the days of the mighty printing press, or a text that you're reading in translation (like our friend Aristotle). In those cases, you will have a publication date for the particular edition or translation, not necessarily the work itself. Don't confuse a translator with the author!

### 2. How was it originally delivered?

Consider **how the original work was experienced.**

This kind of information can really change your understanding of a text. Thinking about *Hamlet* as **it was** performed in a raucous, rowdy theater, as opposed to something you associate with drooling on your desk and the smell of cheap paper, can remind you to look for the humor and *pathos* in the play, to react to it as a human beyond your life as a college student, and to fully understand how different the original audience was from you in taste, shared knowledge, and experience.

### 3. What is the cultural background of the writer and audience?

Which leads us to the **cultural background** part.

With *Hamlet*, for example, it's not just that Shakespeare might not be addressing people who hate plays, or who don't respond to lyricism and intense characterization. There's also the fact that, you know, you don't speak to your mother in allusions to Greek myth: people nowadays don't know Greek myth as well as they used to (because of course, if they did, you'd totally make a speech about it in your next fight with your mom).

But if you could argue with your parents using Aristotle's airtight logic and cool-headed objectivity, you might have a better chance of winning. Something to consider.

## So Now What?

You did it. You read out loud. You circled all the words and looked them up. You annotated your copy of the text. And now, at last, you're finished. Time to put the text away and go watch YouTube videos.

Okay, fair enough. Take a break. But you're not done yet. Your instructor didn't ask you to read Aristotle, or Shakespeare, or Chekov, or fifteen pages of academic argument just because she's mean. She wants you to think about what you read and then *do* something with it.

If you read a *primary* text, like *Hamlet* or Aristotle, then you can start thinking about the text's place in the rhetorical situation.

But if you read a *secondary* text—an article *about* other works, like an academic article about the history of the zombie genre or an analysis of gender roles in *Hamlet* or a think-piece about Twitter humor, you want to start thinking about connections between that article and other texts.

We've already given you advice on figuring out *what* a given text means. You even know something about its purpose and *why* it makes the choices it does. But now you need to think about the text as part of a larger conversation—fitting into the "story" of your class, or even of your discipline at large.

## (Re)reading With Purpose

You need to have a bit of an agenda when you enter into a secondary text, some questions to keep in mind when reading: for example, does it describe genre conventions in a way that you can apply to your section's main text? Can it help you piece together your argument about the history of hill tribe citizenship in Thailand? Reading with purpose will help you find the best pieces from a variety of secondary texts in order to make your *own* meaning.

Of course, you can't go in hoping to twist a secondary text to fit your own assumptions and preconceptions: as you'll read in the 39B chapter on finding your place in the conversation and acknowledging alternative views, you need to have a give and take with the secondary sources you plan to use. As much as you go in with a purpose, you must still be open-minded.

See Chapter 3, "Citing and Integrating Sources" for more information on secondary sources.

After all, we don't have riveting (or even useful) conversations when we're inflexible.

Reading and using secondary texts in that way is going to be useful in all kinds of classes in all kinds of disciplines: for example, in our program, you'll read texts about genre and about primary texts, and texts about a primary event or social problem. And you'll use them for multiple reasons for background information, for help comprehending the facts of a text or situation, for support for your argument, or for illustration of a fact or argument.

## QUESTIONS TO HELP YOU USE THESE STRANGE CREATURES FOR YOUR OWN NEFARIOUS PURPOSES

1. *How does this article or essay connect to other texts I've read in this class? Does it support, contradict, or challenge ideas I've already seen?*

2. *Does this article explain something about the rhetorical situation of another text I've read in this class? Historical context? Genre protocols?*

3. *What new information does this text give me?*

4. *How does this new info help my understanding of another text (secondary or primary) or idea in this course?*

5. *Note whether and how soon the text begins engaging with other voices and having conversations with other writers (other than with the text that's their subject).*

6. *If you think the author(s) make a claim or announce their purpose in writing, underline it. Make note of where it comes in and what precedes it.*

7. *How can I apply it to the primary text it references? Does it help me understand the background of the text?*

8. *Do I disagree with its argument, or can I use a bit of its argument to extend and respond to?*

9. *Can I find evidence of its argument in a primary text or use it as a theoretical framework through which to read a primary text?*

## More than Just Words: Expanding the Meaning of "Text"

Just when you thought it was safe to close the book and check your Instagram and figure out what you're wearing to the movie later...let's ruin things for you. Books and magazines are texts, of course, as are Facebook updates and Tumblr posts. But *text* can mean more than written discourse, including many different kinds of media, as well: television, film, music, speech, art. Essentially, any act of communication—from *Hamlet* to the clothing you choose for a first date—can act as a text and be "read" accordingly.

## Works Cited and Further Reading

Aristotle. *Nicomachean Ethics.* Trans. W. D. Ross. *The Internet Classics Archive.* Web Atomic and Massachusetts Institute of Technology. Web. 8 Apr., 2013.

Joyce, James, Robbert-Jan Henkes, Erik Bindervoet, and Finn Fordham. *Finnegan's Wake.* Oxford: Oxford UP, 2012. Print.

Shakespeare, William, Barbara A. Mowat, and Paul Werstine. *The Tragedy of Hamlet, Prince of Denmark.* New York: Washington Square Press, 2003. Print.

## CHAPTER 3

# Citing and Integrating Sources

*By Jackie Way*

I'm Jackie Way, a Lecturer in UCI's Composition Program. When I'm not teaching, I research and write about literature and politics in the eighteenth century, which often requires me to work not only with a broad range of sources, but also with different versions of the same sources. I love piecing together the details of historical debates and investigating how important ideas are formed by different writers responding to each other. During my time here, I've taught writing and research at both the lower- and upper-division levels and have helped many students work with sources in all kinds of writing situations. This chapter will explain why and how we use sources in academic writing and give you practical insight into how to cite and integrate sources when you write.

## Sources and Academic Writing

The main purpose of academic work at a research university like UCI is to create and share knowledge. No matter your major, your goal as an undergraduate student is to learn the conventional ways in which scholars working in different disciplines create new knowledge and share it with others. From your English classes, you may be familiar with the technique of "close reading" a text: paying attention to all the choices an author makes in a novel, play, or poem and interpreting the literary significance of these choices. Historians also create knowledge by interpreting texts—in their case, various types of records and how they document or even shape historical events. Social scientists create knowledge by describing and interpreting human behavior using observation, surveys, research studies, and statistical analysis. Natural scientists like chemists and biologists create knowledge by designing controlled experiments to help them interpret the significance of natural phenomena.

Despite the obvious differences that separate these disciplines, we can notice two important things that unite them as forms of academic work. First, scholars in all these fields communicate their ideas and findings through writing; second, these scholars always refer to sources in their writing. The point "everybody writes" is perhaps a no-brainer; but you may ask yourself, why sources? If the point of academic research is to create new knowledge, why must we keep referring back to "old" knowledge?

The short answer is that we cannot know what knowledge is truly new without familiarizing ourselves with what is already known and with what others have previously said about what we know.

The long answer has to do with something called **information literacy**. Information literacy encompasses a broad range of skills that enable you to *find information, understand how and why it was created, assess its value, and then use this information to create new knowledge.* Your mastery of these skills is a major goal of the WR39 series.

The aim of this chapter is to explain how you should cite and integrate sources in different writing situations. Among others, these situations include responding to open questions and presenting individual arguments; analyzing a given text's rhetorical situation and effects; analyzing a political or social issue and advocating a position on it; and reflecting on your own writing process. The strategies described here may seem complicated, but once you understand some of the principles behind them, using sources in your writing should become much easier.

## Different Types of Sources

### Popular Sources

Information resides in sources—check. And of course, different sources contain different kinds of information. For academic writers, the most important distinction between sources involves a given source's rhetorical situation: the kind of authority a source has based on how and why the source was created and for what particular audience. These elements together help us tell scholarly sources apart from popular ones. It can be easy to confuse popular and scholarly sources when researching predominantly online, but the differences are pretty big and easy to spot, once you know what to look for.

**A popular source is any source written for a public audience in order to share information, shape public opinion, or entertain.** Authors of popular sources include creative writers, professional journalists, government officials and agencies, nonprofit organizations and think tanks, lobbyists, and scholars.

In your own writing, you already have and will continue to draw on many kinds of popular sources.

## COMMON POPULAR SOURCES

- Websites, blogs, and most other types of online sources

- Newspaper and magazine articles

- Literary texts like novels, short stories, plays, and poems

- Nonfiction texts like speeches, essays, and histories

- Government documents (intended for the public, hence "popular")

- Think tank reports, policy briefs, and "white papers"

- *CQ Researcher* reports

Notice the broad range of authority represented in the sources listed above—we consider these sources "credible" for various reasons. In the case of newspaper and magazine articles, the authority of journalists comes from the fact that their job is to report the news as objectively and accessibly as possible and that individual journalists covering specific "beats" for extended periods of time develop reliable expertise in the relevant subjects.

In the case of literature like novels and speeches, authority rests in the writer or speaker who has something meaningful to say that audiences care about. Writers like William Shakespeare and Martin Luther King, Jr. have considerable authority as significant historical figures. However, writers like J. K. Rowling and Suzanne Collins also exert authority over their stories and their readers.

Likewise, the authority of government documents depends on the trust we place in the government itself to make reliable information broadly accessible, and the authority of a given website depends on the credibility of whoever created it.

The takeaway here is that the usefulness of popular sources depends on the rhetorical context of both the source itself and your own writing situation. Consider the goals you're trying to achieve in a specific assignment: if you are asked to analyze young adult dystopian fiction, you might use *The Hunger Games* as a source. You will probably not use it if your assignment is to analyze the political significance of ancient Roman gladiatorial games or the social significance of reality television in the twenty-first century.

## PRO TIP: WHY CAN'T I CITE WIKIPEDIA?

Let's be honest—most of us use Wikipedia to learn more about un-known topics. As a crowd-sourced encyclopedia, Wikipedia can be a good resource for gathering background information on a topic. The volunteers who edit Wikipedia are expected to evaluate articles for accuracy and relevance and to enforce standards that privilege objectivity and fairness.

However, the ability of Wikipedia contributors to remain anonymous poses a big problem in academic writing, where it's important to know the writer's expertise as well as who said what. When you con-sult a Wikipedia article, you may notice serious issues of credibility that plague the article. Often (but not always) these are described at the top of the page. If you check the entry's edit history to find out who has altered an article and what changes they have made, you'll often find that the contributor does not have much relevant expertise.

This is why you should NOT cite Wikipedia as a source in your aca-demic writing. However, you can always check the list of references at the bottom of Wikipedia entries for possible sources you CAN cite.

### Scholarly Sources

Scholarly sources rely on other factors to establish authority, in addition to the credentials of the writer and needs of the intended audience. Because the purpose of scholarly research is to circulate new knowledge, the author-ity of a scholarly source also depends on the methods used by the writer to create that knowledge: how data was gathered and analyzed, what previous ideas influenced the analysis and why the writer engaged them, and the in-tellectual worth of the overall argument.

**Peer review is the standard process scholars use to consider whether new knowledge should be considered reliable and trustworthy.** Before a schol-ar can publish her research, her work is sent anonymously to other scholars working in her field, who must verify the knowledge and methodology as original and accurate. These peer reviewers must also evaluate the contri-bution of this new knowledge to what is already known and be convinced of its intellectual value. Only after peer review has been completed does the new research actually appear in the form of a journal article or book, to be read, reviewed, and debated by the academic community at large. You may be surprised to learn that a lot of scholarly research does not pass the peer review process the first time without significant revision before publication.

Sources that pass peer review gain authority by the approval of experts who have the in-depth knowledge to judge a writer's methods and critical thinking by the conventional standards of a specific discipline. Non-experts, who may not have the knowledge or experience to assess these factors, depend on academic peer review to help ensure their own arguments are based on sound information and thereby strengthen their credibility. In the context of your own writing, **a scholarly source is written by a professional academic researcher primarily for an audience of other researchers, cites its sources, and undergoes peer review**.

Of all these criteria, peer review is the most important—if the source is not peer reviewed, you should not count it as scholarly, even if it is written by an expert or includes a bibliography. For example, an op-ed piece in a newspaper written by a university professor is not a scholarly source; the writer's goal is not to produce reliable knowledge, but rather to inform and influence public opinion. Nor is a *CQ Researcher* report a scholarly source, despite the fact that it cites its sources in an extensive bibliography.

## HOW TO TELL IF A SOURCE IS PEER REVIEWED

1. *For books, check the press that published it—any publisher called something like "X University Press" is definitely in the business of publishing academic research and likely practices peer review.*

2. *Has the book been reviewed in a scholarly journal? Read scholarly reviews to find out how professional scholars rate the quality of the scholarship in a given book. JSTOR is a great resource for this.*

3. *For articles, check the journal's website to see if it practices peer review or is "refereed." Many online databases give you the option of searching only for peer-reviewed sources.*

4. *Still not sure? Ask your writing instructor or a research librarian!*

## Reading and Understanding Sources

So—you've gathered some sources and the deadline for your first draft is approaching fast. Now what?

The crucial first step is to read your sources as efficiently as possible. In this context, efficiency is not just about speed—skimming your sources over and over again will not help you understand the ideas contained in them, nor will it help you plan how and where you will use your sources in your essay. Reading efficiently means doing the following.

- Locating the information you need quickly

- Recording and organizing the information in a way that makes sense to you

- Understanding how this information fits into your own writing project

The strategies described here are not intended to help you tackle the readings assigned by your writing instructor! See Kat and Leah's chapter on critical reading for great advice on how to read for literary meaning and rhetorical effect and how to prepare for class discussion.

*Reading Scholarly Books*

It's easy to assume that books are too long and complicated to use in your essays, or that it's not worth your time to find print sources in the library when so many are available online—both these assumptions are wrong.

First, books that you find in a university library are practically guaranteed to be useful—they go through a lengthy editorial and (depending on the book) peer-review process before publication. After that, professional librarians evaluate their intellectual value before adding them to their collections. This process of editing, peer reviewing, and evaluating—all before a book lands on a library shelf ready for you to check out—takes years of careful effort intended to ensure that the information you get from them is reliable, credible, and practical for your college writing needs.

Second, books have a lot more information than articles, all collected in one place. You might think of each chapter of a book as containing a comparable amount of information as an article, and they often contain more details, explanations, and references. In short, books are incredibly rich sources for your research project, especially scholarly books.

The same goes for e-books you find in the university library, which are searchable and can therefore make finding information much easier. In many respects, e-books have the same virtues as print books—a lot of information collected all in one place, careful editing and peer review, etc.

Of course, because books are much longer than articles, the prospect of wading through them to find what you need can be intimidating. When you're choosing books to spend some time with, don't just start reading on page one or skimming the middle bits.

## CHECKLIST FOR SKIMMING SCHOLARLY BOOKS

- **The title**. It sounds simple, but seriously, does the title suggest the book's relevance to your writing project? Pay attention to word choices in the title that match or suggest important keywords related to your topic.

- **The table of contents.** The book as a whole may not be entirely relevant, but it might contain a chapter or two that you can use. Again, pay attention to keywords in the chapter titles.

- **The list of illustrations or figures.** If included, this list should appear after the table of contents. Pay attention to the labels to see if there is valuable information in the form of charts, graphs, maps, images, and so on.

- **The index.** After you check the table of contents, *always* browse the index to see if any keywords on your topic appear there. If so, go directly to those pages and read what the author has to say about your topic. The more keywords that you find and the more relevant the author's ideas about your topic, the more useful the book will be to your writing project.

- **The bibliography and footnotes/endnotes.** Sometimes the bibliography is the most valuable section of a book. Does it include sources you've already found? Find where the author cites them and read what the author says at that point. Does it cite relevant sources you haven't found yet? Note them down and look them up too.

*Reading Scholarly Articles*

Scholarly articles are not only shorter than books (though not necessarily short), but also increasingly accessible in full text through online databases. They are published in periodicals called journals, which are the scholarly equivalent of magazines.

Like magazines, journals are published on a regular schedule: each year a journal is published equals one volume of the journal. For example, volume 47 of *The Journal of Popular Culture* was published during the year 2014. Each volume of a journal contains a specific number of issues. Magazines often publish on a monthly or even weekly basis, meaning that each magazine volume will have twelve or as many as fifty issues. Because peer review takes time, scholarly journals usually have fewer issues—for example, *The Journal of Popular Culture* publishes every two months, for a total of six issues per volume. Some journals publish every three months (or every quarter), for a total of four issues per volume. Some journals only publish once a year, and the one issue equals one volume of the journal.

While journal articles are published on a faster schedule than academic books, they undergo the same peer-review process, and professional librarians likewise evaluate journals for their scholarly value before subscribing to them.

Scholarly articles in the social and natural sciences tend to follow a conventional structure. As when you read scholarly books, you usually don't need to start reading articles from the beginning.

## CHECKLIST FOR SKIMMING SCHOLARLY ARTICLES

- **The abstract and keywords**. An abstract is simply a brief summary. Always begin by reading the abstract and, if included, any keywords (selected by the article's author or journal editor) to help you decide how useful the article will be to your project.
- **The discussion and/or conclusion.** These sections explain the author's interpretation of their findings and summarize the article's main ideas. They may also compare the author's study to other

recent studies or suggest next steps for further research. Don't worry about spoilers—you will make most efficient use of your time by reading the end of the article first.

- **The bibliography.** As when reading books, you should always check the article's references to find additional sources that you can cite in your writing project.

- **The introduction.** If the article's conclusion looks promising, go ahead and jump back to the beginning. This section describes the author's perspective on the specific topic or question.

- **The literature review.** This section usually comes after the introduction and situates the author's study in the context of other relevant research. Read this section to understand what has already been done to investigate the topic at hand and how and why different researchers agree and disagree with each other.

- **The methodology and results.** These sections describe the study itself and the author's findings.

### Sources about Other Sources

In addition to books and articles, you can also consult sources whose main purpose is to compile and organize other sources. These sources can save you time and effort as well as deepen your understanding of the current scholarly conversation about your writing topic.

A **bibliography** is simply a list of sources; each source that appears in a bibliography is called a **citation**. You may be most familiar with bibliographies in the form of "Works Cited" pages that you include at the end of your essays, which list all the sources you used, cited in a particular style format like MLA. As sources in themselves, published bibliographies are curated compilations of sources related to a particular topic or set of related topics; researchers consult these bibliographies to find out what information has been published on a given topic.

If the bibliography is annotated, each citation will be accompanied by a brief **annotation** that summarizes what each source contains and comments on the value of that information. (More on annotations later in this chapter.)

**Literature reviews** are somewhat similar to annotated bibliographies. These sources are synthesized, analytical summaries of a set of published sources on a given topic. Sometimes, literature reviews may also be restricted by a particular time frame. Writing a literature review requires a great deal of familiarity with the published arguments on a specific topic; they usually serve as reports on the state of current knowledge on a specific topic and may appear on their own or as a section within a book or article.

**Book reviews** are just what they sound like. However, book reviews that you find in academic journals are more than just a professional opinion about a book; these reviews usually contain some kind of summary of the book's chapters, an analytical evaluation of the argument's strength and weaknesses, and sometimes a comparison with other books appearing near the same time on a similar subject.

## Keeping Useful Notes on Your Sources

It's impossible to overstate the vital importance of keeping detailed notes that record and organize the information you glean from your sources. Experienced researchers know—often through trial and hair-tearing error—that most little shortcuts taken while writing notes inevitably prolong the time and effort spent completing the writing project. Re-reading passages to search for that perfect quote or to verify that small-but-vital-to-your-argument statistic eats up the minutes to your deadline! In moments of fatigue or frustration, it may feel incredibly easy to neglect what seems like extra, unnecessary work. But the truth is that keeping detailed source notes will ultimately save you time, for several reasons.

First, simply having detailed, well-organized notes means that you don't have to keep rereading your original sources because you forgot what information you read in them, which quotes you want to use, the authors' arguments, or any number of other details you want to use in your essay. Reviewing notes automatically helps you make more efficient use of your time.

Second, numerous studies on cognition and note-taking show that the process of note-taking helps your brain digest your sources more thoroughly, improving your learning. In their review of the scientific literature on note-taking, researchers Annie Piolat, Thierry Olive, and Ronald Kellogg point out that "taking notes themselves can also increase learning by fostering retention and connections of information, as seen in the generation effect...moreover, students also memorize during note taking, particularly when they engage in deep comprehension of the source" (296). The "generation effect" they mention is the idea that people remember and understand the notes they've written for themselves better than notes created by other people (like lecture notes posted by a professor).

Third, source notes can help you plan various parts of your essay before you start writing, including its organization, potential analysis of quotes and other evidence, your preliminary responses to the ideas contained in your sources, and so on. Planning ahead as you take notes not only saves you time, but also tends to raise the quality of your final written work.

So how should you take useful source notes? The good news is that the advantages of any system of note-taking depend chiefly on the person writing and using them. In other words, you are the best judge of what useful notes look like for yourself. You might choose to keep notes in one big Word document or write notes by hand in your notebook. You might write outlines of each source or a paragraph summary. Or you might color code your notes according to how you plan to use each source or which sources are most and least important. If you're a visual learner, you might create a graphic- or image-based system for keeping track of your sources. You might also choose to use bibliographic (or reference) management software like Endnote, Mendeley, Zotero, and so on. Really, the sky is the limit here and you should experiment with different strategies to discover what works best for you.

Regardless of what system of note-taking you adopt, good source notes should be comprehensive and precise, including but not limited to the following information.

## CHECKLIST FOR NOTE TAKING

- Citation information: author names, titles, and publication details
- Summaries (written in your own words) of the author's main ideas and lines of argument
- Paraphrases (again, written in your own words) of key evidence and the author's rhetorical positions
- Quoted passages (in the author's original words) containing significant or striking ideas, expressed eloquently or pointedly
- Definitions of key terms and concepts
- Page numbers of important passages and quotations
- Descriptions of graphs and images you might cite as evidence
- Background information on the author's credentials and affiliations
- Background information on the source's rhetorical situation and genre
- Related sources that the author directly engages in the essay itself or that you've mined from the bibliography
- Your own preliminary responses to the author's ideas
- Your preliminary plans to use (or not use) the source in your essay

### Planning How to Use Your Sources

When it comes to assessing the value of your sources and planning how you will use them in your essay, *you should consider what argumentative goals you want to achieve in your writing and how your sources help you achieve those goals.* There are three main categories by which academic writers understand and evaluate a source's relevance to their writing projects.

**Primary or exhibit sources.** These sources contain information that you will analyze or otherwise interpret in your essay, and they usually comprise the most numerous and/or most important sources you use.

In writing classes that focus on rhetorical analysis, these sources are texts like novels, poetry, films, op-ed pieces, historical speeches, and so on. Essay analysis involves breaking down one or two texts at a time and explaining how each part contributes to the artistic meaning or rhetorical effect of the whole.

In writing classes that focus on research, exhibit sources are typically scholarly sources that report new research findings and popular sources that report current or historical events and public opinion. Information may be qualitative or quantitative or both. Essay analysis will often bring together multiple exhibit sources and explain how the relationships between different studies, experiments, polls, events, etc. create a meaningful bigger picture.

**Secondary or argument sources.** These sources contain other people's arguments and commentary about a problem or issue that you will explain, engage, or otherwise apply in your essay. These sources are the second most important category of sources you will use, after your exhibit sources.

Whatever academic writing situation you find yourself in, argument sources will offer their own analysis or interpretation of the problem, issue, or text you are considering. You may agree or disagree with the author's argument. If you agree, your analysis should show why the author's argument holds up in the situation you're discussing. If you disagree, your analysis should refute the author's argument. You may also choose to refine or complicate the author's argument by adding additional context or by applying it to a new-yet-relevant situation.

**Tertiary or background sources.** These sources offer important, foundational, and generally undisputed information about your topic. This information might be statistical or historical background, a famous saying or quotation that introduces your discussion, definitions of key terms or concepts, any basic knowledge or assumptions that frame current understanding of a topic or issue, or anything else on which you will rely as true in your essay or use to contextualize your argument.

As you gather information from different sources, consider the various ways you might use them in your essay. Keep in mind that some sources can belong to more than one category, depending on what information they contain and their relevance to your writing project. Consult your instructor whenever you have questions about how to use a particular source in your writing.

## Citing Sources

Citations serve an important purpose in academic writing: because they document where the information you've used came from, they enable your readers to track down your sources and verify that your interpretations, analyses, and, ultimately, your arguments are sound and trustworthy. Citations also help connect your ideas to those of other scholars in ongoing critical conversation and signal that your ideas are credible, based on sound knowledge created by others.

*Like peer review, source citations are a major convention of the academic discourse community you're part of as a college student—to be taken seriously as an academic writer and researcher, you must cite your sources.*

Citing your sources according to a particular format might seem like a chore—especially if you've left them to the last moment before submitting your essay. Why does your instructor insist that you use a specific style, with all its rigid rules and arbitrary conventions?

Actually, citation styles are not arbitrary at all. Different styles reflect the different disciplinary needs of researchers. You are probably already familiar with the style of the Modern Language Association (MLA), which you will continue to use in your composition courses at UCI. MLA is the preferred system for literary scholars; it emphasizes authorship and page numbers because researchers who study texts need to know who wrote what and what exactly was expressed. In the context of your own writing in the WR39 series, your readers—which include your peers as well as your instructor—will need to be able to differentiate your ideas from those of your sources.

Many of the online sources you'll find and use in your research will be cited in the style specified by the American Psychological Association (APA), the preferred system for social science researchers. APA style emphasizes publication dates in citations because social scientists want to know what research studies are the most up-to-date. You may also find sources cited in the *Chicago Manual of Style* (or just Chicago) style, used by historians and other humanities scholars who want to know where information comes from. Chicago style uses footnotes or endnotes rather than the parenthetical citations preferred by MLA and APA in order to accommodate more details about the precise origins of specific information.

## HOW TO FORMAT YOUR WORKS CITED PAGE

1. *Your Works Cited page should appear on a separate page at the end of your essay.*

2. *List all sources in alphabetical order by author's last name. Last names always appear first. If a source has no known author, list by title instead (not "anonymous").*

3. *Format your citations by creating a hanging indent. This is easily done in your word processor by adjusting the left indent arrow in the ruler by .5 inch.*

4. *Double space your citations, just like the rest of your paper. Do not add additional spaces between citations.*

5. *ALWAYS refer to the relevant style guide to document your sources properly. You are always responsible for the accuracy of your citations, even when your instructor does not explicitly discuss them. A great resource for MLA is Purdue's Online Writing Lab.*

No matter which particular citation style you are required to use, your bibliography or Works Cited page needs to convey important information to your reader more or less instantaneously. To do so, it must be correctly formatted and contain complete information about the source. Check out the sample Works Cited page below as a model for creating your own documentation.

---

Works Cited

Didion, Joan. "On Keeping a Notebook." 1961. *Slouching Toward Bethlehem*, Farrar, Straus and Giroux, 2008, pp. 131-141.

Dillard, Annie. *The Writing Life*. 1989. Harper Perennial, 2013.

King, Stephen. *On Writing: A Memoir of the Craft*. 2000. 10th Anniversary Edition, Scribner, 2010.

Lamott, Anne. *Bird by Bird: Some Instructions on Writing and Life*. Anchor, 1995.

Smith, Zadie. *Changing My Mind: Occasional Essays*. Penguin, 2009.

---. "Speaking in Tongues." *New York Review of Books*, vol. 56, no. 3, 26 Feb. 2009, www.nybooks.com/articles/2009/02/26/speaking-in-tongues-2/.

Wallace, David Foster. "Twenty-Four Word Notes." *Both Flesh and Not*, Little, Brown & Co., 2012, pp. 261-284.

You should not assume that small mistakes in your Works Cited page or in-text citations don't matter or that your instructor won't notice them. Neglecting these seemingly small details seriously undermines your credibility as an academic writer: if you do not pay attention to simple citation guidelines, why should your reader trust that you paid proper attention to the ideas you discuss in your essay? Details matter at every level! Avoid these common mistakes:

- Confusing the name of the database and database provider. "Academic Search Complete" and "Science Direct" are databases; cite database names as needed for electronic sources. "ProQuest" and "EBSCO" are names of database providers—companies that provide paid access to specialized types of sources. These names are almost never required for a source citation.

- Repeating the same information unnecessarily in the citation. If two or more elements of the citation are the same, decide on the most relevant place to put that information.

- Leaving out sources you cite in your essay from your Works Cited page (or vice versa). Although it is sometimes accidental, this mistake comes dangerously close to academic dishonesty. Make sure ALL sources you use in the essay appear on your Works Cited page.

- Pasting citations directly from a website or using automatically generated citations without making sure they appear correctly. These may look close enough but are often incorrect.

- Using "n. p." (no publisher) and "n. d." (no date) in lieu of the proper information. Sources that don't provide this information are probably inappropriate to cite in your essay. The updated MLA style guidelines no longer permit these abbreviations.

## Annotating Sources

An **annotation** is simply a brief explanatory note commenting on the value of information contained in a source. Academic writers read and write annotations in a variety of contexts. In a published annotated bibliography, an annotation appears beneath each citation and briefly summarizes important arguments and evidence; the writer of the annotation may also comment on any striking features of style or methodology in the source. Annotated bibliographies also appear in college classes as a resource created by the instructor or as an assignment to be completed by students to demonstrate independent inquiry into particular topics.

However, annotations may also describe the marginal notes you write in your books as you read, which comment on specific passages, ask questions of the text, and make connections to other ideas. "Annotated editions" of literary and historical texts contain copious explanatory notes written by an editor to offer context and possible interpretations of specific passages.

There's no particular standard format for annotating sources—the content, style, and length of an annotation depend entirely on the context in which it is written. However, as a general rule when writing annotations, you should always consider the intended audience first and foremost: what information does the reader (yourself or another person, like your instructor) want or need to know about the source?

## Integrating Sources

When we integrate sources in our writing, we are directly engaging other people's ideas in order to develop our own. This process of source integration is arguably the most important and complex aspect of working with sources. The steps outlined below are not complicated in themselves, but performing them successfully requires your careful consideration and judgment from beginning to end.

### SIMPLE STEPS FOR INTEGRATING SOURCES

1. *Introduce and frame the source.*
2. *Summarize, paraphrase, or quote the source.*
3. *Analyze the source's evidence or ideas, and connect it to your arguments.*

### Step One: Introducing and Framing Your Sources

The first time you use a source in your essay, you must offer your reader some context for understanding the credibility and reliability of the speaker/writer or the significance of the information itself.

> ▶ *"In just about all cases, you should never stick a quote in your essay without some framing from you, as shown in this sentence."*

In the above example, the quotation marks indicate that some specific person said those words, but who? When source introductions are absent, your reader has little idea of how to interpret the relevance of the source to your ideas.

> ▶ *"Adding a parenthetical with the author's last name at the end doesn't solve this problem"* (Smith).

In this second example, who's Smith? Why should the reader care about what this person has to say? To avoid confusing your reader, you must introduce your sources whenever you use them with some kind of contextual information: how does the information contained in a source relate to your own ideas and argumentative purposes?

## PRO TIP: INTRODUCING SOURCES EFFECTIVELY

- For primary sources, explain how the source connects to your own ideas. Depending on the source and your writing situation, you might describe relevant historical background, summarize meaningful content, or clarify rhetorical purpose.

- For secondary sources, begin with a brief description of the author or publication's credentials, written in your own words. Include both first and last names as well as the author's expertise or significant affiliations. You might emphasize the publication instead if it is particularly well-known or significant.

- After you've introduced a source the first time, you can refer to it again using just the author's last name, either in the body of your sentence or in parenthetical citations. However, you must continue to frame the source so that your reader understands the relevance of the information to your own ideas each time it appears.

### Step Two: Summary, Paraphrase, or Quotation

After you introduce your source, your next move is presenting the material itself. How you present the actual information will depend on your specific goal in a particular paragraph.

A **summary** is useful for presenting the main point(s) of a long passage or even an entire source; this type of information often provides a background to your own argument or relevant commentary on your topic. Keep in mind, however, that the best summaries accomplish a specific purpose—they are not merely arbitrary collections of facts or trivia. When you summarize a source, consider what information your reader must know in order to understand the point you are trying to make.

A **paraphrase** is a more direct way of presenting source material, in which you express another writer's ideas using mostly your own words. Paraphrase is useful for communicating information more clearly and concisely than it appears in the original source, while still expressing the original meaning as closely as possible. When you consider different ways of paraphrasing someone else's idea, experiment with sentence structure as well as with word choice.

A **quotation** is the most direct way of presenting source material, in which you reproduce the exact wording of the original source. Selecting appropriate quotations is actually something of an art and depends on—you guessed it—your argumentative purpose at a particular moment in your essay.

Generally, you should only quote when the actual wording of the original idea is important to your discussion; the most effective quotations record an author's ideas or analysis, not their examples or background commentary. There are three situations in which a quote is better than a paraphrase:

- When the quote expresses an idea that you cannot clarify or otherwise improve using your own words

- When the quote contains specific words or phrases that are important to understanding the idea itself

- When you want to refine or refute the argument made by the author and need to represent their ideas precisely and fairly

### PRO TIP: QUOTING EFFECTIVELY

- Keep your quotations short and sweet—that is, only quote the words you plan to analyze directly.

- Long block quotations are only necessary if you plan to discuss the entire quoted passage. Indent the block quotation .5 inch on the left side and omit the quotation marks. Place the parenthetical citation at the end, outside the final period.

- Quoted material needs to be grammatically consistent with the words you use to frame the quote; number and tense must agree throughout the entire sentence. You may need to insert words that don't appear in the original quote by enclosing them in brackets.

- To cut down a quote, use an ellipsis to replace the omitted material.

### Step Three: Analysis and Interpretation

After introducing a source and presenting its relevant information, the final step is to analyze or interpret the information and connect its significance back to your own ideas. How you do so depends on the source information and the purpose it serves in your argument. Revisit your notes to decide whether the information should be presented as undisputed fact, as evidence to analyze, or as argument to interpret, refine, or refute.

See Emily's chapter on drafting and Loren's chapter on argumentation for additional advice on how to use other people's ideas to develop your arguments.

### PRO TIP: GET THE MOST OUT OF YOUR SOURCES

- While you should beware of relying too heavily on only one or two sources, do not be afraid to cite your most useful sources more than once in your essay.

- Also, try to avoid cramming all of your secondary sources at the end of the essay, which makes it seem like you didn't know what to do with them. Instead, plan carefully where you will integrate each source and try to spread them evenly throughout the essay, so that you're bringing important outside information to bear on your argument regularly and when your ideas can benefit from that outside support.

*Patch Writing and Plagiarism*

**Patch writing** is a form of plagiarism in which a writer takes a passage from someone else's work, changes a few words, and then uses it in an essay as if it was his own writing, without quotation marks. Patch writing may be accompanied by a parenthetical citation, footnotes/endnotes, or even a source introduction, but this doesn't actually save the writer from committing plagiarism.

While patch writing may sometimes result from deliberate cheating, there are also other, more understandable reasons why patch writing occurs. Sometimes the writer has not achieved full understanding of the material and cannot supply his own words to express the ideas. Other times, the writer's inexperience with college-level academic writing may lead to half-finished paraphrases, the result of misunderstanding how to properly integrate source material. Sometimes, writers who lack confidence may try to disguise what they perceive as flaws in their writing with someone else's more polished writing. In all these contexts, we can regard patch writing as an expected part of learning how to write well.

Visit the webpage of UCI's Office of Academic Integrity and Student Conduct (OAISC) for further information on what constitutes plagiarism and the university's plagiarism reporting procedures.

However, *patch writing is never acceptable in final essay drafts. It is always your responsibility as an academic writer to detect and revise all such instances—that is, to ensure that all of your paraphrases chiefly consist of your own words and all of your quotations are purely the words of the original author.*

Patch writing is both serious and common, and you will need to practice vigilance to keep it out of your writing, especially your final drafts. Frequent instances of patch writing in final drafts can negatively affect your essay's grade and possibly cause it to fail.

# Multimodal Sources

## *Multimodality in the WR39 Series*

Practicing information literacy within a rich digital environment means that not all sources you use will be purely written words—sometimes the information you need will be expressed through images, audio, or video. Scholars call such texts that combine words with images, sound, and video **"multimodal,"** though you may be more familiar with the related term "multimedia." You likely already have experience with a range of multimodal texts, especially those that appear online.

In the WR39 series, you will be asked to produce multimodal texts not only in the form of essays and other predominantly written genres, but also oral/visual presentations and digital portfolios where you'll compile your writing and reflect on your process. For these assignments, it is important to remember that multimodal elements are not merely decorative. To communicate effectively, you must consider them as sources containing information, which you will engage in order to develop your own ideas. As a rule, *the multimodal elements you choose should communicate specific information that is directly relevant to your argument, in a way that words alone cannot express.*

Avoid generic images like clip art and stock photos, which are unlikely to produce a useful rhetorical effect in your writing. Instead, choose multimodal elements according to how they will help you achieve your rhetorical and argumentative goals.

### WHEN TO USE MULTIMODAL EVIDENCE

- Clarifying or emphasizing a complex idea more efficiently than written words
- Convincing your reader with compelling visual evidence
- Evoking an emotional response in your reader
- Following the conventions of a specific genre

## *Integrating Multimodal Sources*

To integrate multimodal sources properly, you should rely on the same principles as described above for traditional written sources. Use the three-step method to introduce, present, and then analyze each graph, image, or audio or video clip you cite in your project.

Keep in mind that multimodal elements often present a lot of information that can be confusing to readers who don't know immediately what to focus on. You may also find that some parts of an image or video are more important to your argument than others. As you compose, consider the following principles of design to help your reader make sense of the ideas you're trying to convey and to ensure that your multimodal projects are both attractive and persuasive.

## BASIC PRINCIPLES OF DESIGN FOR ARRANGING VISUAL ELEMENTS

- **Balance** is the way you choose to align or distribute different elements on the page. Symmetrical balance tends to draw the reader's attention toward a specific place. Asymmetrical balance can direct the reader's attention to different places on the page in a particular order.

- **Emphasis** is the way you choose to highlight specific elements in order to call attention to them.

- **Unity** is the way you create a sense of wholeness or completeness in your project. Unity can be achieved through **repetition** and **placement** of certain elements, consistent **similarity** and **contrast** of specific elements, and **proportion** of size and number.

### HOW TO CITE VISUAL EVIDENCE

1. *Graphs, charts, tables, and images should be big enough to read clearly and placed next to the paragraph where you discuss them so that the reader can easily move their eyes back and forth.*

2. *Create a caption using the settings in your word processor. Label each graph or image as Figure 1, Figure 2, etc., then follow the label with the appropriate MLA citation for the graph or image. If complete information about who created the graph or image is missing, cite the source where you found it instead. You do not need to repeat this information in your Works Cited page.*

3. *In the paragraph adjacent to the graph or image, refer explicitly to the figure and state the specific information you want the reader to notice. The key is to be brief and specific—your goal is to direct your reader's attention, not to translate your visual evidence into words.*

4. *Complete your analysis of visual evidence by explaining its significance and relating it directly to your own arguments.*

**Works Cited and Further Reading**

Apostel, Shawn. "Prezi Design Strategies." *Kairos: A Journal of Rhetoric, Technology, and Pedagogy*, vol. 18, no. 1, 2013, http://kairos. technorhetoric.net/18.1/disputatio/apostel/.

Bizup, Joseph. "BEAM: A Rhetorical Vocabulary for Teaching Research-Based Writing." *Rhetoric Review*, vol. 27, no. 1, 2008, pp. 72-86.

*Framework for Information Literacy for Higher Education.* Association of College and Research Libraries, 2 Feb. 2015, www.ala.org/acrl/standards/ ilframework.

George, Diana. "From Analysis to Design: Visual Communication in the Teaching of Writing." *College Composition and Communication*, vol. 54, no. 1, Sept. 2002, pp. 11-39.

Hocks, Mary E. "Understanding Visual Rhetoric in Digital Writing Environments." *College Composition and Communication*, vol. 54, no. 4, June 2003, pp. 629-656.

*MLA Handbook.* 8th ed., Modern Language Association, 2016.

Piolat, Annie, Thierry Olive, and Ronald Kellogg. "Cognitive Effort During Note Taking." *Applied Cognitive Psychology*, vol. 19, no. 3, 2005, pp. 291-312.

Russell, Tony, et al. "MLA Formatting and Style Guide." *The Purdue OWL.* Purdue University Writing Lab, 2 Aug. 2016, www.owl.english.purdue.edu/ owl/resource/747/01/.

## CHAPTER 4

# Discovering Sources

*By Stacy Brinkman*

I'm Stacy Brinkman, and I'm a librarian at UCI. As a librarian, I think a lot about the process and power dynamics behind how information is created, discovered, spread, used, and preserved. We live in a world filled with bad information, and so the ability to find high-quality information is a valuable skill. One of the things I love about being a librarian is that I get to empower students like you in learning the research skills that will help you to be successful in your coursework and beyond. This chapter gives an overview of some of these skills and tools, but if you ever need any help, just ask us! (www.lib.uci.edu)

## Sources and the Scholarly Conversation

In the previous chapter, you learned that scholars communicate through writing and that they include and refer back to sources written by others. They do this to clarify what is already known about a subject and to provide context for the new information they have discovered and wish to share. In this way, scholarly writing is a conversation, where new information comes into dialogue with what other scholars have said in the past. An important task for any researcher is to learn to listen in and learn about what has already been discussed in the scholarly conversation about a topic, and then to consider how you will add your own voice to the conversation.

We typically call this art of listening in to a scholarly conversation "research." The goal of this chapter is to help you become more comfortable with the process of conducting research. This involves explaining some mechanics—tools and techniques—that will help you find many different voices in the scholarly conversation. However, becoming successful in conducting research also involves developing a way of thinking about information. This is where we will begin.

## Research is a Process

*Imagine that you are a detective, and someone has asked you to look into a possible crime. You have some vague pieces of information to start with: something happened, and someone was hurt. What do you do first? Presumably, you wouldn't immediately jump to a conclusion and make an arrest! Instead, you would probably start to gather evidence, and in doing so, you would have a clearer idea of what actually happened. You might interview people. You might analyze a site. You might examine forensic evidence. You might look into a person's background to try to identify a motive. In other words, you would try to collect many types of evidence. Each piece of evidence you examine should help you clarify what the crime actually was and give you a path toward what you need to examine next. After conducting this process a number of times, you should (hopefully!) have enough evidence to build a case and take action.*

Research is not that different from being a detective. At first, you probably only have a vague sense of what your topic or research question is. Don't worry. This will become clearer to you as you start examining the context around that topic. Many people will start by conducting a simple search in Google or Wikipedia. This helps you establish some background facts and gives you an initial sense of what people are saying about your topic. Questions to ask yourself here include the following: Who? What? Where? When? How or Why? Pay attention to subtopics that keep coming up, or particular stakeholders.

After doing some of that background investigation, you can think about what strategies you can use to hone in on a clearer topic. You might start to use additional tools, such as databases and library catalogs to find out what scholars might have said about a topic area. Follow leads in the conversation. Make sure you stay flexible and keep an open mind about where the evidence may lead you. Don't narrow yourself out of the existing conversation! Instead, ask questions like these: When did the conversation about this topic start? Whose voices are mentioned over and over? Whose voices are included or excluded from the conversation? What subtopics keep coming up? Is there a particular detail—such as a geographic area, a law, or a court decision—that is mentioned often?

Here are a few important takeaways from this analogy so far:

- Don't expect to have a perfectly clear topic or research question at first, just as a detective shouldn't expect to have a perfectly clear suspect and case built up at first.

- Searching for information is part of the process of clarifying your research question, just as collecting evidence helps a detective understand a case.

The detective analogy should illustrate that research is a process and that the process is not necessarily linear. As you learn more, you may find yourself modifying your topic, responding to new information, and refining your research question. Along the way, you will be making decisions about what you are NOT going to look into, and why (just like a detective decides which trails of evidence are very unlikely to be fruitful). Eventually, you will reach a stage where you are pretty sure you have found enough evidence and have heard enough voices to start organizing that information into a paper.

## How Do I Get Started?

Students often report that getting started is the hardest part of the research process, and there is a lot of anxiety surrounding choosing a topic. The important thing to keep in mind is that you do not need a "perfect" research topic or question in order to start searching. Instead, just start somewhere and see what's out there. Here are some ways to get ideas:

### GENERATING IDEAS FOR YOUR RESEARCH

- Think about the theme of your class, and look up that theme in **Google** or **Wikipedia**. What kinds of subtopics or related ideas come up?
  - Example: If your class theme is immigration, look up the Wikipedia article on this topic. You might see a number of hyperlinked (blue) words and subtopic headings, including things like "impact of refugees on the economy" or "immigrants and innovation and entrepreneurship." These are potential topics for you to begin to investigate further.
- Look up the theme of your class in a library topics database like **CQ Researcher**, **Opposing Viewpoints**, or **Global Issues in Context**.
  - Example: CQ Researcher has a "Browse Topics" section, and if your class theme was on climate change, you could select the "Environment, Climate, and Natural Resources" topic. In that topic area, you can locate an entire report on "Renewable Energy," which has subtopics like "carbon tax" or "battery technology." These are also good potential topics for further investigation.
- With the theme of your class in mind, pick up a newspaper or other news source and browse stories for potential topics.
  - Example: Imagine that your class theme is technology. Maybe you were listening to a news radio source like NPR, and you heard a story about a potential solution to the problem that no one reads user license agreements or privacy policies when purchasing apps or software, and therefore people may be giving up more personal information than they realize. This news story itself could be used as a source and also identifies a viable topic of privacy and user license agreements.

While you are browsing through some preliminary searches, make a note of the **keywords** you are using. Ask yourself if the results you're seeing suggest ways to narrow or refine your topic even further. If you are finding articles or studies, see if you can find a **bibliography** that can lead you to other related sources.

Your research process may look something like Figure 4.1, and you may need to go through the process of refining your topic several times. Research is not linear. Instead, it is an iterative process of continually refining your ideas and re-searching as you learn more information.

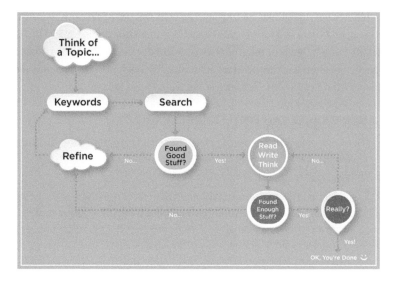

Figure 4.1: Research is a Process.

As you refine your topic, you may find yourself broadening out and then narrowing down again. Eventually, you should be able to define a topic that is sufficiently specific enough that it identifies a particular problem or issue that you might be able to propose a solution to later in the quarter, but also sufficiently broad enough that multiple people are having conversations about the topic. If you find yourself searching but not finding a conversation, it might mean that your topic is a subtopic of a larger issue.

Let's do a quick check. Are the topics in Table 4.1 too broad, too narrow, or just right?

**Table 4.1: Sample Research Topics**

| Research topic | Too broad? | Too narrow? | Just right? |
|---|---|---|---|
| A) Causes of homelessness | | | |
| B) Hate speech on college campuses in the US | | | |
| C) Benefits of solar panels on parking structures at UCI | | | |
| D) Video games and violence | | | |
| E) Food deserts and their impact on children's health | | | |

What did you think? Probably, topics A and D are a little too broad for a final topic, but they are fine places to start your research just to see what's out there. Once you begin, you may see additional subtopics emerge (e.g., mental health as a subtopic in causes of homelessness) and then you can continue to search and refine.

Topics B and E seem reasonably broad enough to find information, while being a bit more specific. Even so, don't be afraid to do some initial searching, and then broaden or narrow down further.

Topic C seems a little too narrow for an initial search. If you have a topic like this, you might get stuck because you can't find any research on this topic specifically about parking structures at UCI. But if you broaden just a little bit and do a general search on solar panels, you are likely to have more luck as a place to start.

## *Sample Topic: Causes of Homelessness*

This topic is still a little broad from a conceptual standpoint. You will probably struggle to advocate for solutions to the cause of homelessness later in the quarter. However, if you search for causes of homelessness in Google or Google Scholar, you are likely to identify many avenues with which to narrow your topic. For example, you may find that there are conversations about the structural causes of homelessness (such as lack of low-income housing), as well as conversations about more individual causes of homelessness (such as disability or addiction). In order to narrow your topic, you should decide which conversations you are more interested in following, and then add those concepts as keywords. A search for homelessness and disability will lead you to another set of conversations, and then you can start to evaluate whether or not you want to narrow further (for example, to homelessness and intellectual disability).

*What Kinds of Evidence Should I Expect to Find?*

Let's take a step back here and think about what kinds of information you might expect to find for any given topic. To do this, it is helpful to think about information production in general.

Imagine that an event happens—the US Supreme Court makes a ruling. Within the next twenty-four hours, you might expect to see a flurry of news stories, opinion pieces, social media posts, and other such activity. In the next few days to weeks, you might expect to see some long-form journalism in magazines and some newspapers, which offer a more in-depth look at the ruling and its historical or social context. Over the course of the next year(s), you may see scholars start to investigate this ruling in academic journals or books. Scholarship may take different approaches, but instead of just summarizing what is already known, you should expect that these academic sources are creating new knowledge. Finally, you may also see individuals, agencies, or advocacy groups publishing reports, data sets, or other forms of information. All of these voices contribute to an ongoing conversation about this Supreme Court ruling. In addition, you also need to remember that there was probably also a conversation happening about the issues in the Supreme Court ruling before that event even took place.

Writing 39C includes an assignment that asks you to consider how these past and present voices interact. However, thinking about scholarship as a conversation is also helpful no matter what you eventually decide to study. Let's say you're working on developing a new treatment for malaria. If so, you would probably want to know (and would need to report on) previous research done on malaria treatment. Academic articles typically include a section called a **literature review** which discusses prior research and context about the topic at hand, and then they cite these previously published papers in their bibliographies. Tracking down these sources is a good way to gain a sense of what the scholarly conversation is, and has been, about a subject. You may notice in your research of the scholarly literature that there are important dates mentioned in the conversation. That might be an opportunity to find out what the general public was saying about that new knowledge by tracking down newspapers or magazine articles. In this way, you can start to trace the historical outlines of the conversation around a topic.

**Table 4.2: Types of Evidence**

| Evidence | Author | Audience | Characteristics |
|---|---|---|---|
| Social media | Variable | General public, usually (popular) | Published within hours or days<br><br>May contain opinion or unverified information |
| Newspaper article | Journalist, usually | General public—can be local, national, or international (popular) | Published within hours or days<br><br>Need to evaluate for bias |
| Magazine article | Journalist or staff writer, usually | General public interested in the magazine's subject area (popular) | Published within weeks or months<br><br>Sometimes more context than newspaper article<br><br>Need to evaluate for bias |
| Scholarly article (academic, peer reviewed) | Scholars | Other scholars (scholarly) | Has gone through peer-review process<br><br>New information<br><br>Often very focused topics<br><br>Bibliographies |
| Academic book | Scholars | Other scholars<br><br>Sometimes general audiences | Has gone through editing and some review<br><br>University or academic publisher<br><br>More context than scholarly articles<br><br>Bibliographies |
| Reports and data by advocacy groups and agencies | Varies—some scholars, some government agencies, some interest groups | General public through academic or professional (may be popular or scholarly) | May be scholarly, may be biased, may be data sets<br><br>Requires evaluation |

In the **Citing and Integrating Sources** chapter, you learned a bit about distinguishing between popular and scholarly sources. The truth is, there are many different voices you may need to engage with when addressing a conversation, and they may not always fall neatly into "popular" and "scholarly" categories (Table 4.2). The important thing is to be aware of how and why a piece of information exists. Ask yourself the following questions as you decide which sources to include in your paper.

## GUIDING QUESTIONS FOR EVALUATING SOURCES

1.  Is the information **RELEVANT** to my topic? Does it further my understanding of important issues or provide me with a new perspective? If so, how?

2.  Who is the **AUDIENCE** for the information? Is it written for students, experts, people working in the field, the general public?

3.  What **AUTHORITY** does the author or organization have to provide information on the topic? What education, training, or experience do the authors have that qualifies them to write on this subject?

4.  What is the **PURPOSE** of the information? Is it to educate, to persuade, to convey factual information, to share opinions, to entertain?

5.  What **EVIDENCE** does the source include? If the piece is factual, what facts does the author include? Where do the facts come from? If it is an opinion piece, does the author offer sound reasons for his or her opinion?

6.  How **TIMELY** is the article? When was it written? Depending on the topic and the use you are making of it, some information becomes outdated when new information is available, but other sources that are fifty or one hundred years old can be relevant.

7.  Does the article include **REFERENCES**? Do the authors include citations to the sources they used?

8.  Is the information **BALANCED**? Do the authors or does the organization acknowledge alternative perspectives or do they include alternative viewpoints?

In the end, there is no magic checklist that tells you if a source is "good" or "bad." Instead, you should imagine that each source you are considering is a voice, and that you are making a choice of whether or not to include that voice in the conversation of your paper. To return to our detective/crime analogy, think of your sources as your "expert witnesses" that can help you support your case.

> **PRO TIP: RESEARCH AS YOU WRITE**
>
> As a librarian, I sometimes encounter students who write their paper first and then go hunting for evidence to support their argument. **This is a bad idea**. That would be like a detective trying to cherry-pick evidence to incriminate a particular person, rather than doing a real investigation. It also often leads to poorly written papers and panicked students trying to find the one magic (and often nonexistent) article that says a specific thing. Instead, gather a bunch of evidence first. Listen to what people are already saying about a topic, and then make a decision on when and how you are going to join in on the existing conversation. When you go to cite sources, you are choosing to highlight the voices that you think will best support and add context to your arguments.

## Finding Sources: Tools and Techniques

In this section, I will discuss some practical tools and techniques that you can use to hone your research skills. I would imagine that everyone already knows how to use a search engine like Google, or even Google Scholar. However, it's important to realize that a lot of information may not be available or may be difficult to find through Google. Reasons might include:

- The information is not free (e.g., it requires a subscription)
- The information is not online
- There is too much information on Google and not enough ways to sort through it

Make sure that you don't short-change yourself by only knowing how to use one tool—the library has a number of additional tools and databases that can help you find relevant information.

### Shopping for Sources

When thinking about research databases and tools, it's often helpful to think about shopping. There are some databases that are very specialized in one particular area (like a boutique store), and there are some databases that are more generalized. Some databases carry content that overlaps with other databases, similar to how some stores carry the same items as other stores.

Many students use Google Scholar (https://scholar.google.com/) to find sources. In our shopping analogy, Google Scholar is kind of like Amazon. It's huge, and carries a lot of things. But let's imagine that I'm looking to buy a sleeping bag. Can I buy one on Amazon? Sure. But depending on how much I already know about sleeping bags, I might be better off if I went to a store that specialized in camping equipment. Just being in that more limited environment might help me choose a better sleeping bag than if I had to randomly scroll through thousands of sleeping bags on Amazon. The same experience is true when searching for information.

The libraries try to make it easier for you to choose the correct database by organizing our resources into **Research Guides** (https://guides.lib.uci.edu/). If we continue our shopping analogy, these research guides are kind of like shopping centers for specific target audiences, meaning that you don't have to go looking everywhere for a particular store (in our case, a particular database). We have research guides for different subject areas, as well as research guides for specific classes. The Writing 39c research guide is prominently displayed at the top of the research guides page (Figure 4.2) (https://guides.lib. uci.edu/w39c).

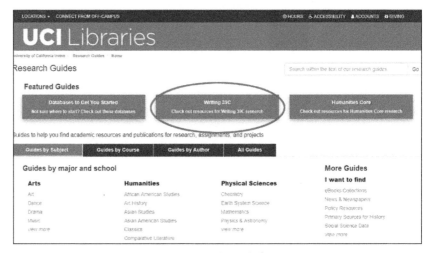

Figure 4.2: Research Guide for Writing 39c.

## Sources to Get Started

When you're just starting out, you can use some library topics databases or encyclopedias in addition to Google searching. Here are three of our favorites:

- CQ Researcher
- Opposing Viewpoints
- Global Issues in Context

These sources can help you develop a strong context for a topic, as well as identify related issues and keywords. They can also help you explore paths for advocacy and understand what individuals or groups are doing work in this topic area. All three of these databases are easily found on the front page of the Writing 39C research guide.

### *Library Search: Discover Books, Articles, and More*

Another easy place to start your research at UCI is to use **Library Search**, a powerful discovery system that searches for books, scholarly articles, news articles, media, and many other resources all at once. Library Search connects you to hundreds of library databases all at once and then lets you filter your results after you search. All you need to do to use Library Search is to enter your keywords into the big search box on the homepage of the UCI Libraries website (www.lib.uci.edu).

Library Search is the best way to discover books or e-books that are part of the UCI Libraries collection. Sometimes, students shy away from using books for their research ("they're too long!"). However, books are great sources when you are getting started with research. They provide overviews and background material and can help contextualize information about a subject. In other words, books can help you gain a broader understanding of what experts know and think about a subject. They can help you understand the historical dimensions of a topic and provide different ways of thinking about it.

## *Try This: Example Book Search*

*Let's walk through an example search for a book on the topic of "video games and violence." This is still a pretty broad topic, but let's start with that anyway. Notice these things about the screenshot below: (1) You are searching "almost everything," (2) You get over a hundred thousand results, and (3) You can refine your results using the filters on the left. Because we want to look for books, let's click on "Books" under the Resource Type section in the left-hand column (Figure 4.3). You may have to click "Show More" to expand the list if you don't see books listed right away.*

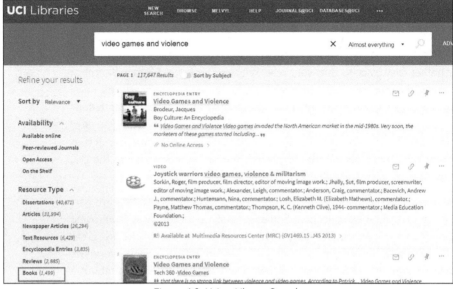

Figure 4.3: Using Library Search.

Use the Resource Type filter to limit your initial search to just books. After limiting your search to just books, you should select a title. Let's click on *Assassination Generation: Video Games, Aggression, and the Psychology of Killing* in order to see this screen (Figure 4.4).

Figure 4.4: Individual Book Record in Library Search

Let's take stock of what we see so far on this screen. We know these things so far:

1. The book has three authors.

2. It was published in 2016.

3. It is available in Langson Library and has a Call number of HQ784.V53 G76 2016. It does not look like there is a link to an online version of this book.

4. There are tools here that might help me cite this book or link to it later.

5. There's a hyperlink to "Call number locations."

Because this is a physical book on a shelf, we will need to go and find it. Click on the link to "Call number locations" to help you out. You will see a table that lists call number ranges, tells you what kinds of books are in that range, and what floor they are on (Figure 4.5).

| Langson Library Books | | |
|---|---|---|
| Call Number Range | Subjects | Floor plans |
| A | General Works | Basement Compact Shelving * |
| B | Philosophy, Religion, Psychology | Basement Compact Shelving * |
| C | General History | 1st floor |
| D-DS 299 | World History | 1st floor |
| DS 300-DX | World History | 3rd floor |
| E | History of the Americas | 3rd floor |
| F | History of the Americas | 3rd floor |
| G | Geography, Anthropology, Recreation | 3rd floor |
| H | Social Sciences | 3rd floor |
| J | Political Science | 3rd floor |
| K | Law | 3rd floor |
| L | Education | 3rd floor |

Figure 4.5: Call Number Locations

Books that start with the HQ call number range are in the social sciences, and are on the third floor of Langson Library. If you go to the third floor, you will find a printed map displayed by the elevator that details where specific call number ranges are on that floor. Then, you need to go to that section of the floor and find the call number range labeled on the ends of each row of books (Figure 4.6).

Figure 4.6: Rows of Books and Call Number Ranges.

The book *Assassination Generation* (Call Number HQ784.V53) will be somewhere in the row HQ774 – HQ799. Once you get in the row, you will need to find the specific book. This is why it's so important to make sure you have the entire call number with you.

## PRO TIP: LOCATING BOOKS ON THE LIBRARY SHELF

- The easiest way to make sure you have the full call number is to take a photo of it on the computer screen with your phone when you look it up.

- You can also email the full record to yourself, and check it on your phone when you're in the library.

- All of the call numbers are in alphanumeric order, meaning that you look for the location alphabetically first, and then they are arranged by number.

- Call numbers actually represent topic areas, so once you've found the book you're looking for, you should browse the titles of books nearby, as you are likely to find related titles. Many people find the "perfect book they didn't know they were looking for" by using this method.

Another way to find related books is to use the **Subject Headings** linked in a catalog record to find other books with the same subject. Subject headings work kind of like hashtags in social media, except that they are much better defined and less random. You can find subject headings toward the bottom

of the catalog record. Figure 4.7 shows some of the subject headings for
*Assassination Generation.*

| Subject | |
|---|---|
| | Violence in video games -- Psychological aspects > |
| | Children and violence -- Psychological aspects > |
| | Violence -- Social aspects > |
| | Violence -- Psychological aspects > |
| | Mass media and children > |
| | Television and children > |
| | Violence on television > |
| | Murder -- Psychological aspects > |
| | Child psychology > |
| | Violence in mass media -- Psychological aspects > |
| | Video games -- Social aspects > |
| | Video games -- Psychological aspects > |
| | Computer games -- Social aspects > |
| | Computer games -- Psychological aspects > |
| | Video games and children -- United States > |

Figure 4.7: Subject Headings in Library Search for *Assassination Generation.*

The book *Assassination Generation* has a number of subjects related to violence, media, and children. The subject headings are all hyperlinked, and
if you click on any of those links, you should see a listing of related books
and topics. For example, "Violence in video games—Psychological aspects"
might lead you to several additional books on the subject, and the broader
subject of "Video games—Psychological aspects" links you to over 700 additional titles.

## Finding Articles

Books are wonderful resources because they provide a lot of context for any
given topic and are usually written for a general audience. However, the vast
majority of scholarly research is not published in book form. Instead, most
scholars publish in academic (or "scholarly" or "peer-reviewed") journals.
These journal articles tend to be written for other scholars and can use very
academic and specialized language. This is one reason why scholarly articles
are not always good places to start your research—you may not understand
enough context to make sense of the article even if you take the time to read
it. However, once you have established a firm grasp of your topic through
initial background investigation (through using web resources, encyclopedia articles, resources like CQ Researcher, and through introductory chapters of books), scholarly articles can add further credibility to any argument
you are making in your paper by presenting validated, expert evidence.

There are a number of ways to find journal articles, and each method has
its pros and cons. Many students simply use Google Scholar to find articles.
Others might use Library Search and select "Articles" as a Resource Filter
instead of "Books." However, as previously mentioned, Google Scholar (and
also Library Search) have so much information that it can sometimes be

difficult to sift through the results to find something relevant—especially if you still have a fairly broad topic.

One of the most common places to start looking for journal articles is in a database called **Academic Search Complete**. It's probably the most generalized database we have, kind of like the Target of databases. It has a little bit of everything, so it's a good place to start. Also similarly to Target, it compiles articles and information with undergraduates in mind, meaning that you are less likely to be hit with scholarly articles that assume you already have a PhD in order to understand the content.

### Academic Search Complete: Search Techniques and Tools

If you don't already have the title of a journal article in mind, your best bet is to start by keyword searching. The important thing to remember is that choosing good keywords takes time and effort. If you try a search and don't find anything, don't find what you expect, or find way too many things, think more carefully about your research topic or question and the keywords you chose to represent the ideas you are thinking about.

## Try This: Example Article Search

*Let's walk through another example, this time on the topic of "homelessness." Imagine that you have already conducted some background research on CQ Researcher and Google, and have started to wonder what happens to the children of families who are poor and face eviction or homelessness. It occurs to you that kids who are forced to move around a lot probably do not perform as well academically. You start to form a topic around the notion of homelessness and performance in schools.*

Before you start typing into a database search box, you might do a quick inventory of your search terms. Databases often work better if you keep your searches organized by concepts, and if you can identify some synonyms for each concept (Table 4.3).

**Table 4.3: Create Search Terms by Separating Concepts and Finding Synonyms**

|  | Concept 1: Homelessness | Concept 2: Performance in schools |
|---|---|---|
| **Synonyms** | Homeless people<br>Homeless children | Academic performance<br>Academic achievement<br>Academic success<br>School success |

You can start to put these concepts into Academic Search Complete's search boxes (Figure 4.8).

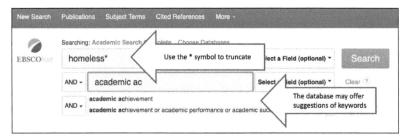

Figure 4.8: Searching in Academic Search Complete

Here are a couple of other strategies: First, you can to use a truncation symbol (*) so that the database will search everything that starts with "homeless…" (this includes homelessness, homeless children, etc.). Then, in your second search box, you can have the database suggest some synonyms for your search, and then allow it to autofill the box.

When you hit "Search," your results might look like those in Figure 4.9.

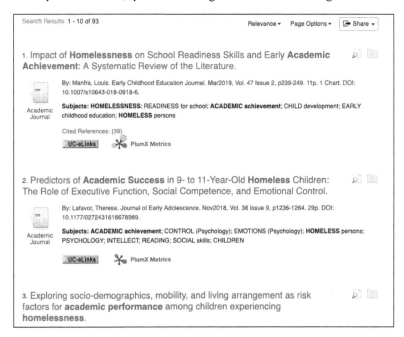

Figure 4.9: Academic Search Complete Results

At this point, it's helpful to stop and reflect. What kinds of search results are you getting? How many results do you have? Is it possible that you are including or excluding conversations based on the keywords you chose?

Look at the subject terms that come up. Do your keywords match any of the subject terms? If they do, it might be wise to actually click on one of the subject terms and use that instead of one of the keywords you initially came up with.

If you scroll through a couple pages of search results, you may notice other ways you can refine your search. For example, you might notice that one of the articles listed in your first page of search results mentions "McKinney-Vento Identified Youth." You might then Google "McKinney-Vento" and discover that the McKinney-Vento Homeless Assistance Act is a federal program that provides funding to states that ensure that homeless children receive transportation and the right to attend a school without interruption regardless of what district the child may temporarily reside in while experiencing homelessness.

At this point, you can make a decision: Do you want to keep searching using your original keywords, or do you want to shift your focus to research surrounding the McKinney-Vento act? This is an example of how one initial search can lead you to other scholarly conversations that you can follow. Remember that research is usually not a straight path; it is natural to do several rounds of searching as you refine your research project.

Once you find an article that looks promising, you should click on it to get more detail (Figure 4.10).

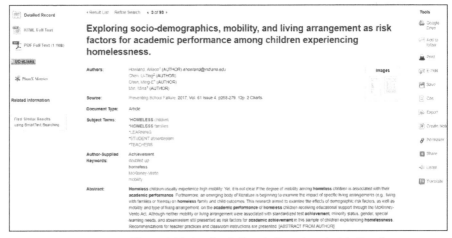

Figure 4.10: Academic Search Complete Article Detail

First, read the abstract to make sure that the article is relevant. Note things like the date of publication, and the title of the journal in which the article is published. Notice also that there is a suite of tools available to you from this database, including tools that may help you cite the article or email it to yourself for future reference. You can also use the "permalink" tool to generate a stable URL to this article so you can come back to it later. In the left column, you may see a linked PDF with the full text of the article. If you don't, you should still see a yellow **"UC eLinks"** button, which will help you locate this article online or in print.

## Once I Find Evidence, What Do I Do?

At some point, you will have gathered a fair amount of evidence, finding relevant voices in the conversation on a topic. Your goal now is to put the voices in conversation with each other, and think about how you are going to add your voice to it. You should be organizing your thoughts and creating outlines of the materials you want to cover and include. You should begin pre-writing—jotting down ideas that come to you or important ideas you want to highlight—without polishing your prose or worrying much about spelling or grammar. The important thing is to put words on a page, so that your thoughts start to take a concrete form.

After you have started to synthesize your thoughts and evidence together, you may want to revisit your research topic or question. Has it evolved in the course of your writing? If so, how? Don't be alarmed if you realize that your original argument has changed or if you find that you still have some areas you need to investigate further. Remember, you are like a detective. Once you have gathered evidence and started to put them together, you may start to see patterns and ideas emerge that you hadn't considered before. It is much better to let your evidence lead your argument than it is for you to stick with an original idea and then cherry-pick evidence to try to support it.

## Need Help? Ask Us!

Remember that librarians are here to help you during any stage of the research process. You can drop by the library, chat with us virtually, schedule a one-on-one appointment, or email us your questions!

https://www.lib.uci.edu/ask-librarian-reference-services

## CHAPTER 5

# Drafting and Crafting

*By Emily Brauer Rogers*

I'm Emily Brauer Rogers, Online and Instructional Technologies Coordinator. I have an MFA in Dramatic Writing. That doesn't mean that I write overdramatically, but instead that I'm interested in conflict—particularly the way it's structured in playwriting and screenwriting. This love of conflict is also why I enjoy teaching argumentative writing and critical thinking: I can help students explore multiple perspectives on issues. I've worked with many students as they craft their papers for various assignments in the Writing 39 series. This chapter will give you some tools to use as you begin to draft your essays and fulfill whatever purpose your writing assignment may ask of you.

## So You Have a Paper Due...

Where do you start? Do you picture yourself thinking about what you have to write, writing it (perhaps proofreading it), and then turning it in? You might see writing a paper like a race—straight from the beginning to the end. However, thinking about writing as a linear process really isn't the most productive way to draft a paper. Writing is more cyclical or, even better, like a spider's web where you have to move back and forth between the elements to refine your message.

Discovering your own process is crucial. We called this chapter Drafting and Crafting because while it's true that writing is an art, writing is also something you design (like drawing up plans for a house) or build (like crafting a piece of furniture). You don't need to follow these steps in the order given here, but if you're going to use this chapter practically, you should probably consider each element as you get ready to tackle it in your paper.

## Invention

Before you can begin to write, you have to begin to think. Invention is the first stage in most writing tasks: that process of gathering ideas, understanding your task, figuring out what you think and feel.

Why should you prewrite? Isn't it just easier and faster to get to the "real" writing? You need a place to explore and invent, and focusing too early on thesis and paragraph construction can prevent that necessary exploration from ever happening. Without it, papers can lack the depth and insight that is required from college writing. The more you invest in this step, the better the results can be when you start putting the paper together.

### PRO TIP: STRATEGIES FOR INVENTION

- **Reread** the prompt.
- **Make annotations** of your assigned reading or of researched material. (See Chapter 2, "Practicing Critical Reading," for how to use your assigned reading to raise questions.)
- **Ask questions** and discuss with your instructor and your peers.
- **Brainstorm** lists of ideas or research leads.
- **Freewrite** some casual but focused explorations of a particular point.
- **Research** additional evidence or for someone else's points to argue with.

When you're thinking through ideas, they don't always come out in an eloquently crafted way. In fact, they rarely do. (And for those who say their writing process works like this, we secretly hate them.) This part of the process needs to be messy while you're getting your thoughts onto the page by any means possible. Don't judge your writing at this point—instead allow yourself freedom; the evaluation of what you write can come later.

### Brainstorming

Starting to write is always the most difficult part, and it's almost impossible if the topic lacks value for the author. There is nothing more crucial than finding a subject that matters to you. The composition process is always more marathon than sprint, so being invested in the topic from the beginning helps when trying to muster the inertia needed to get it going.

Ideally, if you're writing about something that is of consequence to you, then you will have many thoughts on the subject—often even more than you realized until you write them down. Using a brainstorm as an initial invention exercise allows the writer to meander through ideas easily, given that the goal is to merely flood the paper with as many ideas on the subject as you can imagine. When brainstorming, try to avoid making connections between ideas right away. Let as varied a range of concepts get out of your mind and onto the paper as possible.

Once you've jotted down as many ideas as you can, then pull back and think about the subject more broadly, not just as constitutive concepts. Is there any one aspect that you seem to have more ideas about already? Do you see some sort of argument unfolding just based on how you have spread your thinking out in front of you? Make connections between the concepts and draw lines that you can follow. This step is called clustering and it's essentially like looking up at the sky at night and drawing your own set of constellations.

## Clustering

Clustering is a type of free association that often looks like a spider's web (Figure 5.1). It allows you to start with a topic or main idea and then build additional ideas from this by showing relationships to the other topic bubbles. This might be a particularly good way of looking at papers that talk about cause and effect or process because it allows a writer to start making those connections.

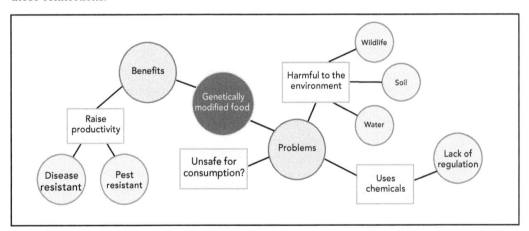

Figure 5.1

With a mapping of ideas, you can now begin to unpack the relationships between them in sentences—explaining with greater detail what links several ideas and how these linkages represent some aspect of your overall aims.

This method can then be repeated multiple times throughout the process of crafting your composition. Especially as you look more deeply into your subject matter, you will develop a broader range of concepts at your disposal, relationships between ideas and thinkers will newly manifest, and your grasp of the nuances of the argument will strengthen.

### Images

If you're a visual person, images might serve as a better way to process your ideas. You can make a storyboard that presents a narrative or argument visually. This is often used in film so that the visuals can be organized along with the writing. Similar to a storyboard is a comic strip, which can present a similar argument and can highlight dialogue from the scholars that you're using. There are a multitude of online programs that allow you to easily create storyboards and comic strips.

If you feel that you like the idea of images or illustrating relationships while exploring ideas but don't want to rely on stick figures, you might use presentation software to organize your thoughts. Tools such as Prezi or PowerPoint can be used to brainstorm your thoughts.

### Discussion

For some writers, the best way to think through topics and prompts is to discuss them with others. Consider bouncing ideas off of your friends, colleagues, classmates, or family to get multiple perspectives on the topic and to refine your points. They may question you, ask for clarification, and help develop your stronger ideas. Even if there isn't much response, talking through these ideas can help you to refine your purpose and message.

### Using Alternative Genres

Starting a paper can be daunting, especially if we feel unsure about how to express our ideas in an academic genre. However, this should not prevent us from getting started: it can be useful to think about these in genres that you use to write every day such as tweets, blogs, emails, and Facebook posts. So perhaps you decide that you're going to inform your friends about a topic or issue through a series of Facebook posts. Or maybe you want to write an email to a close friend about what bothers you about a particular social problem. This allows you to take ownership, be creative, and avoid being too precious with your writing. While you can use these pieces as a private prewriting exercise, you might even send or post your thoughts and see what type of responses you receive.

Here's one example of a writer brainstorming using an alternative genre about his writing process.

# Sample: Brainstorm

*@Emily: Mostly no one gets a perfect essay on his first try. Practice makes perfect. #MultipleDrafts*

*I learned that having multiple drafts are okay because they keep improving as you keep working on them. It's not a bad thing if you don't get your exact idea or topic right the first time and just to keep trying until it improves. Not everyone gets that one perfect essay on the first try, but it is okay because you can gain knowledge to what works and what doesn't. The process can be time consuming, but it is all worth it in the end when the essay improves enormously.*

*@Emily: It is important to organize your thoughts when writing an essay. #Brainstorm*

*On my previous attempts on writing an essay, I always used to skip the step of brainstorming before I actually start writing the essay. I learned that was a huge mistake on my part because that assists you in organizing and coming up with ideas for your essay. If the step is skipped, the essay will lack the right structure and it will be all over the place. It also prevents any repeating of previous thoughts already put in the essay when writing it.*

*@Emily: Peer reviews are an essential part in writing an essay. #GroupWork*

*In almost every day in being in the class, we would work in groups to either correct our essays or come up with a good idea. In the past, I never allowed people to read my essays except the teacher or professor who was grading it. Now I learned that other people have great ideas and that they know how to correct the essay just as well as anyone else. Group work benefits everyone in the group by making everyone improve in the way they write and see different types of ways other people write. This is another form of revising. Like Fitzgerald, multiple revision of one's essay can only bring benefits and make it better.*

## Drafting 101

At some point in the process, you'll have to jump in and write. That may mean thinking about how to organize your message into discrete parts or divide your ideas into paragraphs.

In order to understand how to organize your points, you need to know what your purpose is. You have to figure out what you're trying to accomplish so you can determine the best method to achieve this purpose. For instance, if you want to inform your readers about the results of a lab experiment, a report that clearly states the facts is probably the best method. However, if you want to make a persuasive argument about the solution to the lack of foreign language classes in Californian high schools, an argumentative essay seems more appropriate.

You have to know if you're trying to express, inform, or persuade. While there can be other purposes, these are three of the more common ones that you'll use in your academic writing. Once you know what purpose you have and what message you want to communicate to your audience, you can select the most appropriate genre for your purpose.

If you need a refresher on genre, go back and review Chapter 1, "Introducing Rhetoric and Genre," to help you make a clear plan for your essay.

### Building a Structure

Once you're clear on both your purpose and the genre expectations, you can use this knowledge to determine how to structure your paper. Frameworks, or methods of organization, can help you begin constructing your argument.

There are many ways to structure papers, but you may use some of these common approaches to provide scaffolding for your argument.

### COMMON ORGANIZATIONAL FRAMEWORKS

- **Compare/Contrast:** compares two or more items in order to analyze and make an argumentative point about the items being compared

- **Problem/Solution:** defines a problem and suggests a solution or several possible solutions

- **Cause/Effect:** looks at the determining factors of a particular outcome

- **Chronological:** considers events in order according to when they happened

- **Analytical:** breaks down the whole into pieces so that the pieces can reveal a point about the bigger picture

- **Argumentative:** proves a larger claim with smaller individual claims

## Try This: Map Genre Structures

*Examine models in your genre and map how they structure their arguments. What is the purpose of each paragraph? How does the reader move through the points that the author is making? This can give you a framework that you may be able to follow for your own paper.*

### Outlining Your Ideas

While you may have dreaded those formal outlines with Roman numerals that you had to do in middle school or high school (I certainly did), outlining can serve a purpose in organizing a draft. However, you have to think about your writing process and whether or not outlining will serve you better before or after a draft.

If you are the type of writer that needs to have ideas organized beforehand, then outlining prior to a draft is probably for you. It can be a formal outline if you like that sort of thing, but it can also be a sketch outline of topics or claims. It can be a topic sentence outline with full sentences and evidence included under each paragraph. You should take the information that you have from your prewriting and planning and use whatever method you feel might suit you best.

## Try This: List Individual Claims

*At the top of a piece of paper, write your message and purpose. Then, list individual claims that you want to use to prove your message. These ideas can then be made into complete topic sentences that fulfill your message and purpose.*

### Outlining After Your Draft

You might be thinking, why in the world would I need to outline after a draft? I have a completed draft—this is just more work. If you aren't sure about the organization of a particular paper, outlining after a draft is a great way to check for the soundness of the structure.

## Try This: Summarize Your Argument

*Copy and paste your thesis and topic sentences into a separate document. Then read through your shortened argument. By just reading the topic sentences, you should have a clear summary of your argument. You can then decide if you need to move around topic sentences (and paragraphs) for clarity.*

## Crafting Your Message and Thesis

Just as outlining can be a tool that you use before or after a draft, a thesis can also be developed before or after a draft. Some writers feel that they have to have their message completely mapped out before they can continue with paragraphs, while others find their message and argument as they write.

You might be a little puzzled by this as you may have been taught that you must have the thesis before you can write any other part of the paper. However, if you think about it, a thesis can also be more of a hypothesis—a claim that you're testing and comparing the evidence to in order to see if your original claim suffices or perhaps if it leads you to an alternative conclusion. You might choose to do this for a larger question or two that you want to address rather than having a clear-cut answer already at the beginning.

You should start to analyze your writing process and see what the best way for you to write is, and if you feel that you struggle with one technique, you should try the other to see if it makes more sense in terms of your own writing process. Either way, the process is recursive, meaning that you have to keep moving between paragraphs and your thesis to check that they reflect the same point.

If you choose to wait to find your thesis, you still want to make sure that you have a clear purpose for writing. Think about what you want your audience to get from reading your paper. Then as you write, you'll be able to refine your message based on your original purpose. As you write, you might discover that your thesis should live in the first paragraph to guide the rest of your paper or perhaps it ends up near the conclusion to show how you've come to this overall argument. You should consider what works best for the organization and argument through several drafts.

To learn more about building arguments, visit Chapter 6, "I Came Here for an Argument."

For all thesis statements, you do want to make sure that you have a clear topic, position on the topic, and reasons for that position. You might also include a qualifier that can help limit your thesis or connect to counterarguments you'll address in the paper.

In your revisions, you'll want to continue to check that your claims build to your thesis and that your thesis clearly addresses the claims throughout the paper.

You also want to consider the structure of your paper and revise the thesis so that it indicates the argument in your paper. For instance, if your counterargument will be last in your paper, you may want to move the qualifier to the end of the thesis. If you want to examine an effect and then the causes, you'll need to indicate this in your thesis. These steps give you a starting point for a thesis but not the end result. Remember, in college, you're expected not to repeat arguments that have been made, but instead to gather and add your own insight to existing ideas. Your thesis should reflect this complexity as well.

## Crafting Paragraphs

At some point in your process, you're going to need to think about paragraphs. We all know what a paragraph looks like on the page, but it may be harder to define what a paragraph is. In the simplest terms, a paragraph is a unit of thought, a mini-argument. Each paragraph has its own purpose and claim within the larger framework of an argument.

Each sentence in a paragraph likewise serves a specific purpose in advancing the argument. The **topic sentence** clearly lays out the claims that will be explored in the rest of the paragraph. It should be linked to the previous paragraph by some concept that was introduced near the end of the previous paragraph. Following the initial claim in the topic sentence, **support** from authorities in the field will be needed to underpin that aspect of the argument. Support, however, is not always immediately agreeing with the overall claims of the argument. It is necessary to unfold the argument through the presentation and subsequent destruction of **counterarguments**. In any case, the support should then be connected both to the immediate claims of the paragraph in which it appears and to its broad implications within the argument. *Paragraphs should rarely end with a quote. There must always be some sort of interpretation of the ideas to insure their effective integration into the argument.*

Every single paragraph except for the last one should have a **transition**, that is, a specific idea that compels the reader to continue with the process of understanding the argument. It is important to show the reader that your ideas connect logically and build upon each other. To that end, you also need to think about transitions within paragraphs and how each sentence connects and has a relationship to the one before it.

## Sample: Paragraph

Here's an example of a paragraph written by 39C student, Devin Yaeger, that has a clear topic sentence, strong support, good analysis, transitions, and a purpose sentence:

> *During the era of free trade initiatives and economic prosperity, the Dominican Republic paradoxically cut social spending, compounding the humanitarian strife that led impoverished women into sex work. The low level of government welfare spending, both a historical precedent and a product of the 1980s trade induced austerity measures, is remarkable in Latin America. Whereas other Hispanic nations possess varying degrees of socialist parties and policy, the DR is nearly devoid of left wing political entities due to a long history of the military and social elites suppressing labor movements (Goldfrank 451; Ondetti 49). Gabriel Ondetti, an academic in the field of political science, documents the pitiful amount of social spending the government allocates toward the poor. He deduces that in almost all categories of public welfare spending, from education to healthcare to pension funds, the DR lags behind the rest of Latin America, spending per capita significantly less than even severely impoverished nations such as Honduras and Guatemala (49–51). The lack of social welfare programs deprives Dominicans, including the 40% segment of the population who live below the poverty line, of any social safety net (World Bank). This reality is a significant contributor to women choosing the profession of sex work, a decision of their own free will, as a means to provide healthcare, education, and economic security to their children—the very elements that the government has neglected to provide. As tourism to the Dominican Republic expanded in conjunction with the improved economy, the government made little improvement to these welfare deficits.*

### QUESTIONS TO ASK WHEN ANALYZING PARAGRAPHS

As you read the previous paragraph, consider the following:

1. *What's the argument of this paragraph?*
2. *What evidence or support does the writer provide for that argument?*
3. *Where do you see the writer's own analysis of the evidence? What kinds of conclusions does the writer reach that go beyond merely reporting fact?*

You can also use this to check for the soundness of your own paragraphs.

## Using Sources for Support

Often your support will come in the form of texts that provide credibility. You might not have sufficient credibility to convince your audience directly, so you have to appeal to other authorities to give power to your ideas and increase the likelihood that your audience will agree.

If you're having trouble writing your commentary about the evidence you're using, think about why you chose that quote in the first place. What is it that you want your reader to understand about the quote? Why did you choose to include it? What's important to your argument? If you can't answer these questions, maybe you don't need the quotation.

## Crafting Analysis

Analysis is one of the most important modes of composition for college. The word "**analysis**" generally means dividing something into components, carefully scrutinizing each one, and then seeing how the parts relate to the whole. In an analysis, you break the object of analysis into parts, you closely look at each part (you define, you describe, you summarize), and then you synthesize this information to say something about how the parts work together to produce the whole. In other words, analysis is about describing the relationship between the parts of something and the whole.

Analysis isn't easy, and it takes practice to do it well. The good news is that you've been practicing for a good portion of your life. If you've ever predicted the ending to a movie or a television show, you've practiced critical analysis. What you are picking up on is not so much the content of the story (what the story is about), but its formal aspects (how the story is presented). By the time you are experienced enough to be able to figure out how a story line will end, your analysis tends to be so quick that you are not aware of it as a process at all.

Before you think you will leave all analysis behind when you get out of college, there are whole professions dedicated to nothing but analysis. Systems analysts determine the computer systems and software for a business's particular needs. A business analyst figures out what a client needs and how best to meet those needs. An industry analyst sifts through data and predicts market trends. And of course, a psychoanalyst investigates the underlying, unconscious causes for human behavior and formulates treatment and therapy based on those causes.

## Planning Your Analysis

Academic analysis is a more deliberate version of the same analytical process you use every day. Like all the modes of development discussed in this chapter, it's a way to develop your topic in order to make a critically informed

In order to integrate this evidence correctly and appropriately into you papers, you'll want to see Chapter 3, "Citing and Integrating Sources," about the proper techniques for source integration.

argument about it. Academic analysis can take many different forms. The process you use to craft your analysis will depend, in large part, on your focus and purpose. No matter what the object of your analysis, there are certain steps you must take before you even begin.

### THE FOUR STEPS TO ANALYSIS

1. *Understand the "big picture."*

2. *Break down and select parts of the text you want to examine.*

3. *Describe your selections carefully, including their significance.*

4. *Describe how those parts interrelate to create the "big picture."*

### QUESTIONS TO ASK WHEN PERFORMING ANALYSIS

1. *What is the text's primary message? Is there a scene, sentence, or passage that sums up that primary or controlling idea? How do titles or headings hint at or sum up the message?*

2. *What seem to be the text's primary and secondary purposes? Persuasive? Expressive? Stylistic? Informative?*

3. *Who is the target audience of the text? What textual evidence and other clues suggest that this is the primary target audience? Are there any secondary or additional audiences to consider?*

4. *Has an editor provided introductory notes to the text, and if so, what further information do the notes offer about the text's thesis, audience, and purpose? What research could I do to better understand the author's rhetorical situation?*

## Crafting a Summary Paragraph

**Summary** is a widely used rhetorical tool that isn't limited to book reports and essay exams. Everywhere around us, we can find summary being used to communicate ideas: movie commercials and theater trailers often tease audiences with just enough plot and character information to inspire interest, while the reviewers who critique these films provide synopses that help illustrate the films' strengths and weaknesses. Academic articles are often preceded by abstracts, outlining the whole argument in a few sentences.

However, effective summaries aren't just a random collection of high points. A good summary can (and often does) serve a greater purpose than simply providing a quick overview of the text. The best summaries arrange information around a specific rhetorical goal, often dictated by the purpose, genre, and audience of the particular text.

*Knowing the Purpose of Your Summary*

Summaries usually focus on the most important elements of a text, but what's important is often dependent on what the summary is trying to accomplish. "Previously on..."-style synopses for TV shows don't revisit every character and plot point in the show's history; they usually include only the information and events that are vital to understanding the episode you're about to watch.

Often the genre of the text will dictate the information that can or should be included in the summary. A film review may give a plot synopsis in order to analyze its good and bad aspects, but will almost never give away its ending, since the purpose of a film review is to help readers decide if they want to see the movie. Academic articles often contain another form of summary called an abstract, a brief paragraph containing the writer's primary argument, along with a brief description of its main supporting points. After reading such an article, you may be required to write an annotation in your Working Bibliography, very briefly summarizing the article's purpose, audience, and usefulness in the field.

All of these forms of summary change the information they include based on audience. Movie previews for an action film might spend less time outlining the plot and more time on the shootouts, car chases, and explosions. The audience of a romantic comedy, on the other hand, might be drawn to time spent on the characters and the conflict that keeps them apart.

When composing a summary for your own work, keep in mind not only what your readers want to know, but also what they might need to know. If your reader is unfamiliar with the text you're analyzing, your summary may need to be more comprehensive. Or your instructor may direct you to assume the reader is familiar with the text, so you need only to summarize in order to situate the reader in your argument, to support and develop your point.

In the following example, the student's purpose was to provide an example within her glossary definition of the term **imagery** for the audience of her fellow 39B students. The student uses a text from the class, so she knows her readers are familiar with it. Her summary is light-handed because of this: she's using quotation in her summary just to orient the reader in the text so she can make her real point about one type of imagery. This is a common purpose of summary: using it as a setup for your own analysis.

## Sample: Summary

*An example of auditory imagery can be seen in* Sandman: The Dream Hunters *when "the fox strained to hear another word, but there was nothing." She wants to hear a more human sound, but "all she could hear was*

*the whisper of the wind as it stirred the fallen leaves, the sighing of the trees as they breathed and swayed in the wind, and the distinct ting ting of the wind chimes in the little temple." The peace of the sounds the fox hears after eavesdropping on the conversation of the creatures she comes across signifies the finality of the monk's fate. Instead of hearing what she wants to hear, the fox hears only the peace of the countryside, which serves to worsen, rather than alleviate, her anxiety. The auditory imagery makes the moment more vivid.*

### QUESTIONS TO ASK WHEN WRITING SUMMARIES

1. *Why am I summarizing?*

2. *Which details should I select for inclusion?*

3. *Is the summary accurate? Comprehensive enough for my purpose?*

## Crafting Examples

The concept of "learning by example" isn't new to you. Such learning begins when we are children and continues throughout our lives. We make use of examples every day—in conversations, in emails, in class—and our understanding is enhanced by the practical use of examples. Say, for instance, you wish to rent a room in a hotel; you might go to the website and view a sample room so as to get a better idea of the amenities. Similarly, when it comes to your writing, appropriate examples can help your audience understand your message or concept. Your choice of example should reflect your awareness of your audience and purpose.

### Knowing the Purpose of Your Examples

Aristotle defined rhetoric as the ability, in each particular case, to see the available means of persuasion. Successful rhetoric, then, will require you to choose and to use the right example at the right time. Examples can take many forms, but whatever form they take, their success or failure as support depends upon their suitability to a given rhetorical situation. In your classes at UCI, you will encounter a wide range of rhetorical situations; in each instance it will be up to you, as rhetor, to determine which examples will resonate most effectively with your context, purpose, and audience.

When choosing examples for a given argument you must always ask yourself why you feel that example will be beneficial to your argument and how it will enhance your audience's understanding. If the idea you are discussing is complex, perhaps a simple, expository example would be most beneficial. For example, "America is like a salad bowl: individual ethnic groups come together in one place, yet maintain their cultural uniqueness."

On the other hand, perhaps you wish to complicate your audience's understanding of an idea or challenge biases; an example may do that as well. For instance:

> *While we tend to think of pre-1960s Hollywood films as very conservative in their portrayals of women, before the censorship guidelines of the Hays Code were put into effect in 1934, women were frequently portrayed on camera, in films such as The Divorcee and Blonde Venus, as assertive, street-smart and sexually uninhibited individuals.*

An example can be anything that increases understanding of an idea. In academic arguments, supporting evidence can come in the form of images, graphics, quotations, summaries, or paraphrases from the text you are analyzing. This means that assertions in academic writing need to be supported, illustrated, and developed through the use and subsequent analysis of specific examples.

Like choosing which elements to focus on for a summary, choosing which examples will best illustrate an idea is a complex and important decision—one you can only get better at making with time and practice.

When choosing examples for a given argument you must always ask yourself why you feel that example will be beneficial to your argument and how it will enhance your audience's understanding.

Consider the following example, from a Rhetorical Analysis essay on the great Hindu poem, *The Bhagavad Gita*.

## Sample: Use of an Example

> *The omission of conjunctions provides Krishna with authority and control of his message. Through this technique, the translator is capable of reformulating the appeal of Krishna's message through the direct style of Krishna's voice.*

To support her point, the student must choose the best possible example, one that not only supports her point, but the point of the poem as well. The lines are simple, but the student's point is both illustrated and supported by it:

> *Knowing the Self, sustaining*
> *the self by the Self, Arjuna,*
> *kill the difficult-to-conquer*
> *enemy called desire.*

| QUESTIONS TO ASK WHEN USING EXAMPLES |

1. *What kinds of examples would be appropriate for my point?*

2. *How many examples should I use? Do I show a variety of examples that may support my point?*

3. *Am I choosing the best possible examples from the text?*

4. *Do I adequately set up and analyze the example in light of my point?*

## Crafting Introductions

Introductions serve several purposes in your paper. First, they are there to entice the reader into actually reading the entire paper. So, in your introduction, you want to find a way to hook the reader into your topic as well as show them why it is important for them to learn more about this topic. Your introduction also serves as a way to provide context for the reader to understand your argument. This is where you provide enough information for them to understand the issue that you're writing about and the reason for writing about it. Several strategies can help you introduce your topic and hook your reader into your paper.

### Anecdote

An anecdote is a quick story (whether it is fact or fiction depends on your genre) to describe the context and issue to the reader. Because it heavily relies on description, it allows the reader to relate and even empathize with the situation at hand.

### *Sample: Introductory Anecdote*

*"AHHHHHHHH!" Everyone zoomed past me riding X-2. The trembling noise of metal clashing against metal vibrates through my body, shaking every part of me. Suddenly, I thought to myself, is this true happiness? Is our pursuit of happiness the little things that make us scream and laugh and not the full journey?*

### Statistic

A statistic can be an effective way to illustrate the importance of the issue you're writing about. This quickly allows the reader to understand the reason why you're writing and can draw them in if this is a surprising or shocking statistic.

## Sample: Introductory Statistic

*For over a century, child prostitution in Thailand has become an overwhelming problem plaguing the country due to poverty and lack of education. According to Lisa Taylor from the Coordinator of the Regional Counter-Trafficking Foundation, Thailand has been ranked within the Tier 2 by the U.S. Department of State in the 2011 Trafficking in Persons Report, which indicates that the country has a significant child prostitution problem. It is estimated that over 800,000 children are currently working in the lucrative sex industry that generates roughly 37% of Thailand's GDP generating $22 million of the country's GDP. However, some citizens still live in extreme poverty while others reap the luxurious benefits of the thriving business of prostitution.*

### Example

While you usually want to save your best example for the body of your paper, you can start with your second best example to explore it and indicate how it illustrates the message that you'll be arguing.

## Sample: Introductory Example

*The doorbell of a dim erotic massage parlor breaks the silence on a frigid night in San Francisco, California. The customer is greeted at the door by an elderly woman and escorted inside as the massage parlor manager searches for any sign that he could be part of law enforcement. In another room is the slight pitter patter of a dozen oriental [sic] masseuses positioning themselves and getting ready to be selected. They wait nervously, keeping their eyes on the ground, and hopelessly awaiting their fate. With over ninety sex-for-sale massage parlors stretching across San Francisco, according to myredbook.com, this customer is sure to be the first of many during the night (May).*

*Strategies to Avoid*

There are several strategies that you may have used in the past that aren't good ways to begin a paper. First, you may have been told to start broadly and move to a specific topic. While this can work, you don't want to start too broadly such as "Throughout history." You need to be in the same ballpark as the topic that you're discussing. Similarly, you don't want to use quotes that you find on a quotation website that are vaguely related. If you want to use a quote, it should be from a source close to your topic. And in some cases, a definition of a term or issue is necessary in the introduction, but you don't want to find a dictionary definition online and quote that—instead it is better to build your own definition with research and analysis.

Once you've hooked your reader, you have to move toward your message and/or thesis. But what's supposed to be in between the hook and thesis? Again, go back to your purpose—you need to give enough information so the reader understands where you're coming from and where you're going in order to then understand the message.

## Try This: Setting the Scene

*Consider how movies introduce you to their stories—through movie trailers. How do movie trailers quickly bring you into the world they're creating? They set tone and mood through music and sound. They quickly flash through the main points and present the dilemma that the characters are going to face. For this exercise, describe what a movie trailer for your introduction would look like. What music would you use to set the mood? What images would you show and why? How would you present the dilemma of the paper? What would entice your reader to read the whole paper? Once you've thought about these issues cinematically, think about how you can then transfer this to your writing. For instance, can you describe an important location in full detail? Or can you show particular characters/scholars facing off against each other? How do you show each position? See if you can translate this to an introductory paragraph.*

## Crafting Conclusions

Conclusions also serve a particular purpose and that purpose isn't just to repeat your thesis or what you've already written in the paper. You may have heard the advice "Restate your thesis," but you don't want to repeat yourself. Here are better questions to ask when considering how to conclude your essay.

## QUESTIONS TO ASK WHEN WRITING CONCLUSIONS

1.  *What are the larger implications of this argument? Remind the reader how this argument is connected to a larger conversation in the academy or in the world.*

2.  *Is it important to get your readers to care about this argument? Perhaps you could do that by asking your readers a probing question or by giving them a lasting image.*

3.  *Does this argument demand a call to action? If so, make it clear what that action is and how your reader can get involved.*

You'll have to analyze your writing genre and see how other writers conclude their arguments (with a question, an image, a quote, a warning, a universal statement, or a summary of results).

In general, if you can show the reader why this topic and issue matters, then you can successfully conclude your paper.

## Revising Your Draft

Once you have a fairly solid draft, it's time to start moving to revision. Revision requires you to shift from being a writer to being an editor. You have to actually re-see the paper from a different viewpoint. In order to do this, you need to look at your paper as a whole as well as in smaller parts.

### Global Revision

Global revision requires you to look at the big picture elements of your paper, which normally include argument and organization. You want to check your thesis and topic sentences when you're looking at your argument and make sure that they fit together. You want to check your evidence to see that it supports the claims that you're making.

Check out Chapter 6, "I Came Here for an Argument," for more specifics about making your argument sound.

You also want to make sure that your organization is appropriate for the genre. This might also be a place to use a reverse outline so you can look at paragraph order.

## HOW TO APPROACH REVISION

▷ *The more time you give yourself between drafts, the easier it is to come back to the paper as an editor.*

▷ *Leave yourself next steps before you quit writing, so that when you next sit down to work, you won't waste time remembering what you were doing or what you meant to say.*

> ▶ *Remember that you are always writing to one person at a time. Reading is fairly private: there's a real person at the other end of the page, and your end goal is to communicate your ideas in a way that person can understand.*

## Paragraph Revision

Once you've revised the larger issues of your paper, you want to look at how each paragraph works on its own.

### PARAGRAPH REVISION CHECKLIST

- Do all of the ideas work together within the paragraph? Which ones may need to be revised to make their purpose and message clearer?
- Does the evidence support my claims?
- Are any ideas separate and need to be cut or moved to another paragraph?
- Have you made your sentences work together through transitions?

## Proofreading

This might be the aspect of revision that you're most familiar with. However, proofreading is looking at the small stuff—grammar and mechanics. While it is very important, you don't want to do this until you've fixed the larger issues in the paper. As you proofread, make sure you also look at the citations and properly format your paper accordingly.

**PRO TIP: PROOFREADING**

- **Read the paper aloud.** Hearing the paper allows you to see what you stumble on and what flows well. You can make adjustments when the words and sentences don't flow smoothly.

- **Read the paper backward—no, not word by word, but sentence by sentence.** Read the last sentence and then move to the next sentence. This allows you to stop reading for meaning and focus instead on grammar and mechanics.

- **Use a grammar checker.** You can find a grammar checker in most word-processing programs (and an even more robust one in Turnitin.com). However, you should understand that while grammar checkers can be helpful, there are also limitations to any computer program.

## Crafting a Title

Once you've finished drafting and have a polished final draft, you want to put a title on the paper. The title should draw the reader into your paper, and it needs to be specific to the argument you're making to the reader in the paper. Academics often begin their titles with a creative or catchy phrase, followed by a colon and a clear statement regarding the paper's argument. For instance:

**The Day the Music Died:**
**How California Reduced Arts Education in Elementary Schools**

The first part references a popular song and the second part introduces the reader to the issue and argument being addressed in the paper.

### *Sample: Academic Titles*

**This Is Not a Love Story:**
**How *(500) Days of Summer* Breaks Romantic Comedy Conventions**

**Never Too Late to Educate:**
**A Proposal for Addressing Thailand's Dependency on Prostitution**

**The Long Struggle Continues:**
**The Androcentric Ideology that Influences Scientific Research**

Remember that different genres have different expectations for what's appropriate for a title. Look at different examples of the genre you're writing to see what your options are.

## Now What?

After moving through the required elements of the paper, you're probably ready to turn it in. Of course, it might be that you need more outside feedback from your instructor, peers, or the Writing Center to help refine and revise your paper. It really depends on the complexity of the task and your familiarity with the genre. Keep in mind that even professional writers edit and revise their work obsessively. If you've written more than three drafts of your essay and you're still finding things to improve, then you're in good company. Think of this essay as just one step in a longer journey. What you didn't master this time can be on your agenda for the next assignment.

## What Makes a Good Essay

### Tricks of the Trade

### Clear Argument

Make sure that you have a clear message and purpose for your paper. The paper needs to have a larger claim and smaller claims to help support and add complexity to your argument.

### Strong Evidence

The claims need to be supported by evidence from your texts or outside sources that prove the points you're arguing. Your credibility is judged on the evidence you use, so choose wisely.

### Precise Organization

Your paper needs to connect your ideas together. Organization is about the relationships between ideas. Make sure that you clearly show relationships between your claims, evidence, and analysis.

### Nuanced Analysis

Through analysis you show the complexity of your thinking. Bring new ideas to the table in your writing.

## HOW TO USE THE WRITING CENTER

By Sue Cross

The Center for Excellence in Writing and Communication (or Writing Center for short) promotes effective writing and communication as lifelong skills. Not only are these skills necessary for personal and professional survival, they are also powerful ways in which people think through issues, consider multiple points of view, and become more consciously aware of the world around them.

Located in the Ayala Science Library, the Writing Center is the best place to get feedback on your drafts, outside of your class and your teacher's office hours. Here are some of the services you can get at the Writing Center:

- **Appointments:** Set up an appointment with an experienced Writing Specialist if you want to get in-depth feedback for any kind of writing you're working on, or if you just want to toss around some ideas. This is best done well in advance of deadlines to maximize redrafting time and effectiveness. Note: It is also possible to receive a consultation on a walk-in basis, but only if a Writing Specialist is available. Appointments are your best bet.

- **Online Consultation:** When submitting a draft for an online consultation through our website, be sure to email us your prompt along with the paper, and please indicate no more than two specific things you would like us to look for when reading it. The Center's response time will depend upon the volume of papers received.

- **Peer Tutors:** Drop in during the evening at one of four locations to see a peer tutor and get advice about overall writing strategies, general editing, and research strategies. No advance appointment is necessary. However, it is best to come early in the evening in case a number of students are seeking tutoring at the same time and location. For more information about how to schedule appointments, submit a draft online, or view the times and locations of the Peer Tutors, visit http://www.writing.uci.edu/.

### What Happens After a Consultation?

After a consultation through the Writing Center, you should be able to do the following:

- Identify the rhetorical situation evoked in an assignment prompt. You need to understand what you are being asked to compose, and to whom, before you can effectively communicate. After a consultation, you should be able to identify both the genre and audience called for in a specific prompt and should be more aware of differences between genres and audiences.

- Develop self-guided revision strategies. Revision is more than just correcting mistakes. Most successful writers use it to take a closer look at what they really want to say. After a consultation, you should be able to articulate and execute a plan of action for revision or development of specific writing projects.

- Build flexible writing processes, strategies, and habits. Over time, and with practice and experience, you should be able to transfer strategies and habits for generating, developing, and revising writing from one context to another, even as you recognize that different writing and communicating challenges might require different strategies and ways of thinking. After a consultation, you will be prompted to reflect on what you have learned about your own writing processes, strategies, and habits.

The Center for Excellence in Writing and Communication supports the educational mission of the university by giving students the tools they need to become better writers. While we will discuss issues we see and ask questions, we have a general rule not to edit or mark up your paper. We highly suggest proofreading your essay prior to visiting us.

## CHAPTER 6

# I Came Here for an Argument

*By Loren Eason*

I'm Loren Eason, a Lecturer in UCI's Composition Program, and I study and write about the rhetoric of video games and how they relate to other media. (I get to study video games? How cool is that?) Because my work bridges two very different areas of study, I often find myself explaining work written for one specific group of readers to another group of readers with different interests, knowledge, and ways of seeing things. I'm writing this chapter on argument for you in the hope that it will help you, too, to understand how you can understand other people's arguments and their own purposes for writing them, explain those arguments to others, and use them to support your own claims and purposes.

## We've All Been Here Before

It's the fifth week of the quarter and your professor has assigned an argumentative paper for Marvel's *Black Panther*. You used to love that movie, but now you are beginning to think it may kill you (six pages of writing = doom!). You've been working for days (well, minutes a day, in between all the rest of your classes and necessary college activities), trying to put together your paper, going over your notes, asking questions about the prompt and summarizing all of the things you remember from the class discussion and any outside readings that you were forced at gunpoint to collect. It's getting down to the wire and you are still not at all sure how to put it all together and make it work. Despite your efforts, all you have are a few rambling paragraphs of truthy facts and a vague idea of what you want to say, and somehow you are also supposed to find two outside sources to include. You know you are supposed to integrate those sources and to use them to support a claim of some sort in your paper, but you aren't even sure what that really means.

Something is still missing . . .

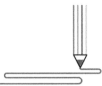

Note how the primary text (*Black Panther*) is woven together with the secondary sources that talk about the film using the method outlined in Chapter 3, "Citing and Integrating Sources."

### That Something Is an Argument

Pay attention to these next three paragraphs because in them I take two outside sources that analyze *Black Panther* and begin building bridges between them and the subject of the paper assigned in the last section.

In Marvel's *Black Panther*, we are introduced to T'Challa, the super-powered king of the fictional African nation of Wakanda that has, for centuries, used its advanced science and its deposits of a mystical metal, vibranium, to hide itself and keep colonial powers away. But in this film the threat to T'Challa's power comes not from outside the country, but from within his own family history.

As Christopher Orr notes in his review of the film in *The Atlantic*, *Black Panther* sets up three different views of the role that the fictional African nation of Wakanda should play in the world. The first one, subscribed to by T'Challa's father, T'Chaka, is that Wakanda needs to stay hidden from the rest of the world to protect its status as an African utopia unspoiled by colonialism. The second one, put forward by T'Challa's ex-lover, Nakia, has Wakanda sharing its mineral and technological wealth with its neighbors as a way to fight against exploitation by colonial powers. And the third vision for Wakanda comes from T'Challa's rival, Erik Killmonger, who says that that Wakanda should use its mineral and technological wealth to promote worldwide revolution against colonialist oppressors with Wakanda at the head.

And that's just the central arguments for T'Challa as leader of Wakanda. Another film critic, R. Eric Thomas, argues in *Elle* that the central debate about Wakanda is never settled because T'Challa's and Killmonger's personal histories get in the way, and that the real argument of the film is between Nakia and Okoye, asking if a citizen's duty is to support the good leader (Nakia's claim) or to support the government regardless of the leader (Okoye's claim). The two of them have several minutes of uninterrupted dialogue in the middle of the film where each puts forward her argument and the evidence that supports it. And it is this argument's resolution in the climax of the film (complete with CGI explosions and war rhinos!) that allows the film to resolve itself.

All the polished writing and good summary and careful integration in the world will not make a successful argument. This is a good start to writing an argumentative paper about the film, but it's not yet an argument because it has not yet told us how you intend to change our view of the film, or why these different articles are important to our understanding of what the film means. You will not have a full, functioning paper until you can figure out what it is that your readers think about the subject you are writing about (listening) and figure out what you are trying to say that adds something new to the "conversation" (some additional information of your own or a new perspective from which to understand the conversation) that all adds up to a better, more productive way of understanding the topic.

## Argument Starts with Listening

In college, the most common situation we face is one in which we are presented with a text that we are meant to decode—to read, understand, and find the significance of. And after we have done this, we are often asked to write an essay in which we reevaluate our own understanding of the text to account for how our understanding of the world is changed by seeing the world through the perspective of the text. This means that before we begin to send our own message in response, we should take the time to **listen rhetorically** to the message we are responding to.

We need to work to understand the significance of our shared messages before we begin to respond and change the situation. Krista Ratcliffe, the person most responsible for promoting the concept of "rhetorical listening" writes:

> ...this sort of understanding means more than simply listening for a speaker/writer's intent. It also means more than simply listening for our own self-interested intent, which may range from appropriation (employing a text for one's own ends), to Burkean identification (smoothing over differences), to agreement (only affirming one's own view of reality). Instead, understanding means listening to discourse not for intent but with intent—with the intent to understand not just the claims, not just the cultural logics within which the claims function, but the rhetorical negotiations of understanding as well. (12)

To listen rhetorically we must decode more than just the meaning of the text that we receive; we must also decode the context in which the communication was sent and attempt to understand our own relationship to both the rhetor who sent it and to the context—the world or culture or circumstance—that prompted the sender to attempt to communicate. This means:

- We need to consider what we know about the sender of the message and the circumstances that prompted the sender to send their particular message in that particular moment.

- We need to consider the sender's purpose in sending such a message.

- We need to think about how our own context might differ and how this difference might change the way in which we understand the message.

It's not quite that we are trying to put ourselves in the place of the communicator so much as it is that we are trying to develop a fair and accurate understanding of what, precisely, the sender is trying to say and what that message tells us about the way the sender sees the world.

As you can see, rhetoric is much more than just the application of a bunch of special techniques to make communication more persuasive. We often look at rhetoric in that way, but the success or failure of any particular technique depends entirely on whether or not it is appropriate to the audience receiving your message at the time they receive it and within the context that connects the rhetor with the audience. The techniques you might already be familiar with from your previous study of rhetoric (especially the use of diction, imagery, syntax, and tone to achieve a particular goal) are not magical nor do they work automatically in every given situation. Rhetorical know-how needs to be employed with a thorough understanding of the purpose behind creating a particular text and of the likely audiences who will encounter and engage with the text.

Returning to our first example of Marvel's *Black Panther*, this rhetorical listening might consist of thinking about and trying to understand:

1. The history of the comic book and the people who have read and loved the character,

2. The current audience for Marvel films and the expectations that they have,

3. The importance of *Black Panther* as a superhero for African American communities and for people of color, and

4. (If you are writing the paper for an academic audience and aiming to impress) the history of postcolonial studies or of Afrofuturism.

Knowing these things will help you to understand the film and also what arguments are being made about the film and the contextual reasons why people consider those arguments important.

But there is also a second layer of listening that you need to do—not for your own understanding of the film (or whatever it is that you are writing about), but rather for understanding your potential audiences and their reasons for wanting to read your text. Think about your own rhetorical situation and the attitudes or understandings that you wish to change with your text. Try to understand what the people you are writing to already believe about the topic, why they believe what they do, and why it is important to them. Once you do these things, you will be ready to start crafting an argument.

*Having a Plan*

Too often the novice college writer finds him or herself following a plan that looks like a famous internet meme:

**Phase 1: Research a "Theme"**     **Phase 2: ?**     **Phase 3: Paper**

Without an argument—something that connects your own thoughts or the thoughts of your sources together—you have no way to profit from having done all that collecting of sources. All you have is a big pile of evidence in the middle of your room.

But putting everything together in a way that makes sense—logos—requires more than just a pile of relevant evidence. You need to understand how to put that evidence together in a convincing manner to show your readers not just all of the pieces of your evidence, but how they fit together, what they build, and why this new information you have built is important.

Chapter 4 of *The Anteater's Guide* should give you some idea of what is going on in Phase 2 so that you have *something* other than a question mark.

---

**PRO TIP: BUILDING ARGUMENTS THROUGH RHETORICAL LISTENING**

An argument is a way of presenting new information (or old information in a new way or new combination) to an audience in order to build a bridge from their old way of seeing things to the new way that you are showing them. Think about what part of their existing worldview you need to change in order to convince them they need to change their opinion.

---

## The Steps of Argument

Classical arguments, following the pattern outlined by Aristotle in ancient Greece, are formal arrangements of terms that combine together like a geometric proof to lead the audience from a first step that they agree with through a series of reasoned steps to a new conclusion. The classic example of this is:

| Statement 1 | Statement 2 | Conclusion |
| --- | --- | --- |
| All men are mortal. | Socrates is a man. | Socrates is mortal. |

There can be more steps in the process and the conclusions can build on each other, but this is the basic idea. As it developed, lots of rules grew up around it as well that you see referred to in guides to argument that use Latin terms like *post hoc ergo propter hoc* to describe errors in the logic that work like bugs in computer code to break the sequence and keep the argument from reaching its intended conclusion.

While it is good to know the classical method of argumentation (and reading works like Aristotle's can help you to become much more systematic in your approach to thinking through a problem or analyzing what you are reading), the classical method is also fairly complex in structure and requires a degree of formality that you don't often find outside of academic sources. Most everyday forms of communication approach argument more casually, operating on informal rules, loose definitions, and commonly accepted notions of how the world works.

## Arguments: Claims Based on Data, Supported by Evidence

Stephen Toulmin, a mid-twentieth-century British philosopher, came up with a flexible system for thinking about all sorts of arguments, without having to get into a lot of technical jargon and details, that's rigorous enough to get you through most sorts of college writing that require argumentation. In Toulmin's influential 1958 book, *The Uses of Argument*, he argues that we can outline most arguments as having a Claim based on specific Data or Grounds, supported by further Evidence or other Backing:

*It's better to have a fire axe in a zombie apocalypse than to have a shotgun because the axe is more versatile. It never needs reloading and doesn't make noise.*

Hovering in the background of these arguments are many unspoken or unwritten assumptions that the people involved tend to take for granted. Toulmin calls these assumptions Warrants. (The warrants here are that zombies exist, are dangerous to humans, and are attracted to noise.)

Of course, few arguments worth the energy required to debate come without at least one other side that needs to be considered, and for this reason Toulmin also includes two other useful and important categories in his system: Qualifiers and Rebuttals (or Reservations, depending on how you decide it is most useful to frame your argument). We can define these elements this way:

### TOULMIN'S SYSTEM TO OUTLINE ARGUMENTS

**Claim (C):** The conclusion to which the writer wants to lead the readers: the thesis or main point in an argumentative paper. [*For a paper, this is your thesis and not another author's thesis: their claims become either Backing or Reservations, depending on whether they support or undermine your claim, respectively.*]

**Backing (B) or Evidence (E):** The examples, statistics, analogies, or findings that the writer uses to convince the readers that they should agree with the claim. [*Bringing in other voices or your own experience.*]

**Grounds (G) or Data (D):** The beginning foundation for the proposition. What the reader must know in order to understand why the claim is being made. [*This is shared between you and your reader. If they don't see and* understand these grounds they will not understand what you are claiming. Why are you making your claim?]

**Warrant (W):** The more general reasons or assumptions that are associated with the Claim and Data. The premise. [*Tricky, because your audience may not agree with them or you, and your audience may not see them because they assume them automatically.*]

**Qualifier (Q):** Used by the writer to narrow down the claim in order to specify the case in which the claim is most probable or applicable, or to highlight an uncertainty in your own case. [*Are there cases in which your evidence does not apply? Is there disagreement over data? Do we need to keep options open?*]

**Rebuttal or Reservations (R):** Counterarguments or counterexamples that the writer puts forward on his or her own of necessity or in order to build his or her own *ethos* as a trustworthy person.

## PRO TIP: S.T.A.R. EVIDENCE

Please note, here, that when we are dealing with evidence in the Grounds, Backing, or Rebuttal, this evidence should always be *Sufficient, Typical, Accurate,* and/or *Relevant*—S.T.A.R. If the evidence you want to use is too limited in scope or number, too unusual, inaccurate, or too tangential to your claim, it will not further your argument and should not be included. If the example or evidence is so cool that you feel your life is diminished by not including it, then either put it in a separate file to use in another work, change your claim so that the example is relevant to the claim, or put it in a footnote or endnote where it doesn't disrupt the central argument but still shows the world just how mindblowingly cool you are.

Also, it's important here to remember how crucial it is for you to develop your ethos as a fair and reliable rhetor. Pay attention to all of the evaluation you do for any outside sources (see Chapter 4 if you need a refresher) and make sure not to misrepresent, distort, or ignore any problematic areas just because they make your argument more difficult. This is what Qualifiers, Grounds, and Rebuttals are for.

When it is all put together in one place, Toulmin's system looks like this:

| Grounds | so...**Claim** | assuming that...**Qualifier** |
|---------|----------------|-------------------------------|
|         | since...**Warrant** | unless, of course...**Reservation** |
|         | because...**Backing** |                               |

Don't worry if all of this sounds a bit abstract. It's easy to get hung up on the names of the different parts of an argument or to get distracted trying to figure out how to break down a writer's argument into the different parts above. Truth is, though, that the names are far less important than understanding what we are trying to do with an argument. *The most important things to take away from Toulmin's explanation is that we need to base our claim on clear grounds and back it with solid evidence, and that we need to consider and include the exceptions our audience will raise and the situations in which our arguments do and do not apply. Like this...*

## Argument in Action

Let's go back to the thesis statement above about weapons in the zombie apocalypse:

*It's better to have a fire axe in a zombie apocalypse than to have a shotgun because the axe is more versatile. It never needs reloading and doesn't make noise.*

In it I'm making a claim about fire axes. My claim is that if you are caught in a zombie apocalypse and have to choose between a shotgun and a fire axe, the fire axe is a better choice. I then offer three pieces of backing for that claim.

Oh, crap...that thesis *looks* a lot like a five-paragraph essay thesis. What I need to do here is think about how all of this information goes together and why I might need all those pieces to convince my readers.

First off, while it might look like my thesis has three points, when you look at the structure, you'll notice that the claim is that the axe is a more versatile tool. That's not *actually* three pieces of backing—it's a claim and two pieces of backing for a separate, but related, comparative claim. If I wanted to turn this into an actual piece of writing, one written for a real audience that I can't converse with, I'd need to make the pieces of my argument a lot clearer.

What I am really doing here is imagining a conversation and thinking about all the points that could be made then selecting the most important ones. Why did I choose to emphasize that the axe is quiet and that it doesn't need reloading? What is it about the world of the zombie apocalypse that makes these things matter? That is to say, what are the Grounds on which these facts become important?

**Grounds:** *In a zombie apocalypse world, both stealth and scarcity matter. You can't just go out and buy the stuff you need—you have to scrounge for supplies. Moreover, because zombies are everywhere and they are attracted to noise, you have to sneak around when you are looking for those supplies.*

Now that we have those two defining points, we can begin to think about a better structure for this argument. We know that we are arguing about shotgun versus fire axe, so what are the strengths of the shotgun? What makes all your friends go "oooh!" when they think about fighting zombies with one? It's a powerful weapon that does a lot of damage and requires less skill than many other weapons.

So what is a shotgun good for in a zombie apocalypse? You can use it to kill zombies. You can use it to hunt game for food. Drawback? In both cases you make a lot of noise while doing it, and noise attracts zombies. And a shotgun needs shotgun shells to work. Using the shotgun means that you will also need to scrounge more for supplies to replace the ammunition that you use, which means you will need to go to places where zombies gather to get those supplies.

Why is a fire axe a useful tool in the zombie apocalypse? You can use it to defend yourself from zombies *and* you can use it to get into places that have been boarded up while you are looking for supplies. More importantly, the axe doesn't use up any supplies in the course of making it work. Drawbacks? One drawback is that it makes noise when you are breaking in. Sure, but you'd need to make that noise anyway if you had to find more ammunition, so you are no worse off than you would be if you had a shotgun. The other big drawback is that the axe can only be used against a zombie if it is close enough to reach you, and that one is not so easy to explain away.

Knowing these things, then, why is it that so many of your friends would pass up the axe for the shotgun? Maybe because they have played a lot of video games or watched a lot of films, and shotguns are more exciting and dramatic than people sneaking around and trying to be quiet.

## Putting It All in the Right Order

Now that we've finally got the whole shape of the argument out, we can better see what's going on here and start to put this all together in a way that makes sense both for us and for readers who can't see all the things that are going on in our heads. An outline might look something like this:

1) What most people think a zombie apocalypse is like [**Rebuttal**]

   a) Zombies chasing people

   b) People shooting zombies with shotguns

2) What a real zombie apocalypse would look like [**Grounds**]

   a) People sneaking around trying to avoid zombies

   b) People having to scrounge for dwindling supplies

3) An axe is better in a real zombie apocalypse because...[**Claim**]

    a) Can be used for more than just shooting things [**Claim/Backing**]

        i) Chopping things for fires [**Evidence**]

        ii) Opening doors and containers [**Evidence**]

    b) Doesn't need ammunition and supplies [**Backing**]

    c) Quieter than a shotgun [**Backing**]

4) But an axe is not perfect [**Qualifier**]

    a) Requires close range to use [**Reservation**]

        i) True. This is a danger

        ii) Shotgun may be more effective early on when supplies are more plentiful

        iii) But the longer things go on, the harder it will become to find supplies and ammunition [**Rebuttal**]

        iv) Attracting fewer zombies means having to fight fewer zombies, so the battles should be smaller [**Rebuttal**]

This is the outline of a paper with an argument. But what's important here is not that I know all the terms for the parts of an argument, but that I have thought through the details of what my audience believes and why (i.e., shotguns!!!); I have shown them why they need to reconsider, given them an alternative, and shown them when and why that alternative is preferable to their previous thought on the matter. And where I saw potential objections to my argument, I demonstrated to my audience that I have considered alternatives and am being reasonable.

### PRO TIP: AUDIENCE EXPECTATIONS

If you know that your audience expects a particular topic or **genre** to be addressed in a particular way, you should take that into consideration in your formal organization. I started the essay outline above with a **rebuttal** in order to set the grounds of my argument early on.

If you know for a fact that your audience is going to view your claim with suspicion, you need to work hard to build some common **ground** before you tackle their opposition and present your own side of the issue.

An argument always needs a claim and backing. An argument with a *complex* thesis (the gold standard of a solid academic paper) will need more than just a claim and backing—it will require some sort of extra consideration of alternative approaches or interpretations along with some demonstration that the writer has weighed these carefully before making his or her claim. Doing this allows us to show our readers why they should consider changing their minds if we know that we are taking on a common belief or if it helps us to build our *ethos* as careful and rational thinkers by showing that we have thought of alternatives that our readers may not have noticed or stopped to consider. All of these are good things.

## Reading for Argument vs. Reading for Content

In order to argue effectively, a writer must be able both to read and understand other writers' arguments and to produce his or her own arguments. Claims are built out of Grounds and Warrants, and both of those things must be shared between the writer and the reader, so they must be established and agreed upon before the argument begins for the argument to make any sense. This is the argument's history. Whatever Backing, Grounds, or Warrants you use—whether in support of your own argument or as Qualifiers or Reservations to be accounted for in the building of a consensus—you have to understand how they are being used in your sources' arguments before you can use them convincingly in your own. This means reading not just for facts and information that can be used as Backing or overcome as Rebuttals, but understanding how the author of a particular source is using that fact or bit of data his or herself: reading for argument as well as for content.

When reading for content, we tend to scan the page looking for definitive claims, facts, and concrete details that support those claims, and especially for the conclusions drawn from these claims. Most qualitative tests that you are given are designed to check reading comprehension and not critical thinking. If you can identify and remember concrete facts and the conclusions that are drawn from them, you will usually do well on multiple choice and short answer exams. But this method of skimming can create misunderstandings and lead you to misinterpret the writer's purpose when you mistake the role these concrete facts play in a writer's overall argument. What appears to be a definitive statement of facts may actually be a writer's presentation of someone else's backing for a claim that the writer of the current piece of writing is preparing to refute. Mistaking Reservations or Qualifications for Backing can lead you to claim that the writer believes the opposite of what he or she actually argues. Doing this can wreck whatever trust you have established with your reader.

When reading for argument, on the other hand, we scan the page looking for clues that track *who is making which claims* as well as *the writer's attitude toward the claims that are being made* (since the writer may not agree with all of the claims—rebuttals, right?). While writers sometimes state these attitudes explicitly within the text as a formal evaluation of another person's claims or evidence, quite often writers use much more subtle clues to indicate their attitudes toward the claim (for example, by using phrases like "While writers sometimes state...," or "quite often writers..."—I used a Qualifier there). The evidence used in these claims is important, but no less important than the words that the writer uses to link together his or her phrases. We call the practice of using these linking words **signposting** because the words act the same way that signs do to show the reader where the writer's argument turns or takes a detour so that the reader does not get lost in all the details.

## SOME COMMON SIGNPOSTS AND TRANSITIONS

- **Backing** (cause and effect): accordingly, consequently...
- **Backing** (related point): furthermore, in addition, likewise...
- **Qualifier** (concession): although, even though, in spite of, despite...
- **Reservation** (comparatives): conversely, in contrast to, on the other hand...
- **Reservation** (evaluative): alternately, rather than, in lieu of...

### Try This: Mapping an Argument

*Try mapping out an author's argument using Toulmin's system: Identify which sentences function as Claim, Grounds, Backing, etc. Then go through and look at what, if any, linking words and signposting the author used to signal to the reader what part of the argument the sentence functions as.*

## Building Your Own Arguments: The Rhetorical Situation

Writing instructors talk a lot about how writing a paper is like joining a conversation that started before you got there, and this sense of joining a conversation already in progress holds just as strongly when we are talking about arguments—especially when we are talking about academic arguments and research papers. As writers, we are never starting from scratch; we are always building onto or branching off of other people's words and arguments. In a way, then, the rhetorical triangle (rhetor, text, audience) that we use to think about our relationship to our audience is misleading and incomplete because we ourselves are already a part of other writers' triangles.

> ▶ "You're not really getting anywhere by trying to enforce your opinion heavy-handedly. But if you can get your reader to at least consider your argument, then you're getting somewhere."
> —*Writing Program award winner Julianna Reth*

Say, for example, that instead of the essay about choosing a weapon for the zombie apocalypse, I am instead writing a paper about how many modern zombie films play on our fear of losing control of our lives, and to talk about this I am bringing in Naomi Klein as an outside source, using her book *The Shock Doctrine: The Rise of Disaster Capitalism*. Rather than thinking about my paper simply in terms of a single rhetorical triangle, it might make sense for me to begin thinking about myself as the middle point in two (or more) triangles: one triangle to describe my relationship as a reader to the other writers whose voices I will feature in my paper and the second triangle for myself as a writer in charge of providing my own readers with enough context to understand my argument.

The reason that I want to think about this in terms of two triangles rather than one is because my own purpose in writing what I am writing is not necessarily the same purpose that Naomi Klein had when she wrote her book and my own audience may differ significantly from Klein's audience.

I have to help my audience understand both what Klein meant in her own context and how it fits with the new context I am creating in my paper. This might look something like Figure 6.1.

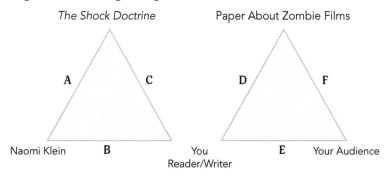

Figure 6.1

Using two triangles rather than just one allows me to begin to think about how I relate to my sources as a reader and take those things into account when I then begin to add my own voice to the conversation as a writer. My first job will be to lay out how my sources fit with my own argument and purposes (the first triangle).

## SAMPLE CRITICAL QUESTIONS ABOUT MY SOURCE

1.   *What is Klein trying to tell her audience about how powerful people manipulate us into giving up our own power out of fear? (Logos)*

2.   *B.   Do I believe that Klein is presenting her evidence fairly and accurately? Why or why not? (Ethos)*

3.   *What does Klein do in her book that resonates with my own values and sentiments? (Pathos)*

Once I have a good sense of this I can begin to make a much clearer argument in which my own voice in the paper is distinct from the other voices found in my source material (the second triangle).

### SAMPLE CRITICAL QUESTIONS FOR MY OWN PAPER

1.  *How much of what Klein writes in The Shock Doctrine do my readers need to know before they will be able to follow my argument about the appeal of the zombie film?*

2.  *How can I best present Klein's work to my audience in order to show my readers that they can trust my judgment?*

3.  *What part of what Klein writes will resonate most strongly with my own readers while also serving my own purpose in writing?*

The other writers who are present in our sources provide us with the material out of which we build our own arguments, but it is up to us to explain how these sources connect to each other and what new tools or perspectives these connections give us to help equip us to live better, and better informed, lives.

When I put this all together, then, what I need to do is decide how I am using Klein in my own paper. If I agree with the parts of her writing that I am quoting or paraphrasing in my own paper, am I using it as backing for my own claim or as a rebuttal for someone else's competing claim? If what she claims contradicts what I claim, am I trying to rebut her argument or am I showing how her claim does not apply in the particular case I want to discuss [Qualifier]? In all of these cases I will need to explain to my reader, accurately and fairly, what she writes and what her original context and intent for writing it was, but once I do this, the way that I unpack it for my own audience depends on how she functions in my own argument and on the signposts and connecting words I choose when I transition from summarizing her writing to furthering my own claim.

- **Backing:** "Klein's discussion of how disaster capitalism stirs up fear and mistrust in order to sell us a sense of security helps to explain why most zombie films include scenes where..."

- **Qualifier:** "Although Klein's 'Disaster Capitalism Complex' gives us a powerful tool for understanding modern, contagion-style zombie films, it does not work as well to explain earlier films where..."

With skill and practice, a writer should, in this way, be able to guide the reader through both examples and counterexamples without the reader becoming confused as to who wrote what or which side of the argument the writer is on. The transitions help the reader to keep it all straight.

# Exercise: Building an Argument Using Toulmin

Whenever a film, TV show episode, or other piece of audiovisual media recorded in one language gets purchased for use in a market with a sizeable population that does not speak one or more of the languages spoken in the recording, the producers have to decide how to make the material accessible to that population. The main two ways in which they accomplish this task are either to subtitle the work in the other language or to rerecord and replace (or "dub") the original spoken dialogue with new dialogue spoken in the target language.

Many people have a strong preference for one or the other of these methods of translation and in some fan subcultures (e.g., Anime) the debates in favor of one side or the other can become quite heated.

## *Try This: Build an Argument Using Toulmin*

*Construct an argument in support of each of the two following Claims: [C] Dubbing is better than Subtitles; [C] Subtitles are better than Dubbing.*

*Start by considering when and why we use dubbing/subtitles on video.*

1.  *Consider how each of these translation features work (reading vs. hearing) and for what groups of people these methods either work or do not work.*

2.  *Think about the genres of video for which one or the other of these methods might be preferable based on the purpose or content being shown.*

3.  *Think about Toulmin's model and work to put the parts of your argument together in the appropriate sections (Claims, Backing, Qualifiers, etc.)*

*Once you have the argument mapped out using Toulmin's model, try writing topic sentences for each step of the argument that include transitional phrases that identify what role the sentence is fulfilling in the argument.*

## Works Cited and Further Reading

Alexander, Jonathan, and Margaret M. Barber. *Argument Now: A Brief Rhetoric*. New York, Pearson Longman, 2005.

Aristotle. *Rhetoric*. Trans. W. Rhys Roberts. Aristotle's Rhetoric: A Hypertextual Resource. Lee Honeycutt and Alpine Lakes Design, rhetoric.eserver.org/aristotle/.

Orr, Christopher. "*Black Panther* Is More Than a Superhero Movie." *The Atlantic*, Feb. 16, 2018, www.theatlantic.com/entertainment/archive/2018/02/black-panther-review/553508/.

Ratcliffe, Krista. "Rhetorical Listening: A Trope for Interpretive Invention and a 'Code of Cross-Cultural Conduct.'" *College Composition and Communication*, Vol. 51, No. 2, December 1999, 195-224.

Tomas, R. Eric. "The Most Important Debate in Black Panther Is, Unsurprisingly, Between Two Women." *Elle*, Feb. 26, 2018, www.elle.com/culture/movies-tv/a18370982/black-panther-okoye-nakia-debate/.

Toulmin, Stephen. "From *The Uses of Argument*." *Teaching Argument in the Composition Course*, edited by Timothy Barnett, Boston, Bedford St. Martins, 2002.

Young, Richard E., Alton L. Becker, Kenneth L. Pike, and Carl R. Rogers. "From *Rhetoric: Discovery and Change with Communication: Its Blocking and Its Facilitation*." *Teaching Argument in the Composition Course,* edited by Timothy Barnett, Boston, Bedford St. Martins, 2002.

## CHAPTER 7

# WR39A & WR39AP: Introduction to Writing and Rhetoric

*By Kat Lewin*

Welcome to the 39A/AP chapter! I'm Kat Lewin, the Course Director of 39A/AP. When I'm not writing homework assignments or AGWR chapters, I write novels and short stories. As a writer, the day I learned about rhetoric, it was like a firework went off in my brain. I've always known when I write fiction that one tiny change (a word here, a dash there) can make my writing come alive by adding a necessary pause or a jolt of emphasis. The beauty of rhetoric is that it gives you a framework for noticing and talking about those tiny yet powerful decisions, which, in turn, allows you to develop more control over them. Rhetoric makes the invisible visible.

## Writing with Purpose: Goals and Routes
### *Using Rhetoric to Make Your Map*

Imagine that you are in Irvine and you have a simple goal: to get to San Francisco. What's the best route?

There are many options:

- You can drive to Los Angeles and take a two-day cruise to San Francisco.
- You can fly from the Santa Ana airport to San Francisco International in about an hour.
- You can drive the fastest route, from the 405N to the 5N, and get there in 6.5 hours (depending on traffic).
- You can drive the long, scenic route up the California coast (twelve hours of stunning ocean views).
- You can spend a week bicycling, camping overnight in various state parks.
- You could walk there . . . or do cartwheels the whole way . . . or get your pilot's license and fly yourself by helicopter . . . or fly by way of Hawaii with a week-long layover . . . or—well, you get the point. There are a lot of routes.

**Question**: Which route is the most effective?

**Answer**: That was a trick question. There *is* no one best route. It all depends on the *situation* you're traveling in.

Maybe you want to get there are quickly as you can, so it makes sense to fly. Or maybe you know you'll need a car while you're in San Francisco and you don't care much about how pretty the drive is, so you drive the direct route. Or maybe you have a friend in town who has never seen California, so you'd prefer to take the longer, more beautiful drive so you can enjoy yourselves. Maybe you love whale-watching and the feeling of the ocean underneath you, so you'd rather sail on the cruise ship. Maybe you have a week to spare and want to challenge yourself to get into shape, so that long bicycle ride is the best option.

There are a lot of potential routes, and you can understand logically that choosing the best one depends on a lot of factors—like who you're with, what your purpose is, and what you value (e.g., getting a good workout, spending time with a loved one, reaching your destination quickly or cheaply).

Writing works the same way: We know from Chapter 1 of this book that when you write you always have a goal (a purpose to achieve and a message that you want to send your reader). But in order to figure out the best route to achieve that goal, there are a lot of other factors to take into consideration: who you're writing for (and what they expect from you), what type of writing you're doing, the context (i.e., when and where) you're writing in, and how you want to present yourself.

## THE MYTH OF "GOOD" AND "BAD" WRITING

There is no such thing as "good" or "bad" writing. **All communication is situational**. And you understand this logically: writing that makes a great text message to a friend (like, for example, "hey bro" followed by eighteen emojis) makes a terrible email to the president of UCI (seriously, don't try it). Sometimes it's tempting to think that there's just one good type of "college writing" or "academic writing." But that's simply not true.

Some of you may have been taught in high school that the five paragraph essay (introduction with thesis statement, three body paragraphs with one example each, and a conclusion that summarizes the entire essay) is a good way to write—yet when you get to 39A/AP, your instructor will tell you that five-paragraph essays won't succeed in this environment. So what's the truth? Are five-paragraph essays good or bad?

Well, neither. It depends on the situation you're in.

Five-paragraph essays might be a very good option when you're writing for an audience who has to read quickly and is primarily interested in the content of your writing—say, for a standardized test like the SAT or for an in-class final for a professor who asks for that style of writing. But for your final essay in Writing 39A/AP—where your goal is to imitate models of complex, academic writing and to help the reader understand and believe your claims—that organization structure simply will not do.

Similarly, in 39A/AP, you may be imitating models that use personal anecdotes or narratives, or rely on lyrical, poetic language and lots of metaphor. And that might be a great decision for that particular essay . . . but that doesn't mean that those same decisions will still be appropriate for the specific writing tasks you're assigned in 39B or 39C.

Writing is all about decisions, and there is no objective "good" or "bad" or formula for great writing. Instead, you have to do the hard work of understanding what your purpose is, what genre you're writing in, and who your audience is and what they expect from you. Only then can you figure out the best decision for that particular situation.

Before you take on any writing task, it's a good idea to have your purpose and message in mind. For example, if I'm writing a persuasive essay, my purpose will be to convince my audience of my argument. My message would be the argument itself—the new, original, interesting opinion that I am explaining and defending.

From there, you need to understand the **rhetorical situation** (i.e., the situation that you're writing in). All writing is an act of communication, and all communication is situated in the real world, and before we start writing, we need to ask questions about that situation that will help inform our decisions.

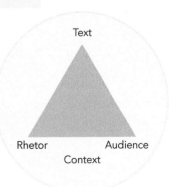

Text

Rhetor          Audience
        Context

Figure 7.1

Here are examples of some of the questions you might ask about your rhetorical situation in order to help you determine the best route to achieve your goal.

AUDIENCE: Whom am I writing for? What do I know about their background that's relevant and will help me make good decisions? What might this audience already know/assume/believe about my topic? If the audience has little to no knowledge about my topic, why is this the case? What does this audience think is important? What do they expect from me?

TEXT: What is my primary purpose? What other purposes might some parts of my text have, to help me achieve my primary purpose? What message am I sending?

MEDIUM AND GENRE: What type (or *genre*) of writing am I participating in? What does this type of writing usually look like? What types of content does this type of writing usually contain? What style decisions do writers tend to make in this type of writing?

RHETOR/COMMUNICATOR: What is my relevant background for writing about the topic? How will I establish my *ethos* (i.e., how will I convince the audience that I am an authority)? What *persona* will I try to create? What style will I write in to help me create that persona?

CONTEXT: When and where is my writing going to be read? Are there any issues, events, or discussions going on in that time/place that relate to my topic? What might the audience have already heard about my topic?

## GUIDING QUESTIONS FOR TRANSFORMING RHETORIC

*If you want to see how dramatically a message can change when you alter part of its rhetorical situation, try an experiment with rhetorical transformation. Let's test it with the simple message:* I don't like this food.

*For each situation below, how would you express this message?*

**Audience:** *How would you say it to your best friend? To your grandmother? To a waiter who has been very rude to you during your meal?*

**Purpose:** *How would you communicate the message to a chef if your goal was to make her feel a strong emotion? Would you express it differently if your goal were to simply convince her to change her recipe?*

**Genre:** *How would you express that you didn't like food as: A restaurant review on Yelp? A caption for an Instagram picture? A humorous text message to a close friend? A formal email complaint to a restaurant, asking for a refund? Wordless body language to someone sitting across the room from you?*

*Your answers for each question probably look pretty different. That's rhetoric in action. In each different situation, you considered factors like audience, purpose, and genre in order to make successful decisions.*

## Try This: Transform a Text on Your Own!

*Choose a paragraph you've written in this class and revise it three different ways. Keep the content the same, but change your audience to:*

- *College students*

- *Elementary school students*

- *Professors*

*For each of these versions, you'll need to ask what each audience already knows about the subject, what vocabulary is most suitable, and how to best keep their attention.*

Once we understand the *situation* we're in, then we can start to decide the most effective choices to make in order to achieve our goals. Rhetoric is the art of effective communication. Whenever we write, we make a million tiny decisions about our writing, and rhetoric is how we use our understanding of the situation we're in to make those decisions successfully.

### How to Use This Chapter

In this chapter, we're going to be thinking about rhetorical situations in two different ways.

For the first section of the chapter (Writing 39A/AP: An Overview), we're going to think about the very specific situation you're in: taking Writing 39A or 39AP at UC Irvine. This section of the chapter aims to help you understand the goals and methods of the course and will give specific tips about how you can set yourself up for success.

The second section of the chapter (Writing in 39A/AP: Imitation and Innovation) gets more in-depth about how you can teach yourself to succeed as a writer in a wide variety of rhetorical situations—including the types of writing tasks that you may encounter in Writing 39A or 39AP. This half of the chapter will include activities that you may wish to try on your own as you write and revise your major assignments throughout the quarter.

# WRITING 39A/AP: An Overview
## Course Goals and Assignments

Writing 39A/AP is an intensive course designed to help students write with confidence and develop versatile reading, thinking, drafting, and editing skills to use in a wide array of rhetorical situations. Each section of Writing 39A/AP is quite different, so the best way to understand the course is to listen to your instructor and pay close attention to the syllabus. However, there are some key elements that all sections of Writing 39A/AP have in common:

- Each section of 39A/AP is built around a sequence of Major Assignments designed by your instructor. The types of writing you do will depend on the section you're in, and these assignments can vary from short stories to academic essays to speeches to analyses of poems—the variety is tremendous! What all of these assignments have in common is that they are designed to guide you to develop your skills in **critical reading**; successfully navigating **a variety of writing styles**; developing and defending **original, complex arguments**; adapting your writing to **appeal to an audience**; and showing ownership in identifying your own strengths and weaknesses so you can improve your own writing with **rigorous revision**.

- For each Major Assignment, you will produce a minimum of **three globally revised drafts**. Global revision means editing your *whole* draft by reconsidering every sentence, paragraph, and section. You'll do more than change a word here and there and add a couple of new paragraphs; you'll push your writing skills by close reading your own work and, over the course of the quarter, using **critical thinking** to challenge and improve your own writing—from choices as small as punctuation and individual words, all the way up to entirely rethinking your central ideas.

- At the end of the quarter, you will compile **an ePortfolio**, in which you will include **a wide array of your work from the quarter**: not just drafts of Major Assignments, but also homework assignments, in-class writing, peer reviews, and more. (Your instructor will give you a prompt with their requirements.) The portfolio is a big deal: *100% of your grade in the course is determined by the work in this portfolio.* (Read the next section for more information about the Final Portfolio and how it's graded!)

- The Final Portfolio will include a **Final Portfolio Introduction**. In the Final Portfolio Introduction (or elsewhere in the portfolio) you will make an argument about the skills you have gained in the course, using your own writing from the quarter as evidence.

## KEY TERM: CRITICAL THINKING

**Critical thinking** means being able to improve your own thinking by analyzing, critiquing, breaking down, and rebuilding your own ideas on a given subject. Critical thinking takes many forms, and one of those forms is being able to think about ideas from *multiple* perspectives (from your own, from the reader's, from another writer's, etc.) and question those ideas deeply, then answering those questions and using your new understanding to make your ideas even stronger.

Writing doesn't just mean sitting at a computer and making words appear on a screen. To grow as a writer, you need to develop your skills as a **reader**, a **thinker**, and an **editor**. These identities are interconnected. In this way, writing is a little like swimming: when you try to swim, if you just kick or just move your arms or just breathe...you'll fall to the bottom of the pool. You can't leave out a single one of those steps because each one helps the others. For a writer, the same is true of the relationship between reading, thinking, and editing: unless you do all three of those things whenever you write, you will sink. Writing 39A/AP is intended to help you grow as a complete writer, and so the assignments in the course develop all three of those skills.

### *The Final Portfolio: Evaluation and Common Questions*

All of the work you do in this course—reading, thinking, writing, and revising—has one very important goal: to allow you to develop control over your own writing, from coming up with original and interesting arguments all the way down to successfully proofreading and polishing a sentence. Make no mistake: the work that you do and the skills that you gain are the most important things you will get out of this course.

But you might also care a little bit about your grade—and, in particular—how you will be graded.

**There is but one grade in 39A/AP. The final grade.** At the end of the quarter, you will compile all of your work into an electronic portfolio, and then the work in that portfolio will be holistically graded according to the 39A/AP rubric. "Holistic grading" means that your grader is going to use the rubric to assign you one overall grade, rather than giving individual grades to each piece of writing in the portfolio.

### Why the portfolio model?

This portfolio grading is useful for students as they develop mastery of a variety of writing skills. Because Writing 39A/AP students come into the course with different strengths and weaknesses, the Final Portfolio sets students up for success in a number of ways:

- **You can continue revising all of your work until the day that portfolios are submitted.** Take a big risk on a draft and then realize it didn't work out as planned? Try again. Reread the work you wrote in week three and realize that, after another month of 39A/AP, you could do it *way* better now? Great, revise it. You can keep revising assignments as your skills develop, **so your work can grow with you**.

- You can identify the skills that you most need to focus on, and seek feedback (from your instructor, from other students, from the Writing Center, etc.) in order to strengthen those particular skills. This model lets your instructor see, concretely, the work that you've put into your growing mastery of writing, and it should motivate you to go above and beyond the technical requirements of the course—pushing your work toward no-holds-barred *excellence*, rather than settling for mere technical proficiency and writing the minimum number of required drafts. (Why settle for competent when you can be awesome?)

- **Your grade is not penalized for weak work early in the quarter.** Because you will be undergoing so much writerly growth in this course, your early work will simply not be as strong as your work near the end of the quarter. Wherever you are as a writer when you walk in, you'll be stronger when you walk out. The holistic grading of the 39A/AP portfolio gives you room to struggle early in the quarter and allow those struggles to build your writing muscles. Instead of spending the first few weeks trying to bang out perfect products, you can focus on mastering the concepts and skills that will lead to great writing later in the quarter.

- Feedback can take the form of a *conversation* between you and your instructor, rather than the model in which your teacher makes a bunch of red marks on the page and you go make the corrections they suggested. When you have the length of the quarter to revise work and build skills, your teacher has the freedom to be more targeted and selective with their commentary. This means your instructor likely won't give you feedback on every single thing that can be improved in an assignment—and that's good. You'll prioritize issues together to find the skills that you need to focus the most energy on, target those issues in your revisions, and then seek more feedback (and give *yourself* feedback) to keep improving. You'll have plenty of time to absorb your instructor's feedback, work with it, and come back for another round.

## PRO TIP: TAKE NOTES ON YOUR WORK TO TRACK YOUR PROGRESS

In the Final Portfolio, you'll be making an argument about the skills you've gained in the course—so track that skill growth! After each revision, while the essay is fresh in your mind, take five minutes and write a reflection about what you improved and what you need to work on. It doesn't need to be fancy! Even a quick list will help you in the end of the quarter. Or if you want to be extra, try inserting comments in the file itself to write your analysis of sections that are successful (and what you did, how it affects the reader, and why) and give yourself advice or ask targeted questions about sections that still need work.

### Does anything other than the final drafts of essays affect my grade?

Yes. Yes. Yes. Please do not make the mistake of thinking that you can skip all of the other work, as long as you write passing-level essays. You will be very disappointed! **The Final Portfolio rubric evaluates not just your essays, but also your work throughout the quarter.**

Your final grade is determined by the Writing 39A/39AP Final Portfolio Rubric. While the rubric does include evaluations of your Major Assignments, Final Portfolio, and Final Portfolio Introduction, it has *many* categories. Homework assignments, rough drafts, participation in class, attendance, and in-class writing are all accounted for on the rubric! Just as all of these things impact your learning, so too do they impact your grade.

## PRO TIP: SAVE EVERYTHING

Different instructors have different requirements, but you will be asked to include a wide variety of work in your portfolio, not just Major Assignment drafts. And if you don't save it, you can't include it! Save each draft separately, save your class notes, the editing and brainstorming you do—everything. Snap photos of in-class writings, peer review activities, notes you take in tutoring sessions, and extra editing you do for your essays. If you receive handwritten feedback or write notes on printed copies of your paper, scan them into a PDF. Keep everything organized in a file on your computer so it's all ready when you start assembling your portfolio!

### But how do I know what grade I'm going to get?!

The portfolio model might take a little getting used to, but here are some things to remember: **You will be in constant communication with your instructor about your strengths and weaknesses as a writer.** You'll hear praise and criticism. You'll hear both frequently.

In fact, if you feel that you have no idea how you're doing in the course, that means you likely need to be showing more initiative in discussing your work with the instructor. Visit them. Bring a copy of the final rubric, and plan to go over it with them. Tell them where you think you are, skill-wise (and have evidence to back that up!), and find out where your instructor thinks you are. Have a lively conversation!

### PRO TIP: REFER TO THE RUBRIC FREQUENTLY

The rubric is a great tool to use throughout the quarter, to see what skills you should focus on. If you're stuck while revising a draft, print out the rubric and fill it out about yourself, to see how your skills stack up. Don't forget to take a photo for your portfolio!

### What do I do with my work once it's in the portfolio?

Once your work is in the Final Portfolio, it is your responsibility to make effective choices to **show off the skills you have developed** over the course of the quarter. Whereas your other Major Assignments may have been drafted over the course of a month or longer, with frequent feedback from your instructor, your Final Portfolio Introduction is an opportunity to show ownership and demonstrate the skills you developed as you worked on those Major Assignments!

### KEY TERM: OWNERSHIP

For a writer, **ownership** is the ability to take control of your writing. Writers with strong ownership are able to read their writing and identify what they need to improve, then make a plan for how to create those improvements. If you rely on an instructor to give you feedback about your writing and you only make the changes that they suggest, then you are letting them be the boss of your essay. If you are able to make your own decisions about how to improve your writing, then you are the boss and demonstrating great ownership.

In many sections of Writing 39A or 39AP, your instructor will ask for a Portfolio Introduction that serves as a tour through the Final Portfolio: it's your opportunity to present evidence of the work you've done and make a compelling, well-supported argument for what skills you have developed in the course—which means convincing the reader **what you have learned, how you will use these skills**, and **what you still need to improve**. After ten weeks in Writing 39A/AP, you will have learned a lot about how to make precise, complicated claims and how to support them with well-chosen evidence—all while writing in a *style* that is well-controlled and appropriate for your writing task. The Final Portfolio Introduction is your space to put all of those skills into practice.

Your instructor will give you specific instructions for the Final Portfolio and the Final Portfolio Introduction. They might request certain style or content choices (such as specific types of evidence included in the Introduction, close readings of passages of your own writing, annotated revisions of certain Major Assignment drafts, a particular genre or format for the Introduction, specific types of organization or design choices, etc.), or they might ask you to show **ownership** in making these choices for yourself. But whatever you do for the Final Portfolio and Final Portfolio Introduction, remember this: the Portfolio Introduction is your final opportunity to demonstrate the skills you have mastered as a writer, so to convince your reader that you have improved as a writer, it's not enough just to say that you have improved your skills. You have to be able to *show* it.

> ## PRO TIP: PAY ATTENTION TO YOUR INSTRUCTOR'S REQUIREMENTS
>
> Just as there's no one "correct" way to write, there's no "correct" way to assemble a portfolio. You have to make good choices for your specific situation. So even if you've taken another class with a portfolio or portfolio introduction, or if you're retaking Writing 39A/AP, pay attention to your instructor's specific prompt and requirements.

If you argue that you've learned how to use evidence to support a claim, but don't use any evidence to convince us of that? The reader won't believe you. If you argue that you've learned how to write stylish sentences that come alive on the page—but make that argument in short, repetitive sentences that don't contain a single detail? Not very credible. It's your last opportunity to show your reader (and grader!) what you're capable of, so leave yourself plenty of time in week ten to do your best. Don't run a ten-week race just to fall down at the finish line!

## WRITING IN 39A/AP: Imitation and Innovation

### The Imitation Model: What and Why?

While the writing assignments in 39A/AP vary from section to section, the course as a whole is based on imitation: the idea that reading exceptional writing from amazing authors in a variety of genres will expose you to rhetorical strategies that you can analyze, understand, and learn how to incorporate into your own writing.

You're going to do a lot of writing in your life. Career writing (like grant proposals, lab reports, emails to clients and managers, progress reports, all kinds of stuff) and personal writing (emails, text messages, dating website profiles, social media posts, Yelp reviews). Here's the deal: your lower-division college writing courses can't teach you how to do all the types of writing you'll need do in life.

"Why not?" you ask. "Isn't that why I'm going to college? To get the skills I'll need for the rest of my life?"

Yes, absolutely. College is great. (Do all the reading. Ten years from now, you'll regret the readings you skipped.) But there are good reasons we can't teach you how to do every single type of writing you'll ever need to do. First of all, Writing 39A/AP is only ten weeks long and we're not wizards. But more importantly: *You will be doing types of writing that your instructors have never done. In fact, in your life, you will be writing in styles and genres that DO NOT EVEN EXIST YET.*

Take social media, for example: You may use Instagram now (or WhatsApp or Tumblr or Reddit or whatever app you use that I'm not cool enough to know about), and you may be very good at it. You'll notice that the social media apps you use require a different type of writing than you use in other parts of your life—maybe there are certain restrictions to the writing (character limits, for example) or certain types of etiquette that only apply on certain apps (like on Venmo, it's customary to use emojis instead of words) or certain emoji or phrases that are popular only on certain sites.

You weren't born knowing how to use these apps, because they didn't exist when you were born. You didn't learn how to use them in school. So how did you learn? Chances are, you used imitation. You probably read a bunch of examples of how *other people* did that type of writing, noticed the choices they made, decided which of those choices you liked (and why) and which choices you did not like (and why not), and then used all of those observations to create your own successful writing style. You may have even kept those other writers' voices in your head and wondered: "How would so-and-so say this?" or "Would what's-her-name think this post was good?"

That's the imitation model in action. It's how everyone learns how to participate in new kinds of writing—it's the most natural possible process. And in real life, when we're writing without having to stop and explain why we make the choices we make, chances are this process feels so natural and invisible that *we don't even see it happening.*

Good news, though: just because you don't notice yourself imitating doesn't mean that you don't already have the basic skillset to do it well. The imitation model in 39A/AP empowers you to take this process of imitation and learn how to break it down into steps, so you have more control of your ability to imitate, you can make better-motivated choices, and you can successfully use imitation to participate in *any* kind of writing, from now until the end of your life. Academic writing! Personal writing! Types of writing that currently don't exist! Types of writing that *shouldn't* exist! Whatever your writing task, once you master imitation, you can go forward with the confidence that you can master any kind of writing.

# Try This: Practice Imitation in Less than Ten Minutes!

*Choose a classic fairy tale (like Cinderella or Red Riding Hood) and rewrite it two different ways:*

- *a movie description (like the ones you see when you scroll through Netflix)*

- *a limerick (a short, funny five-line poem with an aabba rhyme structure)*

*Look up several examples of movie descriptions and limericks, then write your own. Even though the two pieces of writing are similar lengths, you'll have to make very different choices. When you're done, compare the differences between your two versions. Could a stranger easily tell which is which?*

*For the movie description, you likely focused on capturing the hero's main characteristics and creating suspense about the plot. For the limerick, you'll probably have to focus more on creating a humorous mood and choosing words that fit into the rhyme scheme.*

*These differences are evidence of imitation in action! Chances are, you haven't written a large number of movie descriptions or limericks—but after reading some of them, you learned enough of the unspoken "rules" to write your own. And the more you read, the more of the unspoken "rules" you'd learn.*

## Imitation is NOT Copying

### KEY TERM: MODEL TEXTS

**Model texts** are the pieces of writing you read and imitate to learn how to succeed in a certain type of writing task. Sometimes we imitate a model text very closely, to create a text of our own that is similar to the model.

Often, we only imitate some of the choices our model text makes. For example, if you read a short story and think the author writes beautifully complex sentences with exciting verbs, then when you write an essay, you might choose to base your punctuation and verb choices off of the model but make very different choices about organization and message. For any given writing task, you might choose to imitate the writing choices of several different models. Mixing and matching allows you to find your own style!

The goal of imitating a model text is to look at **what** choices an author made, think about **how** those choices affect the audience (and help communicate the message of the text), and consider **why** those choices were successful—then use your analysis of the text to decide how to adapt those choices into your own writing.

Copying, on the other hand, happens when we try to copy an author's rhetorical choices *without* thinking about why the author made those choices and why those choices work. When we copy a text's rhetorical choices, our thought process is something like: "I made this choice because the author made this choice." We don't really have a deeper understanding of *why* the choices are effective, so we don't develop the skills to be creative and logical when we want to make similar style choices in the future.

Remember that your goal when imitating a text is to **learn how to make stylistic choices that you can use in the future.** Your goal is not simply to produce one very good piece of writing for this class—instead, you want to focus on developing a set of skills that you will be able to use in the future. You simply cannot accomplish that goal by copying stylistic decisions without understanding *how* and *why* those choices work.

Let's look at a passage from Kate Chopin's *The Awakening* and illustrate what happens if we copy it without considering her stylistic choices.

> **Original Text:** "The voice of the sea is seductive; never ceasing, whispering, clamoring, murmuring, inviting the soul to wander for a spell in abysses of solitude; to lose itself in mazes of inward contemplation. The voice of the sea speaks to the soul."

> "The ~~voice~~ **light** of the ~~sea~~ **desert sand** is ~~seductive~~ **enchanting**; ~~never ceasing~~ **always changing**, ~~whispering~~ **glimmering**, ~~clamoring~~ **sparkling**, ~~murmuring~~ **glowing**, inviting ~~the soul~~ **you** to ~~wander for a spell~~ **take a peaceful stroll** in ~~abysses of solitude~~ **its golden halo**; to lose ~~itself~~ **yourself** in ~~mazes of inward contemplation~~ **its softly blinding gleam**. The ~~voice~~ **light** of the ~~sea~~ **desert sand** ~~speaks~~ **calls out** to ~~the soul~~ **your heart**."

> **Copied Version:** "The light on the desert sand is enchanting; always changing, glimmering, sparkling, glowing, inviting you to take a peaceful stroll in its golden halo; to lose yourself in its softly blinding gleam. The light on the desert sand calls out to your heart."

My copied version sounds pretty good and was easy to write! All I did was read her sentence, then think of synonyms for every word to tweak the meaning a little. The problem is: **I didn't actually learn anything from copying** her sentence, and I couldn't write another passage like this if I tried. I have no ownership over this passage, because I didn't really write it. Kate Chopin wrote it and I just changed a few words.

Copying doesn't help me, because while I may have noticed **what** choices Chopin made, I didn't do the work to figure out **how** she created her effects or **why** they worked. So I can't recreate this effect, and I can't figure out how to adapt these methods to other types of writing!

Let's try again, but instead of just copying what Chopin wrote, we'll first try to understand the effects she created, so we can learn strategies to apply to different writing assignments. (There's no one right way to analyze a writers' choices and there are no "correct" answers. Table 7.1 records my own personal reactions to and opinions about the text—but another reader might notice totally different choices or have different reactions to them.)

**Original Text:** "The voice of the sea is seductive; never ceasing, whispering, clamoring, murmuring, inviting the soul to wander for a spell in abysses of solitude; to lose itself in mazes of inward contemplation. The voice of the sea speaks to the soul." (Kate Chopin, *The Awakening*)

**Table 7.1**

| WHAT choice she makes | HOW it affects the reader | WHY the choice is successful | Technique to try |
|---|---|---|---|
| **Pace:** The first sentence is quite long, punctuated with frequent semicolons and commas. | The punctuation creates a series of relatively short pauses, giving the sentence a flowing pace. | The "flowing" of the sentence mimics the waves of the ocean. She helps us hear the "seductive" voice of the ocean. | Try describing a moving object in a pace that matches the way the object moves: short, staccato sentences for choppy movement or maybe long, flowing sentences for an object that moves smoothly. |
| **Sentence length:** The second sentence is very brief. It's just a simple sentence with one noun phrase and one verb phrase. | There is a contrast between the complexity of the first sentence and the directness of the second sentence. | Readers tend to focus on contrasts, so she creates emphasis on the second sentence. | Try following a complex, abstract sentence with a short, punchy sentence that captures your meaning in a slightly different way. |
| **Repetition:** Both sentences begin with the phrase "The voice of the sea . . ." | The repetition of "the voice of the sea" might help us refocus on the subject of the description. Repetition also usually creates emphasis. And using the phrase again unites two stylistically different sentences about the same subject. | The repetition helps build a bridge between two sentences that are otherwise stylistically quite different. | Try finding a description that is two or three sentences long and repeat a key phrase at the beginning or end of each sentence. Revise the sentences to make sure they're different enough that the repetition feels intentional! |
| **List order:** In "never ceasing, whispering, clamoring, murmuring, inviting the soul . . ." the items on the list seems to be arranged so they alternate in intensity. | The items on the list seem to go up and down in intensity. "Never ceasing" is moderately intense; "whispering" is quiet and mellow; "clamoring" is loud; "murmuring" is quieter than a whisper; "inviting the soul . . ." is the most dramatic item on the list and the most detailed. | The alternation in intensity is another way she continues mimicking the wave effect, just like she did with the punctuation in the first sentence! And ending a list with the most detailed or vivid image can help that image linger in readers' minds. | Try revising a list in your writing to see how different organizations might change the impact of the list. Try alternating like Chopin or other organizations, like *small to large, simple to complex,* or *least to most intense.* |

After doing all of this analysis, I could write my own description of the desert sand that is *inspired* by Kate Chopin's beautiful sentences, but not a direct copy of them. But better yet, I can also use the techniques I discovered in all kinds of different writing assignments. I could try the repetition technique in an email to my boss, or practice ordering a list in order to write an effective caption of a photo on social media, or vary sentence length in order to emphasize a point in the abstract of a lab report.

When you know **how** and **why** writing techniques work, then you have infinite options about **when** to use them.

To see whether you're *imitating* or *copying* a model text, pause often to check your motivations for making certain stylistic decisions. If you don't understand *why* you're making the choices you make or *how* they might affect the audience, then you've still got some thinking to do.

Let's break down the art of imitation into a few more specific steps, and let's use an example so I can show you what I mean instead of just telling you. Just as your identity as a writer involves being a reader, a thinker, and an editor, so too can you break down the process of imitation into questions to ask as a reader, a thinker, and an editor.

## Imitating Model Texts: Developing Your Reading Skills

### *How Do You Pick an Effective Model Text?*

Ask pretty much any writer who their best teacher was, and they'll point to the shelf of books behind them. (Writers love to hang out in front of bookshelves.) The best writers know that good writing, when you read it deeply, becomes your teacher. If you have a question, you go to the writing and ask it: What did you do? How did you do it? How can I do the same?

But before you let a piece of writing teach you how to make good choices, you have to make sure you've picked an effective model to emulate. You don't want to write your job cover letter in the style of lyrics to a Rihanna song, unless you're applying for a job writing songs for Rihanna.

Fortunately, your Writing 39A/AP instructor will provide you with model texts for all of your Major Assignments. Study these model texts carefully: they can teach you strategies to use in your own writing!

But you are not limited to the texts your instructor provides, and in life beyond Writing 39A, you will have to find your own model texts for writing in your major and career.

Here are some questions to ask yourself to choose effective model texts:

## GUIDING QUESTIONS FOR CHOOSING EFFECTIVE MODEL TEXTS

1. *What is the purpose of this text and how does it relate to my purpose?*

2. *Who is the audience of this text and what do they care about?*

3. *What do I admire about this text?*

### What is the purpose of this text? Is it similar to my purpose?

Does the text primarily try to inform the audience of facts? Convince them of an opinion? Entertain them—make them experience a series of emotions? Everything a writer does is in pursuit of achieving their purpose, so it helps to read writing that has the same goals that you do. You can imitate the author's strategies to achieve those goals.

### Who is the audience of this text? What does that audience already know about the topic? What do they already assume, believe, and care about?

Writing is situational, and because our goal is to create an effect in our audience, we can learn a lot from imitating texts whose audiences have something in common with the audience we are writing for.

For example, there's tons of writing about writing—I've read hundreds of essays about writing, all for different audiences: from elementary schoolers all the way up to folks with PhDs in linguistics. Those linguistics essays have taught me a lot about the subject, but imitating their style would not help me explain writing to college freshmen who don't know (or care) what a *labiodental sibilant* is. To learn how to best communicate with college freshmen, I'd be better off studying the style of college writing textbooks or other forms of writing geared toward young adults.

Choosing model texts for the audience you're writing for is especially useful if you don't have a very good firsthand understanding of your audience or if it's an audience of which you are not a part. If your 39A/AP instructor asks you to write a final essay for an audience of English professors—well, you're *not* an English professor, so how can you know what they already know, what they care about, and what style choices appeal to that group? The best way to learn is by finding texts written for that audience and studying them—figuring out which writerly choices are successful for that audience, so you can emulate them.

### Is this model something I actually like? Do I find some pleasure in it? Does this writer do things that I wish I could do?

Don't underestimate the value of caring about the stuff you write. You know how sometimes you stay up until 4 a.m. writing an essay for your English class, and the whole time you're thinking: "This is terrible. I hate this. I'm so bored," and you just wish you could finish the essay and move on with your life? Spoiler alert: The reader can usually tell that when they read. Find model texts that appeal to you, at least a little. You'll be spending a lot of time taking them apart and figuring out how they work, so you might as well not hate the process. In fact, you might find that you start to really like the process.

Your 39A/AP instructor will be assigning you lots of reading, and you will be able to use these texts as models for the writing that you have to do. But remember as you read essays for your other classes, or books for pleasure, or articles on your phone to pass the time: anything you read can be a model. Look out for choices that writers make that seem cool or unusual or like something you wish you could do. You can make any piece of writing your teacher, and you will be a better writer because of it.

**BUILDING VOCABULARY.** Many Writing 39A and 39AP students say that one of their biggest priorities is expanding their vocabularies. Close reading model texts and looking up the definitions of words you don't know is one of the greatest tools for expanding your vocabulary. But here are a few others to use as you read, write, and revise:

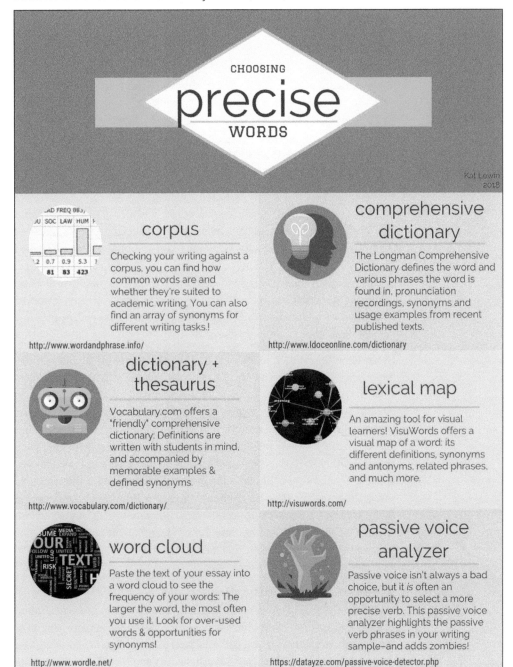

CHOOSING

# precise

WORDS

Kat Lewin
2018

## corpus

Checking your writing against a corpus, you can find how common words are and whether they're suited to academic writing. You can also find an array of synonyms for different writing tasks.!

http://www.wordandphrase.info/

## comprehensive dictionary

The Longman Comprehensive Dictionary defines the word and various phrases the word is found in, pronunciation recordings, synonyms and usage examples from recent published texts.

http://www.ldoceonline.com/dictionary

## dictionary + thesaurus

Vocabulary.com offers a "friendly" comprehensive dictionary: Definitions are written with students in mind, and accompanied by memorable examples & defined synonyms.

http://www.vocabulary.com/dictionary/

## lexical map

An amazing tool for visual learners! VisuWords offers a visual map of a word: its different definitions, synonyms and antonyms, related phrases, and much more.

http://visuwords.com/

## word cloud

Paste the text of your essay into a word cloud to see the frequency of your words: The larger the word, the most often you use it. Look for over-used words & opportunities for synonyms!

http://www.wordle.net/

## passive voice analyzer

Passive voice isn't always a bad choice, but it *is* often an opportunity to select a more precise verb. This passive voice analyzer highlights the passive verb phrases in your writing sample–and adds zombies!

https://datayze.com/passive-voice-detector.php

## Imitating Model Texts: Developing Critical Thinking
*Breaking the Text Down*

Once you've chosen model texts that can effectively teach you about the type of writing you'll be doing, your next task is to think about the texts—analyze the style and figure out what choices the writer made and how the writer created the effects they did.

> ### KEY TERM: STYLE
>
> **Style** is the combination of the millions of tiny choices that a writer makes every time they create a text. These choices encompass every aspect of writing: the writer's tone, word choice, punctuation, organization, etc. Style is the fingerprint of writing: what makes it unique.
>
> You can think of **content** or **meaning** as the **WHAT of writing (WHAT the piece of writing is about)** and **style** as the **HOW (HOW that meaning gets conveyed)**.

When we talk about the "choices" a writer makes, we're talking about "rhetorical devices"—or, as you might know them, "literary devices" or "figurative devices." If you took AP Language & Composition or studied for the SAT after 2016, you may well have some experience with rhetorical devices. (Back in my day, we had to memorize a list of 100 rhetorical devices, in alphabetical order from *anaphora* to *zeugma*!) Even if you haven't worked with many of them, chances are you've had to write essays about a few devices like *diction*, *tone*, and *syntax*.

However, often students are taught that these rhetorical devices are important—but they aren't taught *why*. So even if you think you know what they are, let's take a moment to make sure we're on the same page. **Rhetorical devices are strategies used by writers to provoke responses from their readers.** Some rhetorical devices are *sonic* (i.e., based on sound) like *alliteration* (when multiple words in a phrase start with the same sounds). Other rhetorical devices are focused on the type of logic that you use to create an argument (like *syllogism*, which is a term for the argument that if Premise A → Premise B, and Premise B → Premise C, then Premise A → Premise C). Some rhetorical devices deal very specifically with word choice (like *hyperbole*, another term for exaggeration) or comparisons (like *metaphor*, which transfers the qualities of one object to another object—like saying "his eyes are stars").

There is no shortage of rhetorical devices, and they affect elements of writing that are as small as punctuation all the way up to the entire organization of a piece of writing. While you may not know the technical names for all of the devices you notice, if you pay attention to the style of the writing you read, you'll find yourself noticing these devices and the effects they create on the reader—and then you can learn how to successfully imitate these style decisions.

There are too many types of style decisions to make a definitive list, but throughout the rest of this chapter, you can find boxes defining a few commonly used (and commonly abused!) key terms about rhetorical choices.

## CRAFTING AN ARGUMENT ABOUT RHETORICAL DEVICES

If you write a paper in which you're asked to make an argument about rhetorical devices, remember to argue about what they do. It is not enough to simply point out *that* they exist.

Think of yourself as a chef: A great chef can't just walk into the kitchen and point out every single item in the refrigerator. ("There's a tomato! That's spinach. These are radishes and cucumbers.") That chef would get fired pretty quickly, because she's *not actually making food*. It's not her job to list all of the foods she sees—it's her job to notice them, and then actually do something useful with them. She must take those individual foods and do things with them. Chop up the tomato. Wash and dry the spinach. Cut the radishes and cucumbers into cute little flower shapes. And then toss them with a dressing to make a salad.

Similarly, if you want to make an argument about how a text uses rhetorical devices, you can't just point out the fact that those rhetorical devices exist! That's not a great argument, because you're pointing out the *ingredients* of the writing you're looking at—but not actually making an argument out of them!

You have to *work with* your evidence, to understand it, break it down, explain exactly what effect you think it makes on the piece of writing and why you think that. And then you have to combine that evidence together into a bigger argument that actually says something interesting about what those rhetorical devices are *doing*!

As you notice other writers' stylistic choices, you can analyze them and learn how to imitate them by asking three simple questions.

### *"WHAT Choice Did the Writer Make?"*

Try to get specific in your thinking here. If you're going to learn how to imitate a writer's technique, you have to see the technique clearly in your head—otherwise, imitating them is like trying to draw a picture based on a fuzzy photograph! It doesn't lead to anything but frustration.

So, for example, noticing "the writer uses a lot of detail!" is probably not super useful. Many writers use a lot of details, and yet their styles are totally different. The best way to get a good sense of what the writer is doing is to keep asking yourself questions. If, for example, you notice that a writer uses a lot of details—well, what kinds of things do they describe? Do they give the details simply, in an adjective or two, or in long, complex phrases? Are the details (literal) (describing what actually exists) or (figurative) (making comparisons or using metaphors)? Do the details use our senses, and if so, which ones—taste? sight? sound? smell? touch?

## PRO TIP: HOW MUCH IS "ENOUGH" DETAIL?

Here's the test I use to see if I'm evaluating a writer's choices in enough detail: I ask: "If a writing teacher gave me this advice, would I know how to follow it?" You're trying to become your own writing teacher, so give yourself specific feedback like you'd want from a real teacher.

After all, if you're trying to imitate someone's writing and you just tell yourself: "Use more detail!" then when it comes time to write. . . you're going to spend a lot of time staring at your computer screen and regretting your life. If, on the other hand, you can give yourself specific instructions like: "When I describe people, I should try describing parts of their appearance using short, concrete details that appeal to the senses of sight and touch, and occasionally write a longer, more detailed metaphor about the person as a whole," then even though writing is still difficult, you'll at least have given yourself a very specific to-do list.

### "HOW Does this Choice Affect the Reader?"

One way to think of the rhetorical is: "the relationship between a piece of writing and the outside world." A big part of that connection to the outside world is the relationship between the writing and the reader. Every choice you make as a writer changes your reader's experience.

Some of our choices make a reader read more slowly: like inserting a paragraph break, so the reader can stop, take a breath, and digest what we've just said, or adding a detailed description that the reader lingers over, savoring each word and picturing everything we describe. Some choices make a reader read more quickly: adding a list the reader is intended to skim, for example, or using a comma—instead of a long, dramatic em dash.

Some of our choices can create emphasis on our words or ideas (making them shout in the reader's mind) or remove emphasis (perhaps by hiding the idea in parentheses). Some of our choices help readers understand our ideas, believe our ideas, or care more about our ideas. Choices can make readers laugh or thrill them with a different emotion, or (in the case of typos or confusing grammar) choices can make our reader want to put down our writing altogether.

## KEY TERM: DICTION

**Diction** is perhaps the most slippery "rhetorical device" that you may have encountered. Diction simply means "word choice" and the difficulty of discussing diction is that: every written word is an example of diction. All writing is made up of words, and all of those words are chosen by an author. Therefore, literally every single word in a piece of writing is an example of diction. Imagine how the reader will respond if you argue that a piece of writing uses diction. Chances are, the reader will say: "Yes, I already knew that this short story/essay/poem/play was made up of words. What's your point?"

To think about diction more usefully, a good start is to narrow your thoughts down to a particular type of diction. Of all the words the author chose, which type are you interested in? Poetic? Informal? Profane? Biblical? There are a lot of options—make sure you're being specific so you can narrow your focus and notice something interesting the writer is doing. If you try to make an argument about all the diction . . . well, that's every single word, so chances are you'll just make a series of disconnected observations.

In writing—as in life—our choices have consequences. So as you read your model texts, pay attention to the consequences of the writer's choices.

Writing is a form of manipulation: we put our ideas in the minds of our readers and use style to try to make readers react to those ideas in a certain way. And because the texts we read affect us so skillfully, it can be hard to understand the effects of a choice a writer has made. If you find it difficult to see HOW a writer's choice affects the reader, you might consider trying to rewrite the phrase in a totally different **style** and then pay attention to how or whether the effect changes.

For example, let's say I'm trying to imitate a line from Shakespeare's Sonnet CXXX, in which the speaker describes his lover's mouth:

*"Coral is far more red, than her lips red"*

I might notice WHAT he does—the fact that he repeats the word "red" twice in the same sentence stands out—yet struggle to explain HOW the choice affects the reader. So I could try rewriting the sentence to remove the repetition:

*"Coral is far more [rose], than her lips red"*

And then it's a little easier for me to see: When I reread my new version, I have to read more slowly, because I have to stop and think about the colors "rose" and "red." I stop at the end of the line when I come to "red" and have to consider: "Are rose and red different shades? Which one is redder? What exactly is he saying about her lips? Are they redder than coral or not?!?"

Then I can look back at the original line and realize HOW his repetition affects the reader: repeating the word "red" helps the reader understand the comparison by removing potential confusion from the line. It also gives emphasis to the word "red"—so nice he used it twice!

### KEY TERM: TONE

**Tone** can be thought of as **the speaker's attitude toward their subject**. Consider the following two sentences:

"You are so beautiful!" and "You are not ugly."

They technically mean approximately the same thing (the person that the speaker refers to is good-looking), but the tones are very different. The first example shows an enthusiastic attitude about the subject (and seems much kinder and more sincere); the attitude (and tone) of the second example is insulting.

When we speak, our tone can be a bit of a roller coaster ride, growing more or less formal, polite, enthusiastic, academic, etc., as we continue talking. The same is true in writing: as a writer discusses different subjects (or reveals more about their view on the same subject), their tone can shift gradually or dramatically over the course of a single piece of writing—or even a single sentence. The tone of a text is often not static from one moment to the next, so look out for where and how it changes.

You might be amazed by how much you can learn from just one or two sentences of another writer's work! Check out the process applied in Table 7.2 to just a few sentences of Sojourner Truth's immortal "Ain't I a Woman" speech (as transcribed by Marius Robinson and printed in the Salem *Anti-Slavery Bugle* in 1851):

> **Original text:** "I have as much muscle as any man, and can do as much work as any man. I have plowed and reaped and husked and chopped and mowed, and can any man do more than that? I have heard much about the sexes being equal; I can carry as much as any man, and can eat as much too, if I can get it."

**Table 7.2**

| Style Choice | Original | Rewritten | What Changed? |
|---|---|---|---|
| Pacing: Using "and" between every list item in second sentence (a.k.a. *polysyndeton*) 连词叠用 | "I have plowed **and** reaped **and** husked and chopped **and** mowed, **and** can any man do more than that?" | "I have plowed, reaped, husked, chopped, and mowed. Can any man do more than that?" | The rewritten version has more punctuation and many more pauses. The first version is faster paced and feels kind of breathless. The nonstop pace in the original version emphasizes the amount of work she describes. |
| Repetition: "Any man" in the first sentence | "I have as much muscle as **any man**, and can do as much work as **any man**." | "I have as much muscle and can do as much work as any man." Or "I have as much muscle as any man and can do as much work as one." | The first rewritten version is unclear; we don't understand the muscle comparison until the end of the sentence. The second rewritten version is clear, but ending on "one" instead of "any man" is pretty weak. Ending on "any man" emphasizes the gender comparison, which is her main point! |
| Rhetorical question: She asks a question to create an effect, rather than to get an answer | "I have plowed and reaped and husked and chopped and mowed, and **can any man do more than that?**" | "I have plowed and reaped and husked and chopped and mowed. No man can do more than that." | The rewritten version sounds more like a direct challenge, and like she is giving her own opinion. In the original version, the readers give the answer themselves, so they may be more likely to believe it. (But before the question, Truth gives seven examples of her being equal to a man—and after the question, she gives two more. Even though the reader answers the question, there's really only one way they can answer!) |

## Try This: Rewriting to Understand Style

*Choose a reading from your Writing 39A/AP class that has a great first paragraph. Try making a chart like the one above, where you notice three or four effective choices the writer made. When you rewrite the author's sentences, are they better, worse, or just different? Can you use one or two observations you made to improve the introduction of your essay?*

### "WHY Does the Choice Create that Effect?"

Once you know WHY style choices create the effects they do, then you're ready to think about how you can use this style technique in different situations.

In the Shakespeare example above, once I rewrote Shakespeare's line to remove the repetition, I had a good idea of not only HOW his repetition of the word affected the reader (by helping to clarify his comparison) but also WHY it had that effect (because the reader didn't have to linger over a new synonym for "red" and ponder its meaning—instead of struggling to interpret a new word, they can jump straight to considering the comparison as a whole). When you analyze *why* stylistic choices have the effect they do, then you're one step closer to figuring out when to imitate those choices.

Chances are you won't be writing a ton of Shakespearean sonnets in your life. (Or maybe you will, in which case: I salute you.) But does that mean you can never use this style technique? Of course not.

Once you figure out why a technique works, you can think about how to **adapt this knowledge to different writing situations.** If, for example, you're writing an essay or an email to a professor in which you make a comparison—well, you might not have to worry about rhyme or meter like Shakespeare did, but you can still remember what this poem taught you: "Using consistent terminology in a comparison can avoid confusion." It's good advice that you can use in a lot of scenarios, not just poetry and not just Writing 39A/AP.

Regardless of the style or genre of writing you read, once you understand how and why the writer's rhetorical choices affect the audience, then you can add those rhetorical strategies to your tool kit and make educated choices about how to adapt those strategies to all kinds of writing.

# Imitating Model Texts: Becoming Your Own Best Editor

You won't have a writing teacher for most of your life. So your goal in this class should be to become your own writing teacher—your own best editor. Instead of relying on someone else to make red marks all over your writing, you should leave this class with the knowledge and confidence to read and give excellent feedback on your own work.

How do you do that? By reading your own writing the exact same way you read other people's writing.

You know all the great critical reading you've done so far, reading for style by asking what, how and why? Good news: that is the exact same reading process that an editor does. Only you read your own work instead of someone else's. And instead of reading a Shakespeare play and scrawling, "Seriously, this is terrible, what is wrong with you?!?!?" in the margins, you get to write it in the margins of your own writing! And then you get to change your writing to make it better! (But don't call your writing terrible. Be nice to yourself. Writing is hard for everybody—even professional writers.)

> For more great advice on critical reading, revisit Chapter 2, "Practicing Critical Reading."

## PRO TIP: CREATE DISTANCE FROM YOUR OWN WRITING

Editing is hard, in part because we're often too close to our own writing: we know what we *meant* to write, and it can be difficult to separate that from what we *actually* wrote. Our brains like to autocorrect our own writing, so it's important to learn techniques to turn that autocorrect off. Your instructor will likely teach you several useful techniques for reading your own work for revision, but here are a few to start with.

**Read your writing aloud.** Pretend you are an actor getting paid to read your own writing—and read it slowly, expressively, and *exactly as you wrote it*, grammar errors and everything. You should even consider audio-recording your reading and listening to it again. We read aloud much more slowly than we read silently, and this technique makes it easier to hear every. single. word. (Don't forget: your reader will be reading every word.)

**Read aloud sentence by sentence, backward.** This technique can help you start to improve your individual sentences. Sometimes when we read from beginning to end, the overall logic of a paragraph can cause us to skim over some individual sentences that don't quite make sense. But reading from the last sentence to the first sentence takes away that context and forces you to stare your own writing in the eye.

**Explain your ideas in conversational language—to an audio recorder or to a friend.** It's easy to get so caught up in making your ideas *sound* "fancy" or "academic" that you end up. . . not quite knowing what you mean. But if an idea is truly good, you should be able to explain it clearly and simply—without looking at your writing or falling back on repeating the phrases you've already written. When you start to stumble, you might realize you need to go back to the "thinking" stage and keep building your ideas or explore more evidence.

**Print out your writing and edit by hand.** We do a lot of "skim reading" on our computers and phones—much of our screen-reading time is spent on emails and social media, situations in which we're just trying to figure out WHAT something means and we don't think too deeply about HOW it is written. When you edit, switch it up: the novelty of reading your own writing on paper can trick you into paying more attention!

As you read your own draft, when you find sections that you think could be improved, take notes for yourself: WHAT choice did you make? HOW is it going to affect the reader, and WHY? And HOW do you want to affect the reader instead?

Once you have a clear idea of what problems you'd like to focus on in your writing, then: **Go back to your model texts.**

Find part of a model text you admire that successfully solves the problem you see in your own writing. Then ask: WHAT did the writer do to solve this problem? HOW did their solution affect the reader? WHY? And how can you learn from that writer's experience to try solving your own problem?

Consider making a "What"/"How"/"Why"/"Technique to Try" chart, like the one on page 135.

For example, imagine you're having trouble organizing an essay: In the beginning of each of your body paragraphs, you use really simple transition words like "Firstly," "Secondly," and "In conclusion." You're pretty sure this isn't the best strategy for writing transitions, because none of the essays you've read in class use these words—their transitions seem a lot smoother and more exciting.

Instead of opening Google and typing "How do I write a transition please help me," **let your model texts teach you how to solve the problem.** You might find an essay you think has really beautiful, smooth transitions and then ask WHAT they did and WHY it worked. Find a transition you think is particularly excellent and make a list of style techniques the writer used to achieve that effect. You might ask questions like: How did they choose to order their examples? Is the transition between examples one word, a sentence, a whole paragraph? Do they stop between examples to help the reader understand what they've learned from the last example and what knowledge they will gain from the next example? Does the writer use white space or section headers?

Editing Strategy: Use a reverse outline to revise your organization and transitions.

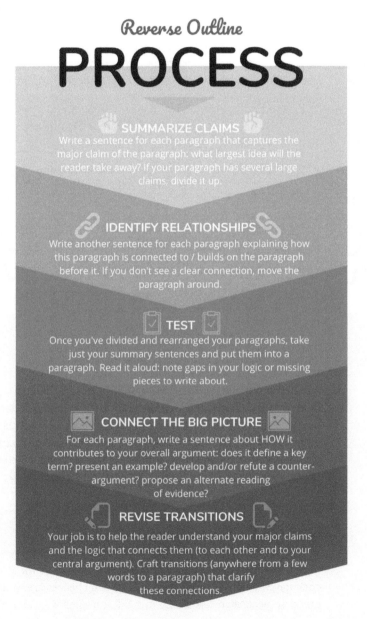

## Reverse Outline
# PROCESS

**SUMMARIZE CLAIMS**
Write a sentence for each paragraph that captures the major claim of the paragraph: what largest idea will the reader take away? If your paragraph has several large claims, divide it up.

**IDENTIFY RELATIONSHIPS**
Write another sentence for each paragraph explaining how this paragraph is connected to / builds on the paragraph before it. If you don't see a clear connection, move the paragraph around.

**TEST**
Once you've divided and rearranged your paragraphs, take just your summary sentences and put them into a paragraph. Read it aloud: note gaps in your logic or missing pieces to write about.

**CONNECT THE BIG PICTURE**
For each paragraph, write a sentence about HOW it contributes to your overall argument: does it define a key term? present an example? develop and/or refute a counter-argument? propose an alternate reading of evidence?

**REVISE TRANSITIONS**
Your job is to help the reader understand your major claims and the logic that connects them (to each other and to your central argument). Craft transitions (anywhere from a few words to a paragraph) that clarify these connections.

*Kat Lewin!*
2019

Once you've spent some time with that example, you can ask yourself: "What advice would this writer give me?" and then give it a try. Even if that solution doesn't work, you'll have gained valuable experience as a reader and as a writer—and you might find you have even more ideas for the next time you edit that part of your essay.

### Wait, I'm Reading The Model Texts Again?! Aren't I Right Back Where I Started?

Writing is an iterative process. Imagine it as a slow spiral upward to excellence: You may feel like you're going in circles, but you are likely moving upward. Because there is always room to improve, writing is never really done—we just have deadlines and eventually force ourselves to stop. But ideally, the process of using imitation to improve your writing looks like Figure 7.2.

## Using Model Texts for Revision

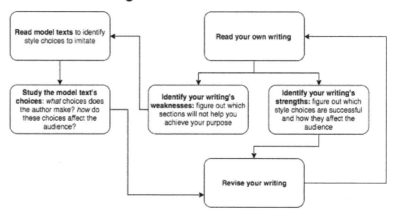

Figure 7.2

And because of the portfolio model of 39A/AP, you have ten weeks to keep refining that process so you can see how far it can take you. Remember also that your identity as a writer includes your skills as a reader, a thinker, and an editor—so as you improve one skill (like writing first drafts), then you may find that when you go to use a different skill (like reading the model texts), you have improved without even noticing it happening.

### Revising Toward an Audience: Empathy + Logic = Effective Rhetorical Choices

Writing is just an act of communication—taking ideas from your brain and putting them in someone else's. You do this *literally all the time*. The most common way we communicate is talking, and chances are, you're already a pretty sophisticated talker who is good at making decisions about, in any given situation, which approaches may or may not be successful. All that talking hasn't been a waste of time! The same logic that you use to communicate successfully one-on-one can help you edit your own writing.

That said, there are some big differences between talking and writing. The biggest, perhaps, is that when we write, *we can't see our audience or their response*s. If you're at a party, talking to a stranger, and you begin to talk so much you get boring, you can tell right away: the person you're talking to may start looking around the room or excuse themselves and join another group or begin frantically texting someone. However, when you're writing an essay, if you're boring your reader—well, they're reading it in a different time and place than you, so you can't see if they're bored. They may be looking around the room or texting. They may even have folded your essay into a paper airplane and flown it to the recycling bin. And you will never know.

Because we can't see our readers' responses, in order to become effective writers, we need to be able to *imagine* our readers' responses by putting ourselves in their shoes. (Another word for this is **empathy**: the ability to share another person's feelings or emotions.)

Once you understand your reader's point of view, then it becomes easier to see places in your own writing that you need to expand or revise. Imagine you are writing for a reader who is very skeptical or critical. If you are writing a persuasive text, imagine a reader who doesn't want to agree with you; if you are writing a text meant to entertain the reader, imagine a reader who is bored and just wants to pull out their phone and check their email; if you are writing an informative text, imagine a reader who may take a while to understand your explanations. Imagine that this reader is intelligent and has their own good reasons for thinking the way they do—and your piece of writing isn't done until you have successfully communicated with this person and made them respond in the way you want them to.

When we assume our readers *want* to agree with us, or that they automatically understand our explanations, we don't have to stretch our brains too much: anything we say will be good enough. But when we imagine a reader who will challenge us, then that makes us challenge and question our own ideas and the way we present them. Considering your own ideas from multiple perspectives like this is an important element of critical thinking. It helps our writing (and ideas) grow stronger.

One way to incorporate a skeptical reader's point of view into your draft is to print out a copy of your essay and read it, pretending to be them. Use those skills you've built up from peer review and give yourself advice. Academic audiences constantly gauge your *ethos* (credibility or authority) and like to ask: "Why should I trust *you*?" As you read your draft, embody this type of reader by stopping at every sentence and challenging yourself to find the objections that reader might make to what you've written.

**Do they understand you?** Where might that sassy reader say: "What do you mean?" or "Can you define that?" or "I think I get what you're saying, but give me an example" or "I know what you mean, but do you know what you mean?"

**Do they believe you?** If you're quoting an expert, will the reader ask: "Why should I trust this person? Why are they an expert on this subject?" (Read the Chapter 3 section about introducing quotes for ideas and how to convince your reader that your sources are credible.) If you're explaining your own idea, where would the reader say: "Prove it!" or "How do you know?" or "Where did that idea come from?" or "Yes, but . . . " Try to imagine the counterarguments that your (educated, intelligent) reader would come up with, so you can account for those arguments in your own writing—before the reader gets a chance to critique you!

**Does the reader care?** Remember that when we think about the situation we're writing in, one of the first questions we have to ask is: "What has the audience already heard about this topic? What do they know/assume/believe about this idea already?" As you edit your draft, take this information into account, and look for places where the reader might say: "I already knew that!" or "That's really obvious!" or "The expert you quoted is making a good point, but what are you adding?" or "So what?"

As you have hopefully absorbed over the course of this chapter, the difficult thing about writing (and the rewarding thing) is that *every choice you make affects whether your communication is successful.* And the Final Portfolio and Final Portfolio Introduction are your opportunity to gather the writing choices you've made in one place and showcase them: to demonstrate to the reader that you have been an active decision-maker and that you have developed the skills to not just satisfy the requirements of Writing 39A/AP, but to continue growing as a writer in your life at UCI and beyond.

## GOALS AND ROUTES: AN ADVENTURE

To return, briefly, to the discussion at the beginning of the chapter: By now, I hope that you understand the goals of this course, and some of the routes you can follow to achieve these goals. Your instructor will determine part of the route you take: they will give you texts to read, assignments to write, class discussion questions to answer. But your instructor isn't the person taking this journey—*you are*. And since it is your journey, you are the one who decides *how* you get there.

As you proceed through Writing 39A/AP, remember that in your life as a student, your choices have effects. Do you want to rush to the goal as quickly as possible, without looking around and asking questions about everything you see? Or would you rather take a leisurely trip, making detours (to the Writing Center and to office hours) and trying to stay in the moment, deeply engaging with the readings and class discussions around you, so that you'll remember your journey?

Your instructor will be there every step of the way, but this is your journey, so choose your route wisely. Bon voyage!

*Sam (Ziwen) Chen is a veteran of Academic English 20C, as well as of Writing 39A, 39B, and 39C. He is also a peer tutor in the UCI Center for Excellence in Writing and Communication, in which role he has presented along with fellow tutors at the 2017 Southern California Writing Centers Association Tutor Conference. Their presentation title, "The Tutor as a Cultural Ambassador," is also a fitting title for this interview, in which Sam comments on differing writing expectations between China and the U.S., and between the Academic English program and 39A. Sam also comments on practices that are useful for all 39A students: imitating professional writers, revising one's own ideas, and soliciting peer and instructor feedback. I interviewed Sam in May of 2017 in my office, and we later revised our conversation to present it in writing here in the AGWR. Enjoy!*
*— Lance Langdon*

**LL:** You are an international student yourself, and you have done research into what it's like for such students to learn writing. What difficulties might international students face in the 39 series, and how can they address them?

**Sam Chen:** First of all, we need to have a consensus that students from different backgrounds are going to have their own embedded writing styles and habits. There's no true or false, there's nothing wrong or bad with international students' writing. But one attitude we want them to establish is to be more adapted to U.S., college-level academic writing.

Within that framework, one difficulty students might have is how they construct their paper. Native speakers often use a lot of transitional words—like additionally, moreover, however, because—to make sentences cohere to one another. But many English learners think that logic has already been implied, has already been embedded, so they can leave it out. From a native speaker's viewpoint, most English learners' essays may be disconnected, not making sense. However, they might make total sense to those English learners.

Also, you might know that Chinese people have circular argumentation, but in an American essay, we want to be straightforward and clearly separate the different points. But Chinese students, most of them think, "I have already told you about this, that's already implicated, so I don't need to further explain it." Or they just explain one thing again and again, back and forth, but don't make further points. So I instruct the students I tutor on proofs, on argumentation.

The last issue is about grammar. English learners don't have systematic pedagogy here in the U.S. They want to adapt to college-level grammar, but college grammar might not be identical to what they learned before. For example, in China, we say, "You help me *to* do the homework." But in our essays here, it's better to say, "You help me *do* homework." In China we say that both of them are fine, but in the U.S., not. So I think the only way that students can improve themselves to make their paper sound more native or more academic is to read more.

**LL:** Let's talk about differences between Academic English (AE) classes and 39A. What should students expect coming out of AE and into 39A?

**SC:** In Academic English the professor concentrates more on the sentence level—for example, the grammar—and on whether or not the student has followed whatever format the professor has proposed. But in 39A, and the 39 series, I feel like the professors have a higher expectation on students' ideas, their initiative, and their own creativity. Students need to focus more on polishing their ideas first, then working on polishing their sentence-level writing.

Students need to understand the writing expectations of the professor. Here, I may want to stand on the students' side, because some professors will not make their expectations clear, which makes students ambiguous in what they are writing. Hopefully, a measurement that can help deal with this problem is coming to the professor's office hours. In the writing series, I think students need to work constantly with the professor.

**LL:** When the professor doesn't propose a format such as the five-paragraph essay, how does a student decide what format to follow?

**SC:** In order to answer that question, let me take you back to two years ago when I was in AE. Although our professor did not encourage us in using the five-paragraph program, that format was still implied. However, when I moved into 39A, that format just vanished. We had the freedom and the power to make our own format. So I believe that students need to know what their professors want them to do. Then the students need to think about their own structure. So what I tell my students in my program is we don't think about 5-paragraph essay. Rather than trying to include everything about one topic in one paragraph, we divide an essay into a couple of parts each consisting of multiple paragraphs. We think about different parts of the essay, then think of the logic connecting the parts to make their ideas stronger.

The second suggestion I would give students to adapt to 39-series writing is to read through the in-class material. Some of my students have very good in-class material that the professor gives them. They have something they can imitate and make reference to.

**LL:** You're absolutely right. Students in 39A learn a lot by reading and imitating professional authors and by reflecting on how that imitation helps them to connect with their readers.

Another cornerstone of 39A is revision. I noticed that for the first major assignment in 39A you wrote several drafts of your poem, "A Lovely Doll." Why did you do four or five drafts, and what changed over those drafts?

**SC:** Professor Abbie Leavens gave us an analysis of another poem, "Lady Lazarus" by Sylvia Plath. Plath was depressed and sad. When we were in class, Professor Abbie gave us many insights in analyzing Plath's poems. For example, she talked about using imagery, using contradiction, using conversation, or using the depiction of the environment to create a feeling in our poem. So I kind of adapted those ideas. When I was doing multiple drafts, I still did the same story, but I tried to fill in those elements I learned in class.

LL: Some students are not sure how much to change from draft to draft. Did you change a lot?

SC: For students, as we finish our writing we have a sense of achievement and accomplishment. We think, "I'm done with this paper, finally. I'm good with it, it's good to go, it's perfect for me." Me too, when I was in the writing series, I felt that my poem was perfect in draft 1.

However, there are two sides to writing. On the one hand, for all of your writing, as long as it's made by you, you should have a sense of achievement, because you wrote it. But, as a rational, conscientious person, you need to admit there are things you need to change, to improve on, so that sense of achievement should not become an excuse for not making further effort in polishing your drafts.

LL: Any tips for when students are editing?

SC: When you do proofreading, you really need to be a third party. Students will have a sense of achievement after they've finished a paper, so although they will do proofreading, they will just read through all the errors because they already have the ideas in their head. Instead, when they do proofreading, they need to have an idea that they are independent, that they are a third party. I'm not saying that they can throw out all their ideas. But they need to proofread their ideas with a critical eye.

LL: We have talked a lot about 39A. But what did you learn in 39A that you could also apply in 39B?

SC: In the RA Essay for 39B, you have to stand in the author's shoes to understand how they use rhetoric to make their idea clear. And in the RIP, which consists of two parts, you need to be both subjective and objective. To make up the RIP project, students are subjective, picking up the rhetorical tools. But the second part of the RIP is the essay. Now they need to be objective to analyze their own story. So they are doing both

LL: How about moving from 39B and into 39C, or upper-division writing. Did you learn a process in these writing classes that you used again later?

SC: When I went into those later classes, I actively did work with my professor. I always attended the professor's office hours and I tried to get both my instructor's and my peer's ideas. If you can hear more voices other than your own, it will make your paper more inclusive and comprehensive. So going to office hours is the first technique, and asking peers to give me some feedback is another technique.

In the end, you're going to submit your essay to the professor, so the paper needs to not only make yourself happy, but also to make others happy, to make sense to others.

## Chapter 8

# WR39B: Critical Reading and Rhetoric

*By Kat Lewin and Tagert Ellis with Elizabeth Allen and Jackie Way*

Hey y'all—I'm Kat Lewin! I earned my MFA in Fiction at UCI, and have been teaching composition here since 2011. Along the way, I accidentally fell in love with rhetoric for the exact same reason I love fiction: it's a way to see the world in terms of choices and the effects of those choices. When I write fiction, I let my characters make a choice (steal that hot air balloon!) and spend the rest of the story exploring the effects of that choice (ugh, your hot air balloon drifted into a volcano?!). Rhetoric works the same way, but with less Grand Theft Zeppelin. As an academic writer, you make choices—like including a credible quote, or using a semicolon, or choosing diction that evokes a particular tone—in order to create certain effects on your reader. And then through the process of revision, you can keep tweaking your choices until you've finally nailed the effect you want.

I'm Tagert Ellis. Just like Kat, I earned my MFA in Fiction at UCI, and have been teaching composition here since 2011. When I'm not teaching, you can find me experimenting with other kinds of rhetorical situations: writing hypertext fiction, playing video games, composing music, laying out websites, photoshopping memes, or writing profile pieces. While I only get paid for some of these tasks (injustice!), the cool thing about rhetoric is that knowing a few simple principles can make you into a jack-of-all-trades. You'll start to see life as it is: a series of rhetorical situations to which you need to find the best possible approach.

When we say "we" in this chapter, we're not referring to the Robotic Rhetorical Hivemind (RRH)—we are just two humans who love teaching rhetoric because we believe that mastering rhetoric gives people the power to change their own lives for the better. And trust us, there's no better training ground than 39B.

## Writing 39B: An Overview

### Writing 39B: What Is It?

In Chapter 1, you learned that rhetoric is the art of effectively communicating by accounting for the rhetorical situation of a text: its *ethos*, audience, genre, and cultural and historical context. In Writing 39B, you'll gain hands-on experience in critically reading texts in order to understand their rhetorical appeals and cultivating your own skills as a **rhetor**: someone capable of successfully communicating in a variety of contexts by analyzing rhetorical situations using that analysis to make focused, effective decisions in order to best communicate your message.

The work in Writing 39B is likely different from work you have done in previous English or writing courses. Writing 39B demands that you shift from an imitator to an innovator. In this course, you will take ownership of your writing by defining the rhetorical situations of your writing tasks and using your understanding of those rhetorical situations to make meaningful decisions about *how* you write.

While the number of assignments in Writing 39B is finite, the **rhetorical know-how** you will cultivate in order to understand and master those assignments will give you the ability to better address *any* future communications—formal or informal, academic or personal—as a skilled and confident rhetor.

### Writing 39B will equip you with the tools you need to:

▷ *Recognize rhetoric at work in the world around you—it's everywhere, once you know how to recognize it!*

▷ *Actively read and understand different types of texts, with an eye to the rhetorical appeals these texts use to communicate their messages*

▷ *Analyze the rhetorical situations of any text in order to help you gain fuller understanding of the text itself and how that text creates meaning*

▷ *Take control of your own identity as a rhetor, and particularly master the academic ethos that you will rely upon to enhance your credibility in every step of your university career*

▷ *Compose sustained, persuasive argumentative essays shaped by strong reason and expert appeal to the specific audience you aim to persuade*

▷ *Master revision so you can become your own best editor, reduce your reliance on instructor feedback, and figure out how to make better choices as a writer, based on the rhetorical situations of your writing tasks*

## How To Use This Chapter

Over the course of your writing life, and over the course of 39B, you will learn small skills, practice using them, and then when you've started to achieve mastery, be asked to use those skills in new, more complicated ways. We have written this 39B chapter with that idea in mind. Throughout this chapter you will find we keep coming back to some of the same ideas. Those ideas grow more complicated as the chapter progresses, just as your own work and thinking will complicate as you proceed through the course.

We have organized this chapter in a modular way, to help you build and combine small skills. Imagine the sections in this chapter as small plates—tapas. A bunch of them together are a fantastic meal, but they're awesome on their own too. You can dive in and out of sections of this chapter as you please, depending on what you're wondering about at a given moment in time. So, please, be inquisitive, jump around, and make the most out of this chapter, compadre. *¡Vámonos!*

## Argumentative Writing: Joining the Conversation

A good portion of the writing in 39B will focus on helping you develop your skills in one specific rhetorical situation: writing analytical, argumentative essays within an academic context and developing the academic *ethos* to make those arguments credible.

Argumentative writing, in 39B and beyond, can be seen as an entry into an ongoing conversation. Let's say you're making an argument about why you think it is important to wear pants. Debates have been raging in the outside world for centuries, eons even, about whether pants are a good idea or not. People have written books, made cave paintings, and written lots of angry forum posts about the utility and social necessity of pants. Sometimes they got into fistfights. Imagine this ongoing conversation as a rowdy but refined cocktail party. You wouldn't just barge into the room uninvited and start shouting at everybody about your opinions (or, maybe you would, in which case, reconsider the decisions you've made about your life). Most likely, you'd make sure you were invited to the party (by having a personality, or *ethos*, that convinces people you're going to add to the intellectual atmosphere). Then, you'd find the people talking about pants, and you'd listen carefully to what they say. Only then would you add your own opinion—and you'd communicate it in a way that was respectful to what had been said before.

Argumentative writing is no different. In order to establish yourself as a credible rhetor, you must listen to what has been said about your topic before, acknowledging and understanding it even if you don't plan to directly respond to it. Then you must make sure that your opinion is backed up by evidence—and that it's intellectually interesting and unique (since, you know, you want these people to think you're interesting, so you get invited to the next pants-or-no-pants party).

To insert yourself meaningfully into a conversation, you need to appeal to your audience by understanding that audience's expectations and meeting or exceeding those expectations. In the case of academic arguments, that means you need to know how to effectively respond to other people's ideas, make sure you have something worthwhile to say, and develop your own credible voice. 39B will help you learn all of these skills.

## How We Use the Rhetorical Triangle in This Chapter

In this chapter, we'll be deepening and expanding the introduction to rhetoric in Chapter 1 of this book. We're still interested in the relationship between the writer (whom we'll call the RHETOR, or the person who creates the rhetoric), the AUDIENCE, and the TEXT (what the rhetor creates and what the audience receives). We also will still consider the way that a text's PURPOSE and GENRE are shaped by its larger CONTEXT (Figure 8.1).

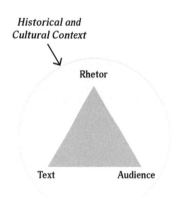

Figure 8.1

However, we'll be expanding this triangle to consider more aspects of rhetoric.

When we approach the TEXT, we'll also be wondering about what MESSAGE or messages it may be sending, and how MEDIUM shapes the text as a whole. We also have the ability think about STYLE choices that the author makes regarding how they compose the text.

When we think about the RHETOR, we'll also ask what sort of *ETHOS* the rhetor adopts.

Finally, when thinking about the AUDIENCE, we have the opportunity to think about how to define the audience based on DEMOGRAPHICS, and (more importantly) how to understand that audience's PSYCHOGRAPHICS, or shared BELIEFS, HABITS, OPINIONS, and INTERESTS (Figure 8.2).

Figure 8.2

## The Writing 39B Assignment Sequence

Writing 39B's assignment sequence is meant to help you think deeply about rhetoric, craft essays that reflect that deep thought, and hone awareness of your own position as a rhetor in every one of your communications—both formal and informal.

The formal work of 39B all builds towards the Final Portfolio. This Portfolio serves as a platform for you to make a meta-argument that you've grown into a so-phisticated rhetorical thinker (Figure 8.3).

This sophisticated thinking begins with **classroom discussion**, which provides the foundation for every-thing that follows. In-class discussions, prewriting, and group work start you thinking about the texts you're examining as a class and about your own devel-opment as a writer and rhetorical thinker.

**Low-stakes writing** assignments and online discus-sion posts will allow you to strike out on your own and focus on building individual skills that you will com-bine for the major assignments, as well as provide you with spaces for **metacognitive reflection**—thinking about your own thinking. This work prepares you for the two major assignments in Writing 39B.

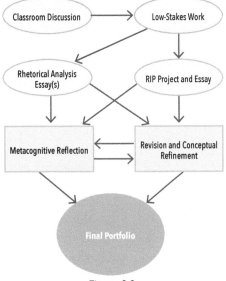

Figure 8.3

## LOOKING TOWARDS THE PORTFOLIO: THE RUBRIC

Your performance in 39B is predicated mainly upon your instructor's eval-uation of the Portfolios you submit. They will examine your accumulated effort and success in the course, as represented by each Portfolio and a handful of other important qualities. The Portfolio Rubrics that your instructor will use to determine your grade don't only judge the Portfolio, but also, to some extent, ask how you've been performing all quarter as a writer and as an engaged scholar. Some of the qualities that the rubric asks about include the ability to make focused and convincing ar-guments, the ability to structure and tailor work in a given genre for a specific audience, and the ability to meet benchmarks throughout the quarter. You should get a copy of the newest Portfolio Rubric from your instructor at the beginning of the quarter and use it to guide your work all quarter as you focus on which skills to build and how to prove that you've built them. If they don't give it to you, ask them for it—it's a fantastic way to show initiative!

One major assignment you'll be asked to complete is the **Rhetorical Analysis Essay (RA)**: a sustained and formal argument about the rhetoric in a particular text. This assignment requires you to collect evidence from a text, build an original argument about the text's rhetoric, and sustain that argument over many paragraphs, assembling a compelling, persuasive essay.

The other major assignment is the RIP, or **Rhetoric-In-Practice project**. For the RIP, you will produce a text that seeks to achieve a certain purpose while targeting a certain audience. You will write an accompanying RIP Essay that explains, in detail, the rhetorical situation of that text: the rhetorical decisions you've chosen to make and how those decisions help you communicate your message effectively.

All major assignments, in addition to other artifacts of your choice, will be assembled into your **Final Portfolio**. In your portfolio, you will curate an electronic document that makes a big-picture argument about your growth and mastery as a writer during your time in 39B. You will compose a rhetorically sophisticated Introduction to contextualize the work you introduce, reflect on your progress, and argue that you've acquired the skills the course demands.

## Why a Portfolio?

Writing 39B runs on a portfolio system. What does this mean? Instead of just plunking an essay draft on your instructor's desk and leaving for the Anteatery (It's avocado toast day, brorider!), you'll be asked to put that major work in the context of the rest of your work from the quarter, writing an incisive portfolio introduction where you reflect on your progress so far, look forward to what's on the horizon, and (most importantly) use evidence to argue that you've reached a certain level of aptitude in the course so far.

Leading up to the portfolio turn-in date, your instructor will have given you targeted feedback about how your work can be improved and strengthened—and your instructor will ask *you* to show the initiative to give yourself feedback. You'll use feedback from your instructor, your peers, and yourself (as well as tutors from the Writing Center or elsewhere) to dramatically and fearlessly revise your work: rethinking your positions, rewriting your arguments, and pushing yourself closer and closer to mastery. By the time the portfolio is due, you'll have drafted each major assignment multiple times.

Because of this, the portfolio process demands a lot of you as a student. It is not enough to write a paper, squeeze your eyes shut, submit it, and pray for leniency. You must look at your work with eyes wide open and be willing to accept constructive criticism. What's more, you must be proactive about seeking this criticism, visiting your instructor during conferences and during regular office hours to ask about your work and how it can be improved. If you don't do this, you're not going to get arrested or anything, but you are going to miss out entirely on the benefits of the portfolio model and sacrifice opportunities to grow as a writer.

## KEY TERM: METACOGNITION

**Metacognition** is a word that we use to refer to the process of thinking about your own thinking. The root meta means "above" and "cognition" is another word for thinking. So "metacognition" refers to thinking that's raised up a level above typical thinking—thinking that's reflexive. This type of thinking about thinking is very important in 39B, and you'll be provided with lots of opportunities to practice it.

It's important to remember that *needing to revise (or even completely rewrite) your essay does NOT mean that you've fundamentally failed.* Do not let it get you down. First off, revision is the hallmark of a brave, confident, intelligent student. It takes bravery and confidence to make major changes to a draft, and intelligence to know where and how those changes should occur. Besides, *every* draft of an essay—even if completely different from the final draft—represents exploratory work that increases your familiarity with the text, deepens your understanding of how its rhetorical gears interlock, and offers valuable practice with fundamental compositional skills. The students who do the best in 39B are willing to revise early, revise heavily, and revise often, frequently visiting their instructors in office hours and tutors in the Writing Center to solicit feedback that they can use to direct their next revision.

Not every revision might make it into the portfolios—lumping all of your major work in the course together thoughtlessly is not a rhetorically effective means of persuading your audience of your success in the course. Rather, the work you select should be assembled carefully: *curated.* Each page should add to your argument that you've become an effective rhetor, a sensitive communicator.

We will discuss this process in more detail later in this chapter. In fact, *it might be a good idea to skip ahead to the portfolio section of this chapter* and get acquainted with what will be expected of you, so that you can keep the portfolios in mind as you approach every assignment in this course.

Metacognitive Checkpoint: Your Writing History

*Throughout this chapter, we'll be providing metacognitive checkpoints. These are opportunities to reflect on your writing, and on your work in 39B, in ways that will help develop your understanding of your growth as a writer and help prepare you for the tasks that lie ahead, including the metacognitive writing you'll be doing in the final portfolio. Write your responses to these exercises somewhere where you'll be able to keep them and access them throughout the quarter.*

*For this first metacognitive checkpoint, reflect on where you are as a writer as you're first entering into Writing 39B. Some questions you may choose to address include:*

▶ *What skills do you have, and what skills do you know you need to work on?*

▶ *What is your past experience in writing courses (what has been rewarding, what has been difficult)?*

▶ *What is your personal connection to writing? Really, how has writing challenged or enriched you in the past?*

▶ *How do you see writing, and maybe Writing 39B in particular, fitting into your greater college experience and into your future life?*

▶ *How has the course so far compared to your expectations of the course before you arrived?*

▶ *What challenges have you encountered in this course so far, and how do you plan to work to overcome them?*

## WHAT IS WRITING 37?

Writing 37 is subtitled "Intensive Writing," and that's what you should expect if you're placed into the course! Writing 37 is an enhanced version of Writing 39B that offers the same instruction in critical reading and analysis, but features additional instruction focused on things like paragraph development and sentence-level mechanics. Several of these areas of focus are borrowed or adapted from Writing 39A. In this way, Writing 37 functions as a sort of middle ground between Writing 39A and Writing 39B, though it may be more accurate to think of it as "Writing 39B *Plus*." Perhaps the easiest way to explain Writing 37 is to examine what carries over from Writing 39B and what sets Writing 37 apart!

### HOW IS WRITING 37 SIMILAR TO WRITING 39B?

Writing 37 features the same primary focuses as Writing 39B. Your assignment sequence will be the same, featuring assignments that deal with critical reading of texts, argumentative rhetorical analysis, construction of your own rhetoric, and metacognitive reflection on your own progress and your own position as a rhetorical thinker.

### HOW IS WRITING 37 DIFFERENT FROM WRITING 39B?

- **More units:** While Writing 39B is a four-unit course, Writing 37 is a six-unit course.

- **More practice:** Because the course is six units, there is more time and space for you to put in more practice with the types of writing the course will expect you to master. You'll spend extra time each week in class. Outside of class, you'll be expected to demonstrate a higher level of time commitment and engagement to succeed in the course.

- **Instruction in style, tone, voice, and mechanics:** Writing 39A focuses more closely on recognizing a writer's style, tone, and voice. Writing 37 allows time for your instructor to lead you through these principles, in addition to prioritizing other concepts from Writing 39A such as effective argumentative structure, thoughtful paragraph organization, and authorial ownership.

- **More focus on building self-sufficiency:** Writing 37 will help you learn how to determine your own strengths and weaknesses, so that you'll be better equipped to build and revise your own work without heavy reliance on instructor, peer, or tutor feedback.

- **A greater focus on iterative drafting:** The increased amount of time spent in class and out of class on writing allows your instructor to put a stronger focus on iterative drafting—asking you not just to write but to rewrite (and rewrite again!) thoughtfully, improving your work incrementally as you gain increasing skill in the abilities the course teaches.

## The Rhetoric of the 39B Classroom: Building Skills and *Ethos*

One of the most important things to remember in Writing 39B is that *you are a rhetor all the time.* Everything you do in the course, from writing essays to emailing your instructor, represents a form of communication that you have the opportunity to rhetorically shape as you see fit. So, before we even get into the assignments, it might be helpful to think about how *you,* the human behind all of this work, can present yourself successfully to your instructor and your peers. This is a life lesson, dude.

We'd like to encourage you in this section to think about how the success of your written work begins with your in-class engagement—and not just whether you're doing the work (or even paying attention!), but whether you're demonstrating a conceptual understanding of the principles the class asks you to grasp.

Let's get real deep for a second and consider your face as a text. Ha ha, yes, but really—your facial expression (and even your posture) can communicate any number of things to people around you: it can tell them whether you're happy, sad, bored, or engaged. It can tell them if you're angry or dejected. If you come into class in a bad mood, disaffected and sullen, your instructor might just think you don't really care about the material. Maybe that's not what you intended to communicate, but it was what you communicated nonetheless. *You are always a rhetor, and your choices determine your ethos.*

Think of *ethos* as broken into two parts: clout (AKA credibility) and persona. The first part of *ethos,* clout, involves to what degree and in which situations people feel like they can trust you based on your past actions or your qualifications.

In the absence of clout, every one of us has the ability to leverage persona. Persona is the face that we're putting on, the mask that we're wearing. Persona is a performance. You can (and probably already do) use persona in many ways. No one wakes up one day as a perfect college student—it's a role you imagine yourself into until you master it. In other words, you fake it until you make it. When you send an email to your professor, for instance, you realize that a professional email includes a salutation ("Dear Professor..."), some social niceties ("I hope this letter finds you well. I have a question..."), and a valediction ("Sincerely, Derek"). Maybe these aren't tools you would use in a casual email to a friend (or a text message to your sister, or a vlog for the senior citizens' home), but they're expected in formal written communication, so you put on a mask for a second and inhabit that role. This persona lets you build clout, and it shapes the way others perceive you.

On the other hand, failures of rhetoric can have catastrophic social consequences. Using bad pickup lines can scare off potential love interests, because those canned one-liners don't account for that person's humanity and intelligence. Cursing and using slang in a job application similarly represents a failure of *ethos*. You won't get the job because you didn't understand the rhetorical situation. *Understanding the rhetorical situation of the classroom environment and of academic professionalism means you've taken the first step to proving that you're able to perceive and utilize rhetoric*—one of the major goals of this course.

---

### PRO TIP: GO TO OFFICE HOURS AND THE WRITING CENTER

You have lots of resources available to help you develop your writing. Among these are your instructor's office hours, the Writing Center on campus (as well as their Peer Tutors division), and regularly scheduled conferences with your instructor. Seeking help in this way is something you should do regularly. The most important reason is that it will help improve your writing. But, as a corollary benefit, imagine your instructor's reaction when a well-mannered, confident student strides through their door, wanting to improve their work without being asked. What a fine ethos you've developed! What a way to meet the benchmarks that the portfolio rubric explicitly demands!

---

*Ethos and the Portfolio*

While each portfolio is primarily a venue for you to show off your written work in the course, it's important not to forget all the things that lead up to (and help you craft) that written work. *The portfolio is an opportunity to assess not only the quality and clarity of your writing, but also your ability to cultivate successful processes for writing and revision.* To create a successful portfolio, you will need to persuasively articulate the skills you have demonstrated in this course. But to build your *ethos*, you should strongly consider how you might also prove skills that the rubric does not explicitly mention, such as initiative (Did you take charge of your own learning or were you merely a passive recipient of knowledge and feedback?), ownership and awareness (Did you understand the feedback given to you, incorporate it well, and take responsibility for your own performance?), and how often (and effectively) you sought help and asked targeted questions. So, when you sit down to curate (and write the introduction for) each portfolio, your written work should not be your only concern.

*Think of your portfolio as a meta-argument—a way to persuade your instructor that you've been successful in the course.* Your written work is strong evidence you can analyze to make this argument, but your drafts alone do not tell the full story of your growth as a writer in this course. You have plenty of other evidence you can bring in as well. Did you have a perfect attendance record? Did you attend office hours every week? Did you participate frequently and thoughtfully in classroom discussions? Did you otherwise make an effort to go beyond the minimum expectations in contributing to the intellectual culture of the classroom?

Right now, as you read this (and as it is early yet in the quarter), *think about the types of claims you want to be able to make about your own engagement, initiative, and ownership once you finally sit down to curate a portfolio.*

**You should also make sure you have a reliable way to collect evidence over the course of the quarter.** While work submitted to Canvas will remain accessible to you later in the quarter, you should also keep your own back-ups of assignments, and find a good way to maintain an archive of work that you don't submit to Canvas during the quarter—notes, reading annotations, and other artifacts.

### *Using Low-Stakes Writing to Build Rhetorical Know-How*

Before you dive into writing a full-fledged essay, you'll hone your skills using low-stakes writing assignments, prewrites, freewrites, and other preparatory work. The key to succeeding in any given task in 39B is to remember that, from participating in classroom discussion to writing weekly discussion posts, **every assignment has its own rhetorical situation**, and the key to your success as a rhetor is understanding that rhetorical situation and using it to craft an effective response.

Before you begin an assignment, consider its rhetorical situation by asking yourself: What is your **purpose**? What *ethos* are you being asked to adopt? Who is the **audience** and what are their expectations of you? What is the **genre** of the assignment, and which conventions of that genre will the audience expect you to follow? What is the **context** of the assignment, and which conversations will your work be adding to?

Let's take, as an example, a discussion forum assignment, where you and your classmates write responses to a central prompt and discuss these responses (Figure 8.4).

In this particular rhetorical situation, the genre of a forum post demands that you and your classmates (and your instructor) switch from rhetor to audience and back again—participating in a collaborative, reciprocal exchange of ideas which may serve as part of the context for your class's future discussions on the same topic. When posting and responding, you'll be (maybe unconsciously) considering the genre

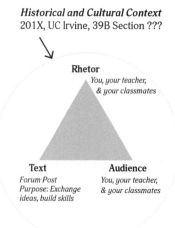

*Historical and Cultural Context*
201X, UC Irvine, 39B Section ???

**Rhetor**
*You, your teacher, & your classmates*

**Text**
*Forum Post*
*Purpose: Exchange ideas, build skills*

**Audience**
*You, your teacher, & your classmates*

Figure 8.4

expectations of forum posts and of academic writing and searching for a way to balance the demands of each genre to achieve the purpose of the assignment. Since you share historical and cultural context with your audience, you might feel free to make some assumptions about their habits and knowledge—maybe you'll discuss current events at UCI without feeling the need to provide much background information, because your audience is part of the UCI discourse community.

**Considering the rhetorical situations of assignments will not only improve your know-how as a rhetorical analyst, but will also help you make more effective choices as a rhetor.** Just as in-class discussion is meant to help you develop ideas and contribute to the intellectual culture of the class without a fear of feeling judged or called out, so too do these low-stakes writing assignments represent a sort of rhetorical charm school—a place to practice thinking rhetorically about *how* to communicate in a given situation, and then honing the composition skills to do so as well as possible. Some assignments may ask you to focus on **critical reading** skills that will later help you perform in-depth rhetorical analysis. Others may focus on **Rhetoric In Practice**, asking you to operate within a real-world (or imaginary) rhetorical situation to achieve a goal, building skills that will be particularly useful in the RIP project. All of the low-stakes work is carefully designed to provide you with skills you can carry forward into the major assignments and into your life and career after the course is over.

Metacognitive Checkpoint: Make An Argument About A Writing Skill In Process

For this metacognitive checkpoint, you'll be choosing a piece of low-stakes work you've completed and making an argument about how it demonstrates a particular course skill.

▶ *First, choose one low-stakes assignment (for example, a CR Exercise, RIP Exercise, or Reflective Writing Assignment) that you believe has been instrumental in helping you develop ONE of the skills of the course. To choose which skill to focus on, it can be helpful to take a look at the course rubric or the learning outcomes.*

▶ *Then, write a reflection focusing on this assignment, where you make a claim about how this piece of writing demonstrates your aptitude in a particular skill. Every good argument requires evidence, and this is no exception; you should include quotes or excerpts of the assignment that demonstrate the skill you're claiming. Make sure to patiently analyze the evidence you've introduced to support your claim about the skill you see in that assignment. This means pointing to specific portions of the assignment and explaining HOW those portions of the assignment represent your aptitude in this skill. DO NOT just summarize what you did in this assignment! Instead, think of this as an argument: you want to prove to your reader that this assignment demonstrates your development in this skill.*

▶ *You can perform this metacognitive reflection multiple times. Try doing it any time you complete an assignment that teaches you something new, surprising, or valuable about writing or about your own writing process.*

▶ *You can also attempt a version of this exercise where you look at two different artifacts (perhaps one from earlier in the quarter and one from later), and compare your performance on the two pieces of work to make an argument about your growth. This is a fantastic form of prewriting for your final portfolio.*

## Reading for Rhetoric: Moving Towards Rhetorical Analysis

When we read, we start with *what happens*, identifying themes, character development, and literary devices. When we start to think about *why* and *how* the text conveys its meaning and its purpose, we are thinking about rhetoric. When we think about how a text communicates within a context, we are thinking about rhetoric. When we think about how a text communicates to an audience, we are thinking about rhetoric. **Rhetoric is a series of decisions that the writer or speaker or artist makes, in order to communicate message(s).** Rhetorical analysis begins when we ask *why* and *how* a text communicates (Figure 8.5).

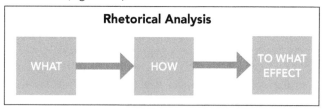

Figure 8.5

We always begin with what is being depicted. What is the plot of the story, or the content of the essay? As rhetorical analysts, **we're most interested in asking *how* that communication is crafted and *what effects* these decisions have.** *How* does the story communicate with its audience? *How* does the essay convey its message? The "how" can consist of word choices, sentence structures, overall structure, metaphor, allusion, citation, and many other specific uses of language.

Let's consider, for example, *how* one could communicate the message, "I'm angry." Telling someone that you're angry by saying, "I'm angry at you" gets the message across simply and directly. Changing your *ethos* by intensifying your word choice to create a sterner tone ("I'm furious with you") will change the message, as the recipient now knows that you're not just angry, you're *very* angry. On the other hand, changing the **genre** to a text conversation and using emoji might tell the recipient that you're not very serious about your anger, since you felt that cartoon emoticons could reasonably express it (and you ended the chain of emoji with a rainbow and a bicycle). Changing the **context** of the communication makes a difference too. Imagine telling a friend "I'm angry at you" in line at Subway, versus saying it to them as you drive them to a funeral. Changing the **rhetorical situation** of a message makes all the difference.

### How Does the Text Interface with the World?

As rhetoricians, we're interested in situating a text in its context. What influenced the **production** of the text? That is, how does the world shape the text? What **reception** does the text seem to be trying to generate? That is, how does the text seek to affect the world (whether directly or indirectly)? See Figure 8.6. **We are interested in the interaction between the text and the outside world.**

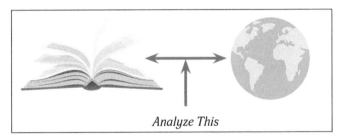

*Analyze This*

Figure 8.6

Note that the arrow in the above diagram points to the interaction between the text and world—*not to the text or the world alone*. If we only analyze the text without considering the wider communicative situation, we lose the sense of the text's purpose. This includes arguments that broadly refer to effects on "a reader" without sufficient support (or attention to who that reader might specifically be—their characteristics, values, beliefs, preferences, and assumptions!). On the other hand, if our argument focuses on the world and attempts to make an argument that doesn't sufficiently involve the text, we've stopped textual analysis and have accidentally moved into advocacy or analysis that focuses on the world itself.

Chapter 2, "Practicing Critical Reading," has a lot of great tips for how to do this—read that chapter, and read it closely. Once you've done that, read on to get our recommendations on how to effectively read for (and subsequently research) each aspect of the rhetorical situation in a text in ways that will specifically help you build a sustained argument in 39B.

The key is to make sure you're examining the way the text was influenced by the world and/or the way the text sought to influence the world. To understand in detail how the text connects with the outside world, we need to research and read about aspects of the world that we may not know everything about yet—whether that's the text's audience, the text's context, or how the text's genre was positioned at the time it was released. This focus leaves a wide variety of possible argumentative strategies at our disposal.

A "text" can be a literary text like a short story or a novel, of course, but everything from TV to paintings, business cards to text messages, can be understood as a "text." Every text communicates within a recognizable genre, conveys meaning within a rhetorical context, has a purpose, conveys a message, and tries to reach an audience. Analyzing texts rhetorically, however, can take practice. So don't worry if it takes time for you to get used to it!

The first step in being able to analyze rhetoric is recognizing rhetoric at work in a text and reading attentively to determine the function of that rhetoric.

## Sample: Arguments

Targeted rhetorical reading not only helps you understand a text better, but also prepares you to develop an interesting, complicated argument based on rhetorical analysis. Throughout this chapter, we have included thesis statements from real 39B students who have chosen to make arguments about these aspects of rhetoric. From these examples, you can see how rhetorical reading transitions into strong rhetorical argument.

As you read through the sample thesis statements provided, **pay special attention to the bolded portion of each thesis—this is the part of the thesis that reaches outside of the text to examine the interaction between the text and the outside world.** Noting what aspects make these arguments explicitly rhetorical will make it easier for you to develop an argument that goes past literary analysis into rhetorical analysis!

### Reading and Researching for Message

In order to read rhetorically, you must ask, *to what effect* does this text seem to have been written? We need to know *to what effect* a text has been written before we can begin to understand *how* that effect was created, and *how* is the heart of rhetoric!

Good news: there isn't just one "correct" message, which means you're not going to get an F for "choosing the wrong message." Most texts have dozens, hundreds, or thousands of messages—some big, some small, some explored throughout the text, and some only emphasized in sections of the text.

Bad news: *thousands* of messages? Stressful. We know.

So how do you find the message you want to write about? There's no single way to go about this monumental task, but here are some ideas to get you started.

| GUIDING QUESTIONS FOR UNDERSTANDING MESSAGE |
|---|

1. *What is the text trying to argue? What does the text seem to believe?*

2. *Why do you think that the text has this opinion? Which particular scenes or events made you believe that this message is in the text?*

3. *Does the text seem to explain why its message is true?*

4. *Does the text defy (or "subvert") any of its genre conventions?*

5. *What is the urgency of this message?*

**What is the text trying to argue here? What does the text seem to believe?** That's really all a message is. You might find on the first try that you come up with a message that's a bit vague or generic, something like "don't judge a book by its cover," or "if you're mean to people, bad things will happen to you." That's a totally fine place to start. Your ideas will get deeper as you continue exploring them through the drafting process.

**Why do you think that the text has this opinion? Which particular scenes or events made you believe that this message is in the text?** Yes, *of course* you'll have to reread at least parts of the text. Making good margin notes on your first read will save you lots of time when you reread.

**Does all this evidence 100% agree with your message?** Probably not! You could just ignore all the evidence that disagrees with or complicates the message you want to argue. But ignoring parts of the text just because they're inconvenient is like running a lab experiment and throwing away or falsifying data just because it disagrees with your conclusion. It's lazy and unethical. Plus, if people realize you're doing it (and they will), your *ethos* goes down the drain. So, how can you reconcile the portions of the text that seem to disagree? How can you use that disagreement to complicate your idea of the text's message(s)?

**Does the text seem to explain *why* its message is true?** One good way to start complicating a thesis is to think about adding a "because." *The text argues that you shouldn't judge a book by its cover because doing so will cause you to miss out on important opportunities.* Not perfect but much better, right?

**What is the urgency of this message?** Is this message being communicated in a context where it is sorely needed, or to an audience that could really use it? The messages that emerge from a close rhetorical reading of a text are rarely as simple as the "motivational poster" messages you may have been taught to find when performing literary analysis. Messages like "Don't judge a book by its cover," or "Success requires hard work and dedication," or "Everyone has their own special strengths" can be developed further and made more specific through close attention to the rhetorical need for such a message.

As you think about the text's message, try to figure out which parts of the rhetorical situation help the rhetor effectively communicate that message. Look out for the decisions made about *how* that message is communicated in the text!

### Reading and Researching for Medium and Form

Medium and form can seem very simple on the surface, and, in some ways, they are: medium is simply a text's means of transmission, and form involves the structure and style of the text.

When it comes to medium and form, your job as a rhetorical reader is to figure out how your text's meaning is tied to (or inextricable from) the means of transmission and the structure of the text. This task will often involve understanding how to properly *read* the medium and form you're dealing with. Some forms and media share reading techniques. Reading petroglyphs, for example, has striking similarities to reading a graphic novel. Reading a poem shares some of the qualities of reading a rap song. But you must also understand the characteristics unique to each form and medium. While both petroglyphs and graphic novels require you to understand the spatial relation of images on a two-dimensional plane, graphic novels place more emphasis on the sequence of the images presented, and they use that sequencing to determine spatial and temporal relationships.

### PRO TIP: RESEARCHING MEDIUM

In your research, look for scholars who specialize in a given medium or form, and learn their techniques for effectively reading these texts. For instance, Scott McCloud, a comic theorist, has written a book called Understanding Comics that has emerged as the contemporary bible for theorists and analysts (such as yourself!) who seek to understand the ways that visual/spatial/graphical meaning (pictures) and lexical/verbal meaning (words) interact in a comic or graphic novel.

### Reading and Researching for Genre

Your instructor may provide readings to help you discuss the genre (and generic conventions) of the texts you're reading, but you may also need to do some of this research yourself. Genre is, after all, just a set of conventions shared among multiple texts. Not every text in a given genre will share every convention of that genre. Not every rap song will feature curse words and misogyny, and not every novel will feature traditional chapter divisions.

First, you'll need to figure out which genre(s) you think your text falls into. Let's say you know that you're reading a horror novel. Well, excellent! You now have two genres: *horror* and *novel*. Are there any others that you think may apply? Does the text follow conventions intended for romance novels? Does the text follow the conventions of satire? Here's where research can come in handy. You can look for academic scholarship on your given genre— perhaps scholars have traced the lineage of your genre over time or suggested texts that they consider to be prime examples of that genre. Finally, less formalized sources, such as the website TVTropes, can help you identify genre conventions and linked texts (particularly conventions regarding theme and subject matter)—although sources like this (publicly editable as they are) are not sufficiently credible to be used as sources for your essays.

## Sample Argument: Genre

*In Sherman Alexie's short story "What You Pawn I Will Redeem," Alexie blurs the line between social classes by not only having Jackson Jackson conform to the picaresque genre convention of the protagonist's low social status, but also by having Jackson diverge from it.* **Illustrating Jackson as a respected member of society despite his low economic bracket allows Alexie to offer a social commentary on judgmental attitudes within civil stratification.**

---

### GUIDING QUESTIONS FOR UNDERSTANDING GENRE

1.  *What are the conventions of each of the genres I've identified in this text?*

2.  *Which of these conventions are present in the text?*

3.  *Are there conventions of the genre that the text does not use?*

4.  *Does the text defy (or "subvert") any of its genre conventions?*

---

If you've identified the conventions of your texts and figured out which conventions are followed and/or subverted, you are then prepared to begin to ask, *to what effect?*

*Reading and Researching for Rhetor*

When we talk about rhetor, it's not enough to know *who* the rhetor is—as you read, consider the rhetor's persona and credibility, and how those factors are communicated through the text.

### GUIDING QUESTIONS FOR UNDERSTANDING THE RHETOR

1. *Where does this text fit into the rhetor's larger body of work?*

2. *Is this text directly reflective of (or informed by) the author's life?*

3. *What ethos does the rhetor adopt in this text?*

4. *To what extent is the author's credibility part of their rhetorical appeals, and how does the rhetor establish that credibility in the text?*

5. *Does the rhetor make herself conspicuously visible as a communicator in the text, or does she remain invisible?*

6. *If there are multiple rhetors, to what extent is each responsible for the content of the text?*

*Reading and Researching for Audience*

Some texts answer this question for us. If we pick up *A College Student's Guide to Surviving Dining Hall Food*, we know its intended audience right off the bat. Other texts may seem to appeal to one audience but actually be targeting multiple audiences. Consider a television commercial for a children's toy. The **primary audience** of the text is children, and the commercial uses one set of appeals to target that audience (bright colors! sound effects!). However, the commercial must also appeal to the **secondary audience**—parents who have the money to actually purchase the toy—and might target that audience through very different appeals (emphasizing the toy's educational qualities or reasonable price).

When we ask about the audience for a given text, we're actually asking a very complicated question. After all, which audience do we mean? Do we mean the **intended audience** (the people that the rhetor *wanted* to experience the text)? Do we mean the **actual audience** (the people who actually ended up experiencing the text)? Was the audience captive (think political propaganda) or self-selected (think a book at a bookstore)? What about audiences in unintended (or unanticipated) times and places? For instance, was it Shakespeare's intention to force high school students across America to read his work five hundred years after his death?

In Writing 39B, when we discuss audience, we're interested in all of these things. Answering each of these questions, and understanding the answers to them, can expand our rhetorical understanding of a text. Typically, though, most of the work we do in 39B tends to focus on *intended* audience. In other words, what audience was the rhetor aiming for, and what choices did the rhetor make in order to appeal to that audience?

The following questions can help you locate the audience of a given text.

## GUIDING QUESTIONS FOR UNDERSTANDING AUDIENCE

1. *Who is the intended audience for the text?*

2. *How was the audience attracted to the text?*

3. *What do the audience's shared concerns, interests, and assumptions seem to be?*

4. *How can your questions about the text lead to a more nuanced understanding of audience?*

**Who is the intended audience for the text? How was the audience attracted to the text?**

Think about how readers were brought to the text. For example, if you're writing about a story published in a particular magazine, who are the actual readers of that magazine? If you're writing about a specific book, how are readers likely to have learned about the book? (Perhaps it was reviewed in newspapers with certain types of readerships? Or the book appeals to fans of the genre or of the rhetor's past work?) Research can help you determine who the initial audience was for a text.

## *Sample Argument: Audience*

*D. B. Weiss's elicitation of ideals which constitute realities accentuates the allurement of video games in his novel* Lucky Wander Boy. **To a subculture of gamers who identify with the enticement of arcades and a culture that prizes practicality over irrational interests, Weiss published his novel centered on the perfected reality Classic video games embodied as to uphold the apotheosis video games represent.** *Weiss manifests the perpetual endeavor for quintessence so as to address its unobtainability and the essence of human consciousness.*

**What do the audience's shared concerns, interests, and assumptions seem to be?**

Consider the issues that the text seems to think are important or which concerns and interests might have drawn the audience to the text in the first place. **Often, shared interests and concerns are in some ways dictated by historical or cultural context.** As you figure out the focuses of the text, do research to consider what the initial audience of the text might have known or believed about those issues. Understanding the context of the text can help you develop a meaningful understanding of what cultural conversations the text's audience may have been listening to or participating in. Once you better understand the audience's backgrounds and shared assumptions, you can analyze how the text attempts to appeal to that audience.

That said, **do not base your ideas of an audience's shared concerns or interests on broad stereotypes.** If you say "Western novels appeal to men because men like violence," you're saying that all men like violence. Is that true? Well gosh, of course not. It's actually kind of offensive, when you think about it. It's good to practice spotting overly general claims about audience now, when you're just in the reading and thinking stage, because when you're writing analytically, making overly large, untrue claims about people or society seriously hurts your *ethos*—it makes you look untrustworthy or like a shallow thinker. If you take care not to rely on these huge assumptions when you're reading, then you won't be tempted to lean on them in your writing!

## *Sample Argument: Audience and Context*

*Although* Pale Fire *portrays Gradus as an incompetent killer throughout the commentary, it is through the multitude of effects Gradus's presence has on Kinbote that* **the paranoia and anxiety become real. The novel's initial audience, Americans in the late 1950s, is called to experience the feelings of paranoia and anxiety caused by the Cold War and thus to reassess the social environment** *that they lived in.*

**How can your questions about the text lead to a more nuanced understanding of audience?**

When beginning to attempt to define audience, it is important to remember one thing: **You may not be the intended audience for the text.**

If you don't enjoy a text, or don't understand it, don't assume it's automatically meant for "the audience of everyone who is not me." In other words, what's important is not to use yourself as the master barometer for audience.

Instead of thinking in binaries (ME and NOT ME), think on a spectrum. If a text seems too difficult, don't think, "The audience has to be smart." Ask, "How much more educated than I would the audience need to be to understand this?" or "What specific body of knowledge would they need?" If a text includes lots of biblical allusions, don't just think, "The audience is religious." Ask, "How familiar with the Bible would the audience need to be to understand these references? Does the audience need to be Christian?" In short, make sure that you're not seeing audience in terms of simple binaries.

*Reading and Researching for Context*

Historical and cultural context involves the world into which the text was released—the specific historio-cultural moment in which the text emerged. Just as no text exists in a vacuum, no rhetor creates their text in a vacuum. Their understanding of the world around them, their concerns (possibly as expressed in their text), their understanding and depiction of social dynamics in their work—all of these things stem from the historical/cultural context in which the text was produced and transmitted.

Basic questions to ask as you read, then, include the following.

## GUIDING QUESTIONS FOR UNDERSTANDING CONTEXT

1. *Where was the rhetor living when they wrote this text? Where was the text released or transmitted?*

2. *At what time was the rhetor creating this text? At what time was the text released or transmitted?*

3. *Of what culture(s) or discourse communities was the rhetor a part when he/she released or transmitted this text?*

4. *What were the dominant social dynamics/hierarchies at the time of the text's release? How does the text use, challenge, address, or reinforce these dynamics?*

5. *What were some major societal concerns and debates at the time of the text's release—specifically those that might relate to the content of the text? How does the text enter or interface with these debates?*

6. *How would the meaning of this text change if it were released fifty years later? What if it were released fifty years earlier? What if it were released into a very different culture, a very different economy, or into a society with a very different set of social codes?*

For example, let's say you're reading a speech from the 1960s about the need for equality among ethnic groups in America. Without understanding the speech in the context of the ongoing civil rights movement, and the debates and societal upheavals that were occurring at the time, you won't have a full understanding of how the text is situating itself in regards to that aspect of its historical/cultural context.

Asking these questions of any text can be difficult if we haven't lived in the time period during which the text was created and transmitted (which we most likely have not, being mere mortals with finite life spans). Funnily enough, though, it can almost be more difficult to ask questions about contemporary texts, since we're living in the context that surrounds the text, and we take it for granted.

Remember also that texts are not produced instantaneously. Writers may spend a decade or longer writing their novel and waiting to get it published—so a novel released in the year 1990 likely reflects the ideas of a writer who has many years of social, cultural, and historical movements resonating in her head as she writes it! And, of course, events that occurred many years before the release of a text can be part of that text's context if those events would have still been resonating in the world into which the text came. Decades after a war, combatant countries may still be recovering from social, political, and economic devastation. And large cultural conversations (like those about race, politics, and social equality) span decades or centuries, gaining complexity and new voices as time passes.

## Sample Argument: Context

*In* Lucky Wander Boy, *Weiss argues that The American Dream is dead for contemporary immigrants, by conveying the daily struggles of Anya and the Mexican Day Laborers. All of these characters resemble the archetypal, contemporary immigrant: one that comes from a poor background, works at a menial, minimum wage job, and struggles simply to survive.* **Weiss utilizes their stories as a representation of the broader immigration situation, one that is starkly different than the romanticized version many still believe.**

## Sample Argument: Context and Genre

*Throughout his work, deWitt* **utilizes the picaresque convention of satire** *to portray a majority of his male characters similarly with regard to several particular aspects, thereby* **mocking the societal masculine "standard,"** *while also developing the complexity and dynamism of these same characters in other aspects in order to demonstrate that masculinity is not limited to any specific definition.* **The obsession with complying with this nonexistent standard ultimately serves as deWitt's primary social critique of the fact that society uses past standards of masculinity to set an unreasonable expectation for men in the present.**

# Crafting A Rhetorical Argument: Welcome to The Jungle

**Writing an argument isn't the hard part.**

**Thinking of an argument is the hard part.**

Two of the most common complaints we hear our students express, when it comes time to write a rhetorical analysis essay, are "I want a thesis that's easy to argue" and "I suck at analysis."

Here's the thing: if you choose an easy-to-argue thesis—an argument that's so obvious and easy to defend that no one would ever argue that you're wrong—then of course you're having a hard time writing analysis. You've given yourself nothing *to* analyze.

## PRO-TIP: PREWRITE

You know that terrible sinking feeling you get when you arrive at the end of an essay draft and realize your thesis has totally changed? Or, worse, your instructor highlights a sentence in your conclusion and writes, "This should be your thesis!"? Prewriting lets you work through your logic and all of your just-okay ideas BEFORE you spend hours writing them with an academic *ethos*.

Consider the relationship between argument and analysis.

### What Is an Argument?

An argument is more or less the use of evidence and data in order to persuade someone of an opinion. You state the central message you will argue (in the case of a rhetorical analysis essay, that message is your thesis), then you present evidence (in the case of an RA, evidence from the text you're writing about and from secondary sources) that you think supports that opinion. And then—the most important step—you *explain **how** the evidence you presented supports your central claim.*

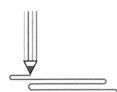

**What is an Argument**

Review Chapter 6, "I Came Here for an Argument," for more information on how arguments work.

### What Is Analysis?

Analysis is the single most misunderstood part of argumentative writing, for starters.

In the context of an argumentative essay, *analysis* of evidence means nothing more than explaining why you think the evidence you presented backs up your argument. If you've written a thesis and have chosen evidence that you think supports that thesis, then you must already have some ideas about why you chose the evidence you chose and how it backs up your argument. Writing analysis just means explaining those ideas clearly and logically, so your reader can understand your thought process behind choosing the evidence you chose.

So if you're walking around worried that you don't know how to write analysis, or your analysis is repetitive, or your analysis is too simple and obvious, or you never know what to analyze, consider, What if there's nothing wrong with your analytical skills? What if the problem is with your *argument*?

## Rhetorical Situation: Writing an Academic Rhetorical Analysis Essay

A rhetorical analysis essay is a sustained, argumentative analysis of a text, analyzing the rhetorical decisions that the text made and *how* those rhetorical decisions help the text communicate.

Even as you analyze the rhetoric of one text (the core text you are making an argument about in your essay), you are *making rhetorical choices* as the rhetor of another text (the essay itself). As with all writing tasks, familiarizing yourself with the rhetorical situation you're entering will set you up for success as a writer. See Figure 8.7.

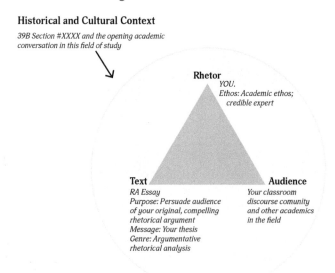

Figure 8.7

The **purpose** of an argumentative essay (like a rhetorical analysis essay) is to persuade. Persuade the reader of what? In an argumentative essay, your **message** is your thesis: an insightful, sophisticated, argumentative opinion about the text's use of rhetoric. The **rhetor** is you, of course, but a specific version of you—you adopting an **academic** *ethos*, establishing your *credibility* (through logic and research) and a particular *persona* (of a formal, articulate, academic expert in your subject).

You'll communicate your message to an **audience** consisting of your instructor and classroom discourse community, while also keeping in mind the potential audience of other academics in the field, who might read your essay in order to learn something cool and insightful about the text. To successfully appeal to these audiences, you must consider **context**: both the context of your particular classroom discourse community and the broader academic context of your paper—keeping track of and meaningfully acknowledging ongoing academic and cultural conversation about the text and subjects that you have chosen to write about.

Finally, the **genre** of the essay is an argumentative rhetorical analysis—specifically, one that follows MLA format. The advice in this section will help you understand some of the genre conventions of a rhetorical analysis. Being able to understand and follow these genre conventions ultimately helps your piece achieve rhetorical sophistication and success by communicating to your audience that you understand what is expected of you when you set out to communicate an idea through formal academic writing!

### Developing Rhetorical Arguments

There is no one way to write a successful rhetorical analysis. If you have been reading your text closely, asking questions, and thinking about *how* the text communicates meaning and achieves it purpose(s), then you are well on your way to developing a successful, effective argument. The following are examples of a few focuses that might help you develop your own rhetorical analysis argument.

### Historical/Cultural Context Argument

A context argument can define a very specific aspect of the novel's historical/cultural context and focus on examining **how the novel responds to, critiques, or otherwise joins an ongoing conversation about culture and society.** Remember that your ultimate goal is to argue about *how* the text uses its rhetorical situation to help communicate its message. Context should help us understand the text, not the other way around. We're not analyzing the world here; we're making an argument about the text.

### Audience Argument

An audience argument that defines a specific intended audience for the text and then analyzes how the text specifically appeals to that audience is one excellent way to frame an audience argument. Alternately, an audience argument might not define a particular audience for the text. Instead, you might argue *how* the text seems intent on eliciting a certain type of response, and what type of response that is, then consider how the text's appeal to audience might support or complicate its other rhetorical decisions!

### Genre Argument

A genre argument will typically focus on one or more conventions of the text's genre(s), seeking to identify those conventions and examine how the text's adoption (or rejection) of those conventions helps the text achieve its rhetorical purpose or communicate its message.

### Arguments about Multiple Aspects of the Rhetorical Situation

As you develop your rhetorical analysis argument, remember that the elements of a text's rhetorical situations all work together to help that text achieve its effect. For example, as you learned in Chapter 1, genre and audience often work together—a particular genre might appeal to a particular audience, and, in turn, an audience's expectations of a text might be defined by their understanding of the conventions of that text's genre.

Your rhetorical analysis argument may well require that you focus on multiple parts of the rhetorical situation and explain how they work together.

#### *Refining Your Argument*

**Think narrow and deep, not broad and shallow.** All of your thinking has likely given you *many* ideas. The biggest challenge before you write is choosing *one* argument that you can sustain and develop meaningfully over the course of an essay. Make sure you have an idea of *how* the different parts of your argument work together, or else you might end up with an essay filled with small, disconnected arguments about different parts of the rhetorical situation. This scattered handful of arguments may fulfill the page requirement, but it will not create a coherent, successful essay.

Academic writing rewards specificity and depth. If you choose a very, very broad topic ("I'm going to look at every use of every convention of the Western genre in every single scene of the book!") it can be hard to narrow down which evidence will be most helpful to you. If your topic is smaller, you will be able to analyze it more deeply.

## Case Study: Birth of an Epic Thesis

Every thesis has to start somewhere! Follow a former 39B student's process, as she came up with what was ultimately an exceptional thesis for a rhetorical analysis essay:

**Defining an area of interest:** The student chose twenty pieces of evidence from the novel and came to this conclusion:

> "Through this process, I learned that corruption is high in a lot of the characters, regardless of age or gender. I think that if I go back and reread some parts of the book that I mentioned in my brainstorm, I would be able to get a clearer picture."

**Prewriting:** The student used pre-writing techniques to narrow her idea further:

> "Both the boy at the duel and the intermission girl are examples of corruption in children."

**Pre-first-draft hypothesis:** The student chose parts of the rhetorical situation but hadn't yet figured out how they communicated message:

> "In Patrick DeWitt's novel, corruption is very prominent among the characters; however, it is also apparent in the young children of the novel as well, such as the boy at the duel and the girl in the intermission. DeWitt uses historical context and genre to convey to his readers this message of corruption in children. The message of corruption in children in The Sisters Brothers gives the readers insight into this societal problem."

**Final thesis statement:** After several revisions, the student finished refining her complex, rhetorical thesis statement:

> "DeWitt exaggerates society's culture of apathy toward what children are allowed exposure to and uses the picaresque genre's convention of a corrupt world to underscore the message of depravity found in children who are negatively influenced by the horrors that they see in their world. Through this message, deWitt gives the reader insight into this societal problem and lends support to the growing culture of recognition that is needed in the world today."

## Organizing Your Argument

Don't wait until it's time to write your draft to start organizing your essay: as you develop and refine your larger argument, imagine how that argument will be organized in the final essay. Planning the organization of your essay can show you which parts of your argument need further development which will, in turn, give you ideas about how to best divide your ideas into paragraphs and order those paragraphs. Continuing this cycle of organization and argument will allow you to develop and reconceptualize your argument until it is as sophisticated and logical as you can make it.

Chapter 6 taught you that arguments are made up of *claims* that are supported by specific *grounds* and supported by *evidence*. Using the concepts from that chapter to separate your thesis statement into its claims will allow you to easily see which ideas you'll need to organize in your own essay.

### How NOT to Organize an Argument: The Five-Paragraph Essay

A five-paragraph essay is not necessarily five paragraphs long. When we say "five-paragraph essay," here's what we mean: an essay with an intro, a conclusion, and a number of small separate arguments, each made in a single paragraph, that do not tie together to make one larger, more complicated argument.

There are many ways to develop a sustained, complex argument. There is one way *not* to develop your argument: the good ol' five-paragraph essay. **Writing a five-paragraph essay is not a rhetorically effective choice for an argumentative academic paper** because the format is incapable of establishing the kind of deep, sustained argument required to succeed in the task.

You can typically tell a five-paragraph essay by the thesis—it often includes a list of three things. Here's an example from a former 39B student:

> *In* The Hawkline Monster, *by having a mysterious setting, supernatural occurrences, and female characters in distress, Brautigan creates a true gothic text.*

In order to persuade the reader of his argument this writer needs to persuade his reader of the following claims:

Claim 1: *The Hawkline Monster* successfully follows the genre conventions of a gothic fiction novel;

Claim 2: Mysterious settings are a convention of a gothic fiction novel;

Claim 3: *The Hawkline Monster* follows the gothic fiction convention of mystery;

Claim 4: Supernatural occurrences are a convention of a gothic fiction novel;

Claim 5: *The Hawkline Monster* follows the gothic fiction convention of supernatural occurrences;

Claim 6: Female characters in distress are a convention of a gothic fiction novel;

Claim 7: *The Hawkline Monster* follows the gothic fiction convention of female characters in distress.

All of the claims are about the same level of complexity, and they interact with each other very little. In this student's essay, each of his body paragraphs used the same organization strategy: defining a convention of gothic literature, then listing examples to show that the novel uses that convention. No individual body paragraph is necessary in order to help the reader understand any of the other body paragraphs.

The logic of a five-paragraph essay is flat: the writer makes a point, then moves on to the next point, then moves on to the next point. While a five-paragraph essay might achieve the appropriate *length*, its format will not achieve superior *depth* in the subject. In this case, the author's argument doesn't manage to achieve a sufficiently rhetorical point—it shows how the author has constructed their text so that it fits into a certain genre, but does not make any larger assertions about the effect of that choice.

### Thesis ➔ Claims ➔ Organization

A sustained, sophisticated argument about a text's rhetorical situation will contain a number of claims—ranging from relatively straightforward to very complex—and, unlike the claims in a five-paragraph essay, the claims in a sophisticated rhetorical analysis will build on one another.

For example, recall this thesis statement from a truly magnificent rhetorical analysis essay by a former 39B student writing about the novel *The Sisters Brothers*, which was published in 2011:

> *In* The Sisters *Brothers , Patrick deWitt exaggerates society's culture of apathy toward what children are allowed exposure to and uses the picaresque genre's convention of a corrupt world to underscore the message of depravity found in children who are negatively influenced by the horrors that they see in their world. Through this message, deWitt gives the reader insight into this societal problem and lends support to the growing culture of recognition that is needed in the world today.*

When we write a thesis statement, we are making a contract with the reader, promising that by the end of the paper we will have persuaded them of our argument. In order to make good on the promise in her thesis, this essay writer needs to convince the audience of the following claims:

Claim 1: The novel exaggerates society's culture of apathy toward children's media exposure.

Claim 2: There actually is a culture of apathy toward children's media exposure in the historical/cultural context of the novel (North America, early twenty-first century).

Claim 3: The picaresque genre features the convention of "a cruel world."

Claim 4: The novel follows the picaresque genre convention of "a cruel world."

Claim 5: The novel sends the message that children who are negatively influenced by horror that they see in the world end up depraved;

Claim 6: The particular way that the novel follows the picaresque genre convention of a cruel world helps it send the message that viewing violence leads to depravity in children.

Claim 7: The novel's message that viewing violence leads to depravity in children ultimately supports a growing culture of recognition regarding what types of media children are allowed to be exposed to.

Claim 8: There actually is a growing culture of recognition regarding what types of media children are allowed to be exposed to in the novel's cultural context (North America, early twenty-first century).

Once you've sorted your whole argument into all of its small claims, then you can begin to think, What is the most logical order to address these claims in, so your audience is most easily persuaded by this argument and doesn't lose track of your logic?

While we can't give you an easy answer, we can suggest *some good questions to ask yourself in order to start organizing.*

## GUIDING QUESTIONS FOR ORGANIZING CLAIMS

1.  *What ideas does the reader absolutely need to understand in order to fully understand my thesis?*

2.  *How difficult will it be to convince my reader of each of these claims? Are there any claims I can persuade the reader of with few examples or in very little space?*

3.  *Which claims are necessary for the reader to understand and accept before the reader can understand and accept the more complicated claims?*

4.  *Which claims will I probably need to keep building throughout multiple paragraphs?*

Let's take these questions and see how the writer of the above thesis statement could use them to effectively organize her essay.

### Giving the Reader Context to Understand Your Argument

In order to write a rhetorically effective persuasive essay, you need to appeal to your audience by giving them sufficient background to understand your argument.

The student whose thesis statement you read above cannot effectively persuade her audience if that audience is not given enough context to understand her thesis's key phrases: "culture of apathy toward what children are allowed exposure to," "picaresque genre convention of a corrupt world" (and the term "picaresque genre," for that matter), and "growing culture of recognition."

This student chose to define the genre convention of a "cruel world" in the introduction to the essay. After the thesis, she included a well-researched paragraph explaining the historical/cultural context of social views, conversations, and arguments about the connection between children and media violence. *Starting the essay by using expert evidence to define key terms not only helped the student appeal to her audience, but also established her ethos as a credible rhetor.*

### Organizing Your Claims to Guide Your Audience through Your Logic

You can't persuade your reader if you get him hopelessly tangled in your thought process. In our example essay, the reader absolutely must be convinced of Claim 4: "The novel follows the picaresque genre convention of a 'cruel world'" before the writer can even start discussing how that convention helps the novel send its message (Claim 6).

Although you may want to race toward the most complicated or interesting claims in your essay, doing so may not be the most effective way to appeal to your audience. As you write, consider your essay from the perspective of your audience and ask, "Have I successfully and thoroughly persuaded the audience of this point?" To you, a small claim might seem too obvious to require evidence and analysis. You have thought more about your own argument than your audience has, however, and *if you don't convince the reader of all the steps of your thought process, then you will damage your ethos as a credible thinker and, as a result, you will fail in your purpose: persuading the audience.*

### Emphasizing Key Claims

As you imagine the shape and logical flow of your argument, consider which claims you might need to keep addressing throughout your essay. *In order to credibly persuade your audience of a particular claim, you may need to support the claim using multiple pieces of evidence or evidence from multiple perspectives.*

In the thesis statement above, many of the writer's claims (and, ultimately, her whole argument) hinge on her successful argument of Claim 5—that the novel is sending a message about the negative effects that viewing violence can have on children. Because this claim is so central to her argument, the student chose to address it in several paragraphs.

### Metacognitive Checkpoint: Reflecting On The RA

For this metacognitive checkpoint, write a sustained and careful reflection discussing your RA composition and revision process in detail.

> ▶ *What assignments best helped you prepare for the RA Essay?*
>
> ▶ *Once you began drafting the RA, what was your process, and how did you move between drafts?*
>
> ▶ *What types of changes did you make between drafts, and why?*
>
> ▶ *What would you continue to revise in the final draft of the RA, if you could?*

To gain practice with using multimodal evidence to make an argument, like you'll be doing in the Final Portfolio, you can try incorporating excerpts of your work (ideally visual artifacts such as screenshots) to make your work visible to the reader. You should be using your reflection to not just summarize what you've done, but to make a convincing argument about how your work and your process prove that you've developed the course skills. You can, and probably should, discuss multiple skills in this response—as long as you're being patient and fully exploring each one.

## The Rhetoric-In-Practice Project: The Cave of Trials

### What is the RIP Project?

Despite the ominous name, many students describe the Rhetoric In Practice Project (RIP) as their favorite of the quarter. It's not because the RIP is the first time that students get to construct their own rhetoric—we hope that if the rest of this chapter has taught you anything, it's that you've been doing that all quarter long, you savvy rhetor—but it's because the RIP allows for almost limitless formal and rhetorical creativity. In many of the assignments you've written in college and before, you've been given very, very specific limitations about what you are and are not allowed to do. For the RIP, you're the one making the decisions. How many of the decisions? *All of the decisions.*

In many ways, this project prepares you for life after the Writing 39 Series. While you may spend a very small portion of your life formally studying rhetoric, you know that every time you communicate, you are a rhetor, and it is your responsibility to understand the rhetorical situation that you enter when you communicate, so you can do so as effectively as possible. The RIP is a way for you to show your know-how and adaptability as a rhetor.

The RIP consists of two sections: Project and Essay.

- The **Project** is a text-based piece of rhetoric (related to the theme of your class) that you will carefully construct in order to target a certain audience and achieve a certain purpose.

- The **Essay** is a written document that analyzes, in close detail, all of the rhetorical choices you made in your Project, regarding each aspect of the Project's rhetorical situation, and how those choices contribute to your Project's effectiveness.

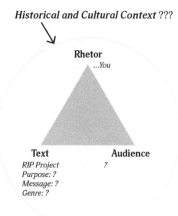

Figure 8.8

By now, you've gotten used to thinking about the rhetorical situation for each of the different writing tasks you've been given. Take a look at the rhetorical situation for the RIP Project, and see if you notice a difference (Figure 8.8).

You've probably noticed that the rhetorical situation for this project is *suspiciously empty.* Don't be frightened. Your challenge is to design the entire rhetorical situation surrounding the text you propose to create: you pick the genre, the medium, the audience, the purpose, and the context.

## RIP PROJECT AND RIP ESSAY: TWIN SISTERS

Once you have a general idea of the rhetorical situation your project will operate within, you should begin to conduct research. This research has three main uses:

1. To help you get ideas that will let you deepen and complicate your rhetorical situation before you start composing your RIP Project;

2. To help you understand the best way to make your choices while composing the RIP Project;

3. To bring into your RIP Essay as support for the decisions you chose to make.

As you perform more research and find out more about your rhetorical situation, you should use that information to build your Project. Once you have begun the RIP Essay, you will likely notice gaps in your research or your idea of the rhetorical situation. This is a great opportunity to return to the RIP Project and make new decisions based on further research, which you can then explain in the next draft of your RIP Essay. Working on one can always lead you back to the other. Don't view these two components separately or sequentially. See them instead as two sides of the same coin, and feel free to build and revise them simultaneously.

In life, the demands made upon us as communicators are rarely as rigid and clear-cut as college assignment prompts—much of your success as a rhetor in the real world depends upon your ability to analyze a broad variety of rhetorical situations and make confident, focused decisions about how to best address those situations. The RIP, then, represents a meaningful culmination of all the skills taught in 39B: it's your opportunity to apply your skills of critical reading, rhetorical analysis, and effective composition to a free-form project, to demonstrate your adaptability as an everyday rhetor.

### Metacognitive Checkpoint: Moving From The RA to The RIP

For this metacognitive checkpoint, reflect on the ways that working on the RA Essay prepared you for your work on the RIP Project and Essay. Tell the story of your process and reflect on what's helped you find success as well as what areas where you can still stand to grow. Think about what skills and techniques you've found to be transferable between these two major assignments.

> *What skills did you gain while writing the RA that have been helpful while composing the RIP?*

> *What skills did you have trouble with on the RA that you've continued to build (or managed to acquire) while composing the RIP?*

> *How has the genre-oriented thinking you did while composing the RA transferred to your work in another genre during the RIP?*

### THE ROAD TO THE RIP

- *Choose a purpose, audience, and context*
- *Define genre, medium, venue, and rhetor*
- *Find and analyze model texts*
- *Conduct outside research*

### Choosing a Purpose, Audience, and Context

Before you can make effective rhetorical decisions about a text, you must define your **purpose** and **audience**. In short, what do you want to communicate, and whom do you want to communicate it to? This is the time to get creative and brave. The more unusual your rhetorical situation is, the more difficult decisions you will have to make in order to effectively appeal to the demands of that rhetorical situation, and the more you'll have to say when it comes time to explain your rhetorical decision-making process in the Essay. On the other hand, choosing a rhetorical situation that already exists and then choosing to copy it wholesale will not leave you with many productive opportunities for rhetorical decision-making.

Your **purpose** should be specific and clear. Are you informing? Persuading? Entertaining? *Remember that many texts have several purposes*—after you consider your primary purpose, consider which other secondary purposes might help you achieve your primary purpose!

Your **audience** is possibly the most important part of your RIP Project. A nuanced understanding of audience (and the ability to use research to define that audience) can make or break your Project. Avoid broad, general audiences ("the public," "men," "scientists") and get as specific as possible ("single engineers who read *Reddit*"). In the section later in the chapter that deals with researching the RIP, you'll find more information about effectively defining, narrowing, and understanding your audience. Whoever you end up choosing as your audience, your goal will be to *make focused decisions in order to appeal to that audience's demands.*

In addition, your **context** is very important when it comes to how your text will be received and understood. Is your proposed project going to be released this year? Ten years ago? Five hundred years in the future? Is the culture you are releasing your text into our own (contemporary American) culture? Is it a foreign culture, or an imagined one? What are the values, beliefs, trends, and assumptions present in the context you've chosen, and how will they inform the way that your audience receives your rhetoric? *You need to understand the context of your project so you can determine which ongoing conversations your text will join and how your text can meaningfully add to those conversations.* Projects taking a past year as their context will benefit from research, and projects taking a future year as their context will benefit likewise from using what we know about today's world and ongoing trends to extrapolate what the future might be like.

## A NOTE ON AUDIENCE: AVOIDING CIRCULAR REASONING

Since you get to invent the entire rhetorical situation for your RIP, you may be tempted to do a very bad thing. You may have a wonderful idea for a Zombie Cola advertisement.

"Superb," your instructor will say. "That sounds just great. Who is your proposed audience?"

A wily grin spreads across your face and you pull your sweatshirt hood onto your head. "My audience is people who want to buy Zombie Cola."

Your instructor's head has exploded. What's worse is that this type of circular reasoning sets you up to struggle when it's time to write your essay.

Remember that the essay asks you to articulate, in detail, why you made the choices you made. The essay can be seen as a series of implied questions: *how did you use medium to appeal to your audience and achieve your purpose? What was the importance of the context you chose, and how did you work effectively within it? How did you use or subvert conventions of your chosen genre to achieve your purpose?*

So, as you sit down to answer the question, *How did you make your audience want to buy Zombie Cola?*, your essay will look like this:

> *I didn't have 2 because they already wanted it lol #YOLO.*

This essay is unlikely to receive a high score.

It's important that you develop a nuanced understanding of the rhetorical situation you create and avoid creating appeals (or a rhetorical situation) that will lead to this kind of simplistic reasoning. This is why an unusual rhetorical situation can work so well for the RIP—you'll need to do more work (and craft more rhetorical appeals) to sell Zombie Cola to impoverished senior citizens on a gluten-free diet than you will need to do to sell Zombie Cola to the Zombie Cola Fan Club (est. 2501 AD).

### *Defining Genre, Medium, Venue, and Rhetor*

Once you've determined your audience, purpose, and context, the real fun begins: deciding which medium and genre(s) would be most effective for delivering your message. Which media would most effectively and reliably reach your audience? Where would they be able to find your text? What genre will appeal to them? Once you've chosen a genre, read up on that genre and gather model texts so you can *determine the conventions of the genre and consider how following and/or subverting those conventions will help you effectively communicate your message.*

Make sure you are not underestimating the importance of **venue**: the place your text will appear. **Ask yourself questions about *how* audiences will encounter the text, so that you can gather the most helpful possible model texts.** For example, if you're writing a script for a TV show, you might find a venue by asking what channel the show would appear on, and in what time slot. Or if you're writing a blog post, will it be published on Tumblr? On a famous existing blog? Which related websites will link to it?

Finally, in the real world, of course, you are **the rhetor** for this project. But you have the opportunity to pretend to be someone else—to either present this text as the work of another person in our world or to invent a fictitious rhetor. If you are positioning yourself as another rhetor in the context of this project, what do you know (or what have you invented) about them? How is this rhetor well-chosen in regards to the rest of your rhetorical situation?

## Finding and Analyzing Model Texts

To help gather ideas and deepen your understanding of your rhetorical situation, you should find models that you can use to help shape your text. If you're imitating an existing rhetorical form, venue, genre, or medium, then closely analyzing the rhetorical situations of those model texts will help you understand what audiences will expect from *your* text and how you can effectively satisfy those expectations.

In addition, model texts are invaluable tools for understanding the conventions of the form you've chosen: conventions of the genre, conventions of the medium, and conventions of the particular venue you've chosen. As you analyze your model texts, pay special attention to genre conventions of **form**, **style**, and **content**.

You can begin your model text research broadly. For example, if you want to write a newspaper article, you might already know that newspaper articles tend to be printed in column form. But once you gather model texts, you'll realize that it will take a lot more than laying your writing out in columns to create a credible newspaper article—and every paper has its own rhetorical situation, making a series of decisions about content, style, and form, in order to achieve its own purpose, for its own audience.

Let's say you decide that the *New York Times* is the best model text for you: it seems to share your purpose and audience, and does so effectively. Now's the time to ask questions about its rhetorical choices. What font does the *New York Times* use, and what effect might that font choice have on audience? (If you're proposing to write an article for the *New York Times*, you'll want to use their font. But if you're proposing to create a fictional newspaper inspired by the *New York Times*, you might choose your own font by deciding what effect the font choice has on the audience, then choosing a font that you think creates a similar effect.) By researching circulation statistics, such as on a website like Alexa.com, you might discover that the *New York Times*'s audience is older, more educated, and wealthier than a median consumer. Look closely at the *New York Times* and try to decide how their diction, syntax, layout, and choice of topics might appeal to this audience directly. What do the articles in the *New York Times* seem to expect their audiences to already know? How explicitly do the articles respond to ongoing conversations in the cultural context? Questions like these will help you best understand the rhetorical situation of your project, so you can act as a credible, expert rhetor. Using some of the questions in the "Reading and Researching for..." section of this chapter can be very helpful when it comes to breaking down model texts.

If you've chosen a more fanciful project—a text that is the first of its kind!—you can still make creative use of model texts to inform your rhetorical decisions. Let's say you set out to create a commercial advertising Zombie Cola to children. You Google "ZOMBIE COLA FOR KIDS COMMERCIALS" and receive startlingly few results. Apart from possibly having gotten yourself added to a government watchlist with this search query, you now realize that there are no model texts in the world that share your exact purpose, audience, and message. Instead of looking for something that *exactly resembles* what you want to produce, you can seek out models that can help you with just one aspect of the rhetorical situation you're creating.

In our Zombie Cola example, you might start by finding commercials for other products that are aimed at your target audience. Which rhetorical appeals do these other media use to capture that target audience? What is the effect of those appeals, and why are they effective? Though a commercial for a Pearlescent Pony Princess Playset might not seem to have much to do with your Zombie Cola advertisement, it might be an invaluable model text for helping you better understand one part of your project's rhetorical situation.

The advice in this section has focused on how to use model texts, but more outside research will also be necessary and should be conducted before you begin composing your RIP Project. Let's explore some possible directions to take as you branch out from models toward other outside sources.

### Conducting Outside Research

To create the best possible RIP, you need to ensure that your decisions are supported by strong outside research. You should return to the section of this chapter that deals with "Reading and Researching For..." different aspects of rhetoric—the questions that those sections ask you to consider will all be relevant as you construct your project. However, since you're now the one crafting the rhetorical situation from the ground up, it may also be useful to adopt new points of view to help you calibrate the way that you conduct your research.

**The questions listed below aim for comprehensiveness; not all of them will be equally relevant to every project.** You'll need to decide which of these approaches seem most relevant and most vital to the mission and rhetorical situation of your particular project.

## GUIDING QUESTIONS FOR RESEARCHING THE RIP

1. *How do demographic and psychographic factors define your audience?*

2. *What do you want your audience to think or do after reading your project? What is your purpose?*

3. *How will following (or subverting) key genre conventions help you achieve your purpose?*

4. *What style and design choices are most appropriate for your rhetorical situation?*

5. *How does your project address a specific context that is relevant and recognizable to your audience?*

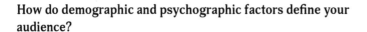

### How do demographic and psychographic factors define your audience?

You will begin by defining an audience you want to reach with your text. You'll probably begin by (consciously or unconsciously) defining them in one or more of the following ways:

**DEMOGRAPHIC FACTORS:** You may define your audience based on demographic factors such as age, gender, ethnicity, income level, geographic location, and education level (e.g., "Korean females from Indiana who are between the ages of 40 and 60" or "college graduates living in Berlin").

> ▶ *CONSIDER ALSO: STAGE OF LIFE:* You may define your audience primarily based on their stage of life and what that might tell you about them and their daily routines (e.g., "retirees" or "middle-aged American workers").

**PSYCHOGRAPHIC FACTORS:** You may define your audience based on BEHAVIORS, PREFERENCES, and OPINIONS. This kind of definition may include things that the audience likes or dislikes, activities they perform frequently, or beliefs that structure their life (e.g., "men who disagree with third-wave feminism" or "Snapchat users").

> ▶ *CONSIDER ALSO: NEEDS AND DESIRES:* You might choose to define an audience that needs or wants something in particular. (e.g., "wheelchair users," "those looking to purchase a home," or "voters who want stronger immigration laws").

> ▶ *CONSIDER ALSO: VENUE OR GENRE:* You may define your audience as people who are frequent consumers of a given genre or people who often visit a given venue (e.g., "Tumblr users," or "members of LA Fitness").

## AVOIDING ASSUMPTIONS AND STEREOTYPES IN AUDIENCE RESEARCH

**What's most important is not to make assumptions or rely on stereo-types when thinking about your audience.** Just because someone is religious doesn't mean they go to church. Just because an audience member is female doesn't mean she likes the color pink. What's also important is the way that you frame this research in your essay. If your audience is "UCI students" and you find data indicating that 75 percent of UCI students take the shuttle bus at least once a week, that does not mean that all UCI students take the shuttle bus. However, that data will allow you **to say with greater confidence** that **the majority of your audience** are **probably** users of the shuttle bus.

After you have your initial conception of your audience, **you cannot stop there.** You may first think about audience in terms of demographics, for example, but that will not give you a complex and nuanced view of audience. It will be necessary to specify and narrow that audience further to help you direct your choices and your research. When you choose a *specific* and well-defined audience, it's easier to find out information that will help you make good choices about how to best target that audience. Consider, for example, making a department store catalogue with an audience of "women." Well, since women are all different from each other, your super vague audience isn't giving you much helpful information to use! If you don't believe us, you can talk to some women.

Instead, you can help yourself improve your research by narrowing down a few factors, like age, geographic location, interests, or opinions. Whichever category you're beginning from (beliefs, opinions, demographics, stage of life...), careful research will allow you to use this initial conception of audience as a starting point to fill in the blanks in your knowledge of the audience, to specify further who you would like that audience to be, and to find out what members of your audience may have in common. *By beginning from one of the approaches above, you will be able to learn more about the information contained in the others.* Thanks to census data from governments, surveys from polling firms, companies, and nonprofits, as well as reports from advertisers and corporations seeking to sell products, there is a lot of information about various audience segments available if you're willing to dig a little. Any one of the categories mentioned above will almost never tell the whole story. But, when you use one category to lead you to others and make thoughtful observations about how these categories seem to intersect, you can start to make more meaningful choices about how to target your very specific audience. Perhaps you're targeting elderly residents of Alabama, and you discover that both Alabama natives and elderly

Americans have rates of church attendance that are higher than the national average. This allows you to be confident that your audience members are likely to be churchgoers.

**Remember that this research allows you to have more confidence, but it is not a guarantee.** Not all women are the same or like the same things! Not all Belgian citizens! Not all middle-aged people! Not all Alabama residents! Just because 90 percent of survey respondents chose a certain response, that doesn't mean every member of that audience segment will respond the same way. But this type of research *will* be able to give you higher confidence in your decisions about how to approach audience.

Of course, as you learn more about your audience, you'll be able to use that information to build out other aspects of your rhetorical situation. Soon you'll be able to answer questions like the following.

▷ *What will make my audience feel welcome, comforted, or appreciated?*

▷ *What might make my audience adversarial?*

▷ *What means of persuasion will be most effective for my audience?*

▷ *Is this audience very receptive to my purpose/message or will I have to do some serious work to get them on my side?*

## What is your purpose? What do you want your audience to think or do after reading your project?

What do you want your audience to do when they've finished consuming your text? Should they go out and buy something? Change their mind about an issue? Write to their congressperson? Whatever you're trying to do, there's no question that someone else has tried to do it before. You can learn from their experience and use the information they've gathered to calibrate your rhetoric. For example, there are dozens of possible ways to persuade an audience. So, what are you trying to persuade them of? Maybe you want them to buy a product—what are some effective ways that that goal has been achieved in the past for your audience or in your context? What are the purchasing habits of your chosen audience, and what income level are they likely to have (determining whether they can afford your product)? Or if you're trying to entertain your audience—what types of entertainment do they tend to gravitate toward and how can you use that knowledge to shape what you're doing? How much free time do they tend to have for entertainment?

### How will following (or subverting) key genre conventions help you achieve your purpose?

Are you using the conventions of that genre thoughtfully or just because you feel like you have to? **Genre research for the RIP will allow you to determine the conventions of your chosen genre and the value of following or subverting them.** If you want to go further, you can consider how your genre has evolved and changed over time, and where your project fits in the history of that genre—are you pushing the genre forward, or perhaps hearkening back to an older iteration of that genre? Which conventions did you choose to follow, and why? Which did you choose to subvert, and why?

In terms of rhetorical intersectionality, you should also consider using research to establish whether this genre is a good choice for your audience—how is it right for them? How does it appeal to them specifically?

### What style and design choices are most appropriate for your rhetorical situation?

This category of research is perhaps the broadest and will vary wildly from project to project. It also intersects with genre research as style choices often base themselves on conventions and expectations. Some considerations include the following.

**Written Work**

What style choices have you made in your written text? What voice and tone(s) have you adopted, and for what purpose? Have you based these choices on instinct (or a wild guess), or have you found sources to help you calibrate these choices? What diction level is appropriate for your audience and purpose and context? How complex should your syntax be? How should you organize your writing with paragraph divisions and white space, and format it with line spacing and margins? How much figurative language should you use as opposed to direct, concrete expression?

**Multimodal Work**

Some instructors may choose to allow RIP projects that work in multiple modalities. If your project is working in more than one modality, you'll want to consider each modality individually as well as considering how those modalities meaningfully intersect. If your project uses visual multimodality, what genre conventions are at play? Can you find genre-specific sources to inform your use of layout, color, and the interplay of text and image? If your project uses recorded speech, what decisions have you made about vocal tone and pacing? If your project is navigable in a tactile manner, how are you asking your audience to handle or move around that text through subtle rhetorical decisions? If your text is electronically navigable (like a hypertext), how are you using that navigation structure as part of your rhetoric?

## How does your project address a specific context that is relevant and recognizable to your audience?

Projects that are working in a past or future context will, as described earlier in the chapter, require research to establish how the project accounts for that context. However, even projects whose context is modern and local will benefit from research on salient aspects of modern context. What trends are currently relevant to your work? What beliefs do people in your context tend to adhere to and how can you account for that? What assumptions do people in your context make about how life should work? Are they assumptions you share or assumptions you'll have to work to understand and empathize with? Just like we want to avoid stereotypes and baseless assumptions about audience, we want to make sure we're seeing our context in full detail—when that context is a context we're living in, it's easy to assume we already know everything. Don't take anything for granted!

---

### PRO TIP: SEEK FEEDBACK FROM YOUR AUDIENCE

As you draft, conduct market research. Seek out people in your life who are used to consuming the type of text you're constructing (your friends who throw Zombie Movie Nights would be a great test audience for the Zombie Cola advertisement) and see how they respond. Or seek out people who are part of your target audience. While their feedback won't be admissible as research in your Essay, you can still use it to gain an outside-the-box perspective on your own work. When you've been staring at the same creative project for weeks, it can be difficult to see every dimension of it without an outside perspective!

## Composing the RIP Project and Essay

If you have a deep understanding of your model texts and have conducted good research, having considered at length each aspect of your rhetorical situation, you should be in very good shape to compose your project.

As you draft and design your project, you'll demonstrate your rhetorical sensitivity by ensuring that *every* choice you make is purposeful. From font sizes to the placement of the text, from tone and diction level to syntactical complexity—every choice should be justified by your purpose, your audience, and the rhetorical situation surrounding your work.

How do you demonstrate that your choices are justified? Why, you write an essay, of course.

Successful rhetoric often works so well that it seems invisible. When we try to influence (or, more cynically, manipulate) people, we're more likely to succeed when they don't even know that they're being manipulated. So, if your RIP Project is doing its job well, the appeals you're using might seem so natural to your audience that they won't even realize those appeals are present. This is why you write an RIP Essay: to show off all the hard work you put into crafting your rhetoric and to *demonstrate your awareness of the rhetorical choices you've made.* In this way, the RIP Essay is perhaps more important than the Project itself. You are, in essence, using the RIP Essay to perform rhetorical analysis on your own rhetoric.

Unlike the RIP Project, the rhetorical situation for the RIP Essay is clearly defined from the outset. You're stepping back from the imaginary rhetoric of your Project and examining your rhetoric to persuade your audience of the following message: *Every one of the choices I made in the RIP Project was careful and deliberate, perfectly calibrated to my rhetorical situation and supported by strong outside evidence.*

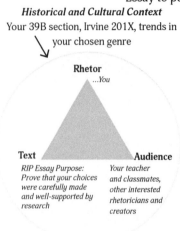

*Historical and Cultural Context*
Your 39B section, Irvine 201X, trends in your chosen genre

**Rhetor**
*...You*

**Text**
RIP Essay Purpose: Prove that your choices were carefully made and well-supported by research

**Audience**
Your teacher and classmates, other interested rhetoricians and creators

Figure 8.9

Persuading your reader of this message will require breaking down your rhetorical situation: the demands of that situation (including how you came to understand those demands—this means including outside research to establish yourself as a credible rhetor) and *how* you effectively fulfilled those demands, as shown in Figure 8.9. You'll want to be very specific about your purpose and message, and then clearly explain how you achieved them, given what you knew about your audience's shared interests, concerns, and expectations. There is room for extensive discussion of genre, medium, venue, form, style, tone, organization, and context. You might also choose to discuss your model texts in order to demonstrate that you've critically analyzed their rhetorical situations, determined their most effective rhetorical appeals, and demonstrated mastery of those techniques in your own work.

In Figure 8.10 we show specific tips for organizing and conceptualizing the RIP Essay. Remember, though, that the work you're being asked to do here is the same rhetorical analysis you've been asked to do already. The skills you picked up from the section of this chapter that deals with rhetorical analysis will be useful here. *Consider returning to the "Reading and Researching for..." sections earlier in the chapter and asking those same questions about the text you produced for the RIP Project.* Which of those questions would be helpful to answer in the RIP Essay? In addition, most of the tips there about strong analysis, effective organization, and other aspects of effective rhetorical analysis should prove useful as you compose the RIP Essay.

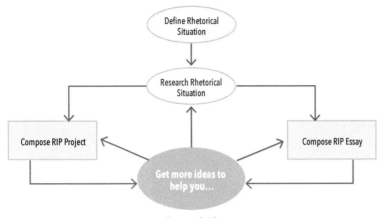

Figure 8.10

The RIP Essay will test your skills when it comes to prioritizing and organizing information.

Some questions you should ask yourself as you prepare to write the RIP Essay may include.

## GUIDING QUESTIONS FOR PLANNING THE RIP ESSAY

1.  *What does my reader need to know in order to understand my explanations?*
2.  *Are there overarching categories or groups of choices I made that I can discuss holistically?*
3.  *What rhetorical moves would my (smart, talented) teacher probably notice without my explaining them? What choices may have been invisible to the typical reader?*
4.  *If this were a text in the real world, where in the production process would it be? What would be the next steps?*

Below, we'll show you how these questions can help you make the right decisions for your RIP Essay!

### What does my reader need to know in order to understand my explanations?

Before you get deep into the essay, it's a good idea to briefly explain what your project is. Specify the audience and purpose you chose and the context you're working in. Specify the genre/medium you've chosen and the venue where you imagine your text appearing. Explain anything else you need your reader to know before you move into dissecting your project.

If you're working in an esoteric genre or context, for example, it might be worthwhile to spend some time contextualizing that for your reader and filling them in on the basics so that they can make an informed judgment about your argument in the essay.

### Are there overarching categories or groups of choices I made that I can discuss holistically?

The meat of the essay should involve a careful breakdown of the rhetoric in your project. But discussing every choice would be silly (*Why did I type the word "the"? Why did the word "end" come after "the"?*). Therefore, it's probably to your advantage to figure out what larger groups or categories of choices you made in your project. For instance, if a student designed a website, their groups of choices may include "layout decisions," "navigation decisions," "image decisions," and "written text decisions." Or that same student may choose a different way to divide their choices, such as "choices made to suit my genre to my audience," "choices made to persuade my audience of my message," and "choices made to keep my audience entertained." What's important when you do this is to make sure the organizational scheme you choose is customized to *your* particular project.

It's very important to consider the relationship between parts of your rhetorical situation. For instance, it doesn't make much sense to talk about your choice of genre in isolation. It will be much more productive to think about how your genre is affecting your message or appealing to your audience. Style choices you made might fit your genre and appeal to your audience. Or a style choice might break the rules of your genre to help achieve your purpose. You should be able to demonstrate that all of the aspects of your rhetorical situation are working together in harmony.

Considering all of the above, you can figure out how much time you think you should spend discussing each group of choices. Two sentences? A paragraph? A page? What level of detail should you provide about research that informed those choices? Should you give examples of specific choices from this group and analyze those particular examples? Choose the right method of persuasion for each claim you make in the essay based on how much support you think readers will need to be convinced!

### What rhetorical moves would my (smart, talented) teacher probably notice without my explaining them? What choices may have been invisible to the typical reader?

Some rhetorical choices will be so obvious that they require no explanation. Choosing to write in English for an American audience is unsurprising and does not display any sort of rhetorical thought—while it might be a good choice, there's no need to discuss it in your essay. Choosing to make links on your website clickable is likewise a genre convention that is almost never broken, and there's probably not much utility in discussing it in your essay. However, many of your highly visible choices will be worth discussing—why did you choose those colors? That font? Why address your audience as "Sir"? If your goal for the essay is to impress your reader with your rhetorical know-how, you'll want to figure out which choices you think they need to be informed about. This may include choices that seem obvious but that you actually only made after careful research and consideration.

However, there are also choices you'll make that a sensitive reader may not notice without your explaining them. Maybe you optimized your webpage's code to make it load faster. Maybe you chose to sell sugar-free chocolate instead of regular chocolate because 78 percent of your audience is at risk for diabetes.

You might think of the goal of the RIP Essay as the following: *impress your reader by making your invisible choices visible and by demonstrating that your visible choices were the result of careful consideration and research.*

### If this project was really being released, where in the production process would it be? What would be the next steps?

An ideal RIP Project is as polished as possible—that is, it approaches the caliber of work that an expert in that genre and context might produce.

Notice that we said "ideal." Expecting complete polish and professionalism from college students working on a seriously constrained timeframe (and taking several other classes besides! Possibly working a job or two!) would be unreasonable. However, that doesn't mean it's not a goal you can push for.

Consider your project in the context of the world you've defined for it— whether that's our world or some distant, imaginary context. Is it finished, polished, and entirely ready for its audience? Maybe not! So, what would be the next steps? Are those storyboards you made going to be turned into a film by a talented director? Is your satirical letter to Congress going to become part of a book, or maybe be published on a blog somewhere? Some students find it helpful to end their RIP Essay by providing their thoughts on the questions like the following: **If your project continued to grow, what work would come next? Where is the project headed, and how would it finally wrap up?**

## Metacognitive Checkpoint: Breaking Down the RIP

*For this metacognitive checkpoint, perform some patient reflection on your RIP composition process.*

▶ *What low-stakes (or major) assignments best helped you prepare for the RIP Project and Essay?*

▶ *What preparatory work went into building the RIP, and how did this preparation aid your final result?*

▶ *Once you began drafting the RIP, what was your process, and how did you move between drafts?*

▶ *What types of changes did you make between drafts, and why?*

▶ *Finally, how do you think the final results reflect well on your mastery of the course skills? Can you explain fully why you think so, and introduce evidence to support your ideas?*

*Note that the type of reflection you're performing here (like the reflection you'll perform in the Portfolio Introduction that focuses on the RIP) is NOT the same as your RIP Essay. The RIP Essay focuses on explaining the choices you made in the RIP Project and demonstrating the soundness of those choices and their basis in research. This reflection has to do with exploring the process of composing the RIP (both the Project and Essay) as well as reflecting on how that work demonstrates your aptitude in the course skills.*

## The Final Portfolio: Metacognitive Strategies

The Final Portfolio is an assignment that asks you to thoughtfully select work from among the assignments you've completed so far in the class, arrange that work in a compelling way, and contextualize that work with careful metacognitive reflection. The goals are to illustrate what you've learned so far and to argue that you've achieved the objectives of the class. No small feat, right?

**Historical and Cultural Context**
201X, Irvine, 39B Section #XXXX

**Rhetor**
*You!*

**Text**
*Final Portfolio*
*Message (implied): I*
*have performed well*

**Audience**
*Your instructor*

Figure 8.11

The audience of your Portfolio is different from the audience of any individual assignment you have written this quarter. Now you're just addressing your instructor (Figure 8.11). During the course, you should have come to know them quite well and to know what they prioritize: careful rhetorical analysis, effective evidence selection and deployment, and effective metacognition, for starters! You are the rhetor, of course, and the Final Portfolio is the text you're composing. You have a lot of leeway in how you choose to put it together, but in any case, the way that you construct and curate the portfolio should communicate that you have performed well in the course, learned the lessons you've needed to learn, grown and progressed as a rhetorical thinker and capable writer, and generally hit all of the bullseyes that have been set up for you.

All quarter, you've probably been using metacognition to learn about your own writing process. The portfolio is your chance to shift the audience of that metacognition—to present the conclusions it helped you reach to your instructor, and to lead them through the logic of that metacognition so that you two are on the same page.

Your portfolio is your opportunity to argue that you've reached a certain level of aptitude in the course skills. Of course, if you stomp into the room and just shout the grade you think you deserve (in all caps: "I DESERVE AN A+++ OK THANX IT WAS GOOD TIMES DUDE"), your message isn't going to be very convincing. (As a rhetor, your *ethos* would leave something to be desired: that tone won't appeal to the expectations of your audience, your lack of evidence will sorely hurt your credibility, and your lack of supporting material woefully ignores the genre conventions of a 39B Final Portfolio.)

You've learned how to argue much more effectively than that this quarter, and the portfolio is your chance to show that you've taken those lessons to heart: a meaningful argument always takes its rhetorical situation into account, and uses a combination of evidence and analysis to give the rhetor credibility so that they can successfully persuade their audience.

## LOOKING TOWARDS THE PORTFOLIO: LOW-STAKES ASSIGNMENTS, METACOGNITIVE JOURNAL

You should make sure to save copies (physically or in the Cloud) of all the work you complete during the quarter as well as materials (like annotations and notes) that are not submitted for a grade but that help you to build and understand your work as you go. When you assemble your Final Portfolio, you may want to bring in a few of these smaller pieces of writing as evidence of skill development or as evidence of a way in which you've surpassed benchmarks. Note that anything that's uploaded to Canvas will be preserved electronically, so this kind of archival work is most relevant when it comes to work you may not submit to Canvas: annotations you've made on your readings, mindmaps you've sketched out on gym towels, or notes you took during group work in class. Of course, it's never a bad idea to save everything in the Cloud anyway—Canvas isn't perfect.

You may also find it helpful, after completing a low-stakes writing assignment, to write a short reflection for yourself and save that as well. In that reflection, make some notes about the skills that each assignment helped you to develop as well as things that the assignment taught you that you did not know before. If certain aspects of an assignment (argument, organization, analysis) seem easier for you than they did before, make a note of that too, and try to figure out why! This kind of reflection is fantastic preparation for the metacognitive reflection you'll perform in the portfolio, and doing little bits of it throughout the quarter could save you a lot of time and stress when it's time to begin assembling your portfolio.

## How to Assemble a Portfolio in WR39B

Portfolios in 39B are not comprehensive—which means you will not include all of your work from the quarter so far. We use the verb "curate" to describe the way that you put together a portfolio because curation implies careful selection, thoughtful arrangement, and harmony—the idea that all elements of the portfolio work together to persuasively deliver your message.

Requirements for what to include in the portfolio will vary from instructor to instructor, and here it is vital to know your audience. However, we can draw some general guidelines about what you should include in the document. You will certainly include the final draft of every major assignment you've completed so far. You should also include evidence of drafting those assignments (both to show your level of engagement in the process as well as evidence of growth from early drafts to more polished work). You will accompany these documents with a thorough and searching **Portfolio Introduction**, which we will discuss in more detail shortly. You will also select specific **artifacts** from the quarter's work that you will introduce in the Introduction and use to support your argument about your progress so far. These artifacts may include (but are not limited to):

- Low-stakes writing assignments, discussion posts, or freewrites
- Additional drafts of major assignments
- Copies of your drafts that your instructor has annotated
- Copies of rubrics you've received from your instructor
- Materials (including written feedback) from the Writing Center or Peer Tutors
- Notes, brainstorms, or reading annotations

- Peer Feedback you've given or received
- Evidence of work you've done without being asked to do it—extra effort that your instructor may not be aware of

There is much space for creativity in the curation of your portfolio and many ways to decide which artifacts may be right for you to include. Do you want to include artifacts that you think show off a single skill very clearly? Do you want to include a pair of artifacts that show growth in a given skill? The suggestions we've provided are basic suggestions, and you are certainly creative enough to go beyond them as you develop a portfolio that distinctly reflects your individual work and your own unique experience in the course.

### The Portfolio Introduction

If the materials you present in the portfolio are evidence of your development as a rhetor, the introduction is the space in which you analyze that evidence to prove the claim that you've done well in the course.

The introduction should ideally work together with your artifacts to support your argument about your own work. Just as you would never put a quote in an essay without taking the time to explain why you've included it and why it is important, *you should not include any artifacts in your portfolio without thoroughly, patiently explaining how they help demonstrate your aptitude as a rhetor and your success over the course of the quarter.* One of the main purposes of the introduction is to demonstrate effective metacognition—that you've been thinking about your own thinking and about your own work. If you've been doing the kind of reflective preparation that was suggested throughout this chapter, you'll be in good shape to begin building your portfolio and composing your introduction, since you will have been recording the development of your own skills throughout the quarter.

As you seek to find a way to convey to your instructor that you've developed the skills that 39B prioritizes, you'll likely want to look at higher-order concerns: effective incorporation of feedback, strong analysis, effective use of evidence, sensitivity to audience, and so on. This often involves using your introduction to directly reference your own work (major assignment drafts and artifacts), describing which sections of the work reflect your mastery or development of these skills (and patiently analyzing exactly how they reflect that mastery). If, instead of looking at higher-order skills that you've developed, you're spending time in the introduction talking about small-scale edits, such as misplaced commas that you've fixed while drafting or misspelled words that you've realized were incorrect, what message will your instructor take away? Well, they very well might think that you haven't learned very much about what revision entails and that you're trying to fill up space in the introduction by talking about issues that lack urgency.

Of course, you also have the opportunity to get *meta-rhetorical* and use the introduction itself to show off those skills. Write it carefully, because your work composing the introduction can be further evidence of your excellence in the course.

In the introduction, you should be able to demonstrate to your instructor that you've used metacognitive thinking throughout the quarter to understand and refine your personal writing process. Your journey through the course is different from anybody else's. While you want to avoid merely summarizing that journey (see below about the Narrative of Progress), you do want to show awareness of your own unique position as a writer. What techniques of prewriting, drafting, and revising have worked best for you? How did you approach incorporating feedback? How did you figure out which course skills you were already fluent in, and which ones you still needed to work on? And, how did you work to achieve that growth once you'd diagnosed what you needed to do?

What's perhaps most important is to be honest with your instructor and with yourself. Your instructor has carefully read your work this quarter and given you feedback on it. Don't stretch the truth when it comes to how you've progressed: if you've dropped the ball in significant ways, don't try to hide it. Acknowledge your shortcomings, and emphasize ways in which you've worked (or will work) to rectify them. Your instructor wants to know that you've been thoughtfully composing your essays with an eye toward the demands of their rhetorical situations—including this introduction!

## AN EFFECTIVE INTRODUCTION: AVOIDING THE "NARRATIVE OF PROGRESS"

Students often have the tendency, when asked to perform reflection in a space like the portfolio, to fall back on what Kimberly Emmons, in her 2003 article, "Rethinking Genres of Reflection," calls "the narrative of progress." This kind of metacognitive reflection stays broad and shallow, and its main focus is to argue that the student made progress—that the student grew a lot and learned a lot of lessons about life. This narrative may include phrases like "I always hated writing until I came to your class," or "Before this class, I had no faith in my writing, but after this class, I feel confident and ready to shout at the world." These narratives are often sincere, and we're not here to tell you to exclude them entirely. However, it will be useful for you to shift your expectations of the portfolio introduction somewhat to avoid focusing on this kind of progress narrative. One problem is that this kind of approach can lead to very broad claims without strong evidential support (or close analysis).

We'd suggest that you think about it this way: there is no one "correct" way to write. "Good writing" and "bad writing" are empty terms. What does exist is a set of genres—each with their own conventions and expectations—that we learn to navigate as writers and as thinkers. You might consider what expectations and conventions are present in the types of academic writing you've been asked to learn during the quarter. How have you learned to navigate and fit into those conventions?

And remember: academic culture is not static, and it's different the world around. We happen to be working in modern American academic culture. What assumptions and expectations come with work in that context? Contextualizing your own work in this way asks you to become more argumentative and more rigorous. You can no longer just say "I've gained confidence in my writing." What kind of writing do you mean? Why have you gained confidence in it? If that's because you've built specific skills or learned to navigate certain expectations, what evidence can you introduce and then closely analyze to support that claim?

The goal will be to make a well-supported, consciously structured argument about what you've learned. This argument should be just as carefully constructed as other extended arguments in 39B. That is, you should make sure that every one of your claims is supported by evidence, and that that evidence is broken down patiently with analysis. You might choose to establish the standards of performance for the course (using the course rubrics) and then try to ensure that you reference these metrics as you argue about your success and your learning in the course.

## Using Multimodality

The introduction should interface closely with your work to demonstrate your fulfillment of the course's requirements and your aptitude with the skills that 39B teaches. Because your portfolio is composed electronically as a multimodal document, there are dozens of ways to get creative with how you make your argument(s) and how you choose to integrate your artifacts into your introduction.

### KEY TERM: MULTIMODALITY

The word "multimodal" is closely related to "multimedia," but refers to *modes* of communication and expression rather than *mediums* of representation. When we ask you for multimodality, we're asking you to communicate in various modes—textual, visual, aural, spatial... and to consider how these modes interconnect to achieve effective communication.

### HOW TO INTEGRATE MULTIMODAL EVIDENCE IN THE PORTFOLIO

1.  *Hyperlink from one part of your portfolio to another. You can use this to develop creative organizational schemes that are tailored to your audience, or that reflect your particular composition process or your unique experience in the course.*

2. *Use a given section of your introduction to discuss an artifact in detail, and hyperlink to that assignment or to relevant excerpts of it.*

3. *Take screenshots of your work that you can insert into your introduction.*

4. *Choose an artifact, highlight every part of the writing in that artifact that reflects a specific skill, screenshot that highlighted excerpt, and insert that screenshot into your introduction for discussion and analysis.*

5. *Use the "Insert Comment" feature on Microsoft Word to make line notes on your drafts, take screenshots of those drafts, and upload those screenshots into your introduction.*

6. *Use the "Compare Documents" feature in Microsoft Word to show the differences between your first and final drafts of an assignment, and upload that document to your portfolio.*

## HOW TO USE MULTIMODALITY TO PROVIDE ANALYSIS

1. *Print out your work and make physical line notes, such as underlining and highlighting significant passages of revisions, drawing arrows between passages, and making informative drawings.*

2. *Create a mindmap or other conceptual diagram that can show the mental connections you're making between concepts and how those connections function.*

## HOW TO USE MULTIMODALITY TO APPEAL TO AUDIENCE

1. *Insert images or videos into your introduction to capture or keep your reader's attention, to establish a certain tone, to provide humor, or to illustrate, challenge, or deepen parts of your argument.*

2. *Insert music that's meant to be played on each page of the portfolio to help establish a certain mood, illustrate a concept, or entertain your audience.*

Multimodality in your portfolio should not be an afterthought, and it should not merely function as decoration. It should be a vital part of the way you're making your argument and the way you're presenting that argument effectively to your audience.

## DIRECTING ATTENTION AND INTERPRETING WORK: YOUR ROLE AS TOUR GUIDE IN THE PORTFOLIO

As you compose your portfolio, remember that it's important to direct your reader's attention effectively. If you turn in a portfolio with one hundred pages of work and fifty links, you'll need to find a way to tell your reader what they should look at and how they should understand it. *Imagine you're giving a tour of an art museum*, and you certainly don't have time to lead your customers through the whole place—it's huge! What are the main exhibits you'd show off? *How can you communicate to your reader where they should go and what they should look at?*

**Finally, remember that it's your responsibility to analyze and contextualize what you present.** A good museum tour guide won't just stand in front of a painting or sculpture and say, "Well, here it is. I'll be at the snack bar." Nah, they're going to *explain why the work is important, what's impressive about it, and where it fits in the artist's larger body of work.* You need to do the same! Interpret your evidence (your work) for your audience (your instructor) and show them what you see in it.

### *Examples of Successful Multimodal Evidence*

I proceeded to focus upon the context necessary in order to understand the meme (highlighted in yellow), while also looking at what features of this meme that contributed to its virality. As I did this, I argued that the mass appeal of this meme derives from the use of simple replication, which allows any individual to easily create their own strain of this meme (highlighted in green). Thus, because the meme is can be replicated easily, the audience becomes broader. In doing so, I state WHAT aspects of this meme make it enjoyable, HOW these features contribute to the spread of this meme, and went over TO WHAT EFFECT these features have on the longevity of this meme (highlighted in blue below).

> The core aspects that makes this meme appealing to the masses, deals with the simplicity of recreating this post and the all-inclusive nature of it, which is not directed to a specific discourse community — only excluding those absent from the internet. The only previous knowledge necessary to understand this meme is that "bon appetit" is a French salutation to a meal, and that all the variants are deliberately misspelling it. If one would like to take part in creating their own strain of this meme, all they would need is the ability to take a photograph and caption that photo with "Bone Apple Tea." Not only can this meme be easily replicated, but it is also a non-offensive and all-inclusive one, creating a neutral humor that can be enjoyed by any person – considering that they have the preexisting knowledge of what "bon appetit" is used for. This vast audience that the meme has taken on invites any individual to appreciate and take part in the spread of this meme, expanding the existence of this image on social media, blogs, and discussion forums, such as Reddit and 4chan. More importantly, the longevity of this meme can be said to be due to the universal acceptance of any variation and the broad audience that it can appeal to.

In her portfolio introduction, this student quoted her previous work and used color-coded high-lighting to indicate different relevant portions of the assignment.

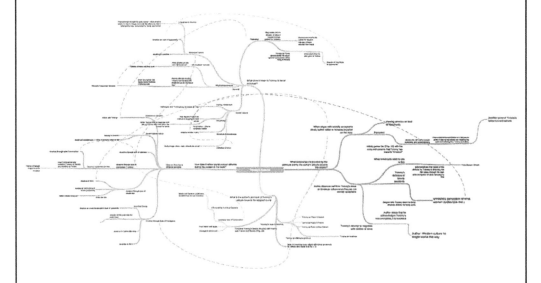

Later, she included this screenshot of a mindmap she'd made while planning her essay. This helped her make an argument about her prewriting process and metacognition.

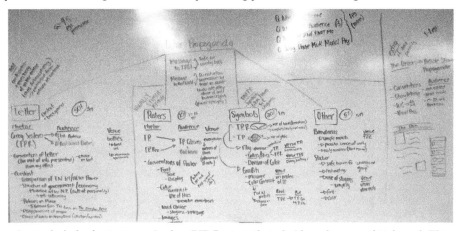

She also included a brainstorm for her RIP Project that she'd made on a whiteboard. This was further evidence of her prewriting and metacognitive skills, and it showed her unique writing process and style. Multimodality like this is a chance to really stress the individualism of your writing process and products.

Each of these images were included in-line with text that contextualized and explained them, and the writer used the images to thoughtfully further the arguments made in her portfolio introduction.

# Final Thoughts

As always, your instructor might have a specific way they want to see your portfolio put together or specific artifacts they'd like you to include. But, if you have a creative idea for how you'd like to curate your portfolio, run it by them. The worst that can happen is that they say no. And if they agree that it's a good idea, you've taken initiative by taking charge of your own learning in order to maximize your potential rhetorical appeal. Basically, you've proven that you know your stuff and that you care about the work you're doing.

At the end of the day, if you've learned one thing from Writing 39B, it should be this: *all communication is rhetorically situated*—whether you're texting your friends, writing an academic essay, editing a cover letter for your dream job, or drafting the final portfolio introduction here in 39B. And no matter what task you face, the skills that you learn in 39B will help you rise to the occasion by being able to critically read the aspects of a rhetorical situation, then to analyze those factors in order to make decisions that will help you communicate your message as effectively and successfully as possible.

*Emile Shehada won the 2016–17 Upper-Division Writing Award in the Humanities and the Arts with the philosophical essay "Moore or Less: Moore's Partially-effective Reply to Humean Skepticism," which arbitrates Moore and Hume's debate about the ability of our five senses to deliver truths about the world. Emile, a private writing tutor, has a penchant for dictating his own writing; this probably made my job easier, as we edited very little of our May 2017 conversation to bring it into the shape you see below. In what follows, Emile encourages student-writers to give themselves enough time to create their best work, and he walks us through his research process for a Humanities Core film analysis essay. I hope those doing similar projects, such as the Rhetorical Analysis essay in 39B, not only take Emile up on his advice but also follow his example. – Lance Langdon*

**ES:** I analyzed *Heroes of the Desert Storm,* a made-for-TV propaganda film about Operation Desert Storm in 1991. The movie was panned by critics and it was also extremely popular on TV. Its Nielsen ratings belied what the critics were saying about it. People loved it. So that's why I picked it. For all that we understand that this was a shameless propaganda event, a lot of people watched it, enjoyed it. So it's worth writing about, it's worth analyzing, because it gives you insight into what people expect to see when they're confronted with war, or with news.

I wrote about how *Heroes of the Desert Storm* was a bunch of baloney. The movie was such a painfully obvious attempt to sanitize and propagandize a war that, like all wars, really did have a human cost.

**LL:** Do you remember where you started looking or how you built up your evidence?

**ES:** We saw clips from that movie in class that established that there was a lot of media sensationalizing surrounding the Gulf War.

I just started Googling "Heroes of the Desert Storm Review Ratings." I found old newspaper articles, old TV guides that had the reviews of it. That was what helped me frame that question.

And there weren't that many critics.

**LL:** And I understand that you looked into the factual discrepancies as well, between the war and its portrayal. How did you do that?

**ES:** Well one, I watched the movie. And then I read a lot of military background, a lot of critiques of bigger theatrical movies. What is it, *Jarhead?* There were a bunch of movies from that period, or that postdated that period, that were very theatrical, very well produced, with lots of money behind them. They attracted critical reviews, which I wasn't interested in. More importantly, they attracted reviews from people who closely follow the military, who like to fact-check military movies. I found what veterans were saying. And they said, "No, this part isn't true. You would never do that and that." And so I was able to apply some of that. Obviously, I don't just go by what the veterans said. I would look up what the veteran said to see if in fact that is how the military did it. And if in fact that is how the military does it, or did it, in 1991, and the movie is showing us something different because the different thing is more theatrical or more uplifting or more whatever you want, then I would make a note of that.

And then there were some elements that don't need extra research. Like the helicopter descending to save the man framed by the sunset, and the shot of the flag as we close the film and the credits roll. Something like that, I don't need to look up other analysis to understand that this is a shameless play for my feelings.

LL: And so you broke down the composition and those elements to think about how they appeal to our emotions?

ES: Yes, exactly.

## Chapter 9

# WR39C: Argument and Research

*By Brad Queen with Rachael Collins, Brian Fonken, Scott Lerner,*
*and Ali Meghdadi, Brendan Shapiro, Alice Berghof, and*
*Keith Danner*

This chapter has been written before, many times in fact, in previous editions of the AGWR. Over the years, numerous teachers have worked together to write the 39C chapter. Their thoughts linger on these pages even as this new iteration of 39C recasts them and reshapes the curriculum. My task has been to weave everything together, to synthesize the approaches and values of our teaching community. We hope this chapter takes you to the next level as a college-level research writer. Good luck!

## Introduction to Writing 39C

*Education reform. The mass incarceration of African-Americans and institutional racism. Violent rhetoric, obscenity, and hate speech on the Internet, across social media, and in video games. Ethical perspectives on animals. Climate change, resource management, conservation, and the redesign of cities and suburbs. Medical ethics and exploratory science. Upward economic and social mobility for oppressed peoples. Issues facing women across the globe...*

This list of topics for 39C could go on, and it will over the course of the quarter as you and your peers study the various social, cultural, and political problems you see around us today. Your task this term will be to describe and analyze one of these problems, to show how it affects individuals and communities, and to research expert perspectives that discuss remedies. Such a rigorous and multi-layered analysis will take you the entire quarter. All the while you'll stay focused on the people most affected by your central problem, those whose stories need to be told.

You're probably already getting a sense for the differences between WR39C and WR39B. You won't leave WR39B far behind. The knowledge and strategic know-how you acquired in B—about critical reading, rhetoric, genres, metacognitive analysis of your own writing processes—will serve you well in WR39C as you move into the complicated and interesting world of research writing, as you move into the broad expanse of nonfiction writing, which is a huge genre that contains many sub-genres within it.

## MOVING FROM WR39B TO WR39C: FICTION VS. NONFICTION

- What are the differences between fiction and nonfiction as genres?
- Why does 39C focus on nonfiction?
- Can you list different genres of nonfiction and their differences?

### Capstone Course

WR39C is a capstone course, which means it's the culmination of a sequence of courses. As such, you'll put to use what you've learned so far in your previous writing classes and take your learning to the next level. Once you complete WR39C, you've satisfied the Lower-Division Writing Requirement!

Writing WR39C deepens your understanding of rhetoric and communication by teaching you how to conduct research and how to evaluate and use various types of evidence. The reading, composing, and researching practices you'll learn in this course and the various intellectual strategies you develop will help you to succeed in your other courses, prepare you to engage in the university community and in your chosen discipline, and deepen your perspective on current issues and the idea of social justice itself.

WR39C asks you to participate actively in and evaluate discussions that shape our cultures and society. You will take part in academic discussions and vital public debates about issues that concern us all.

When you leave WR39C and move on to writing courses in your major, we hope you will take with you a sense of confidence that you can use the following strategies.

### Rhetoric & Composition

▶ *Recognize forms of rhetorical persuasion and understand the functions of various genres, both academic and non-academic.*

▶ *Craft substantive, motivated, and balanced arguments, and use counterarguments.*

▶ *Plan, draft, and revise effectively; develop and skillfully employ a variety of revision strategies that attend to structure, arrangement, pacing, and transitions.*

▷ *Read with understanding and engagement across a variety of genres, mediated forms, and discourses.*

▷ *Write clear, correct, coherent prose.*

▷ *Reflectively evaluate and analyze reading, writing, researching, revising, and organizing processes.*

## Multimodal Composition & Communication

▷ *Understand the distinctive rhetorical properties and effects of delivering arguments in written forms, orally and visually, with particular attention to audience/community, discourses/genres/contexts, and occasions/warrants.*

▷ *Arrange, display, and deliver arguments and evidence clearly and coherently.*

## Research Methods and Ethics

▷ *Comprehend the importance of information literacy, seen as both the act of researching and the skillful evaluation and use of evidence.*

▷ *Understand the definition of information literacy as the ability to discern and critically evaluate source materials of different types, in different media, genres, and discourses.*

▷ *Comprehend the communicative and rhetorical intentions of a source and use such understanding to determine a source's value as evidence.*

▷ *Learn to locate sources using a variety of tools, methods, and databases.*

▷ *Learn research ethics and avoid plagiarism.*

**Information Literacy**

You've already learned about information literacy in Chapters 3 and 4.

Here are some questions for you to consider. (You might even write out your answers.)

1. How is info literacy different from what we think of when we use the word "research"?

2. How does info literacy relate to the broader notion of literacy itself?

---

### PRO TIP: HOW TO DO WELL IN WRITING 39C

• Write to discover! Do all of the writing assignments.

• Complete all of the ungraded assignments. Embrace the opportunity to make productive mistakes.

• Attend every class meeting and participate actively in workshops.

• Respond constructively to the work of others and learn to become a fair and rigorous critic.

• Talk to your teacher, ask for advice. Go to conferences and office hours. Bring your questions and your insights.

• Engage your curiosity and your passions.

*How to Use This Chapter*

The 39C segment of the *AGWR* works together and in close conversation with a number of the other chapters you've already encountered in this book. Your teacher will direct you to specific sections, but you can refer back to them on your own and actively consult key strategies and pieces of advice that have already worked for you.

Keep the following chapters close at hand as you read this one and as you move through your writing process:

- Chapter 3: Citing and Integrating Sources
- Chapter 4: Discovering Sources
- Chapter 5: Drafting and Crafting
- Chapter 6: I Came Here for an Argument

*Overview of the Quarter*

Three major assignments will guide you through the quarter in 39C. They are: 1) The Contexts Project (CP), 2) The Advocacy Project (AP), and 3) The Final ePortfolio. While their due dates go according to the following order—the CP is first, followed by the AP, and then the final ePortfolio—you'll assemble the ePortfolio over the course of the quarter while you work on and then finish the CP and while you generate the AP in the second half of the term.

While the ePortfolio is something quite different from the CP and the AP in terms of what it teaches you, all three assignments work together to give you a powerful array of communicative, rhetorical, and intellectual strategies. Let's think of the CP and the AP as the major elements of the writing process curriculum, and the ePortfolio as the major assignment of the reflection or metacognitive curriculum. Where the writing process curriculum includes the final and graded compositions of the CP and the AP, and all of the ungraded assignments you complete along the way—source evaluations, annotations, a research proposal or prospectus, and drafts—the reflection curriculum includes prompts given to you by your teacher over the quarter that ask you to analyze the strategies you're using as you conduct research and invent arguments, and as you draft and revise your compositions. These two curricula work together to teach you how to craft arguments, to deepen your information literacy, and to enable you to understand and master the strategies you use for research-driven writing, rhetoric, and communication.

**KEEP THE "META" IN MIND**

Remember the definition of metacognition from the WR39B chapter?

Here's something for you to consider: Revisit your 39B portfolio and think about how you might use specific strategies that you used in 39B for the challenges you'll face in 39C.

## The First Steps

On the first day of class, you'll be assigned the final ePortfolio and the CP, and you'll be given your first writing assignment: a reflective self-assessment. The self-assessment asks you to look backward, inward, and forward as you write this first reflective piece, something that you can use as the first artifact in your final ePortfolio. In the self-assessment, you might go back to your portfolio from 39A or 39B, or reach back even further, to offer some initial thoughts about your experiences with writing, research, and rhetoric, and what you hope to learn in 39C.

Over the course of the first week or two, you'll work closely with your core text, other readings, and your section's themes for the first time. As you read and engage in class discussion, take note of ideas that interest you and arguments that elicit a reaction from you. When your curiosity is piqued and your emotions engaged, you are ready to articulate your first guiding questions.

Sometime within the quarter's first few weeks, you'll visit the UCI Library and have the opportunity to talk with a reference librarian about the questions you have and how you might begin researching them. These questions serve as the starting points for the first major project.

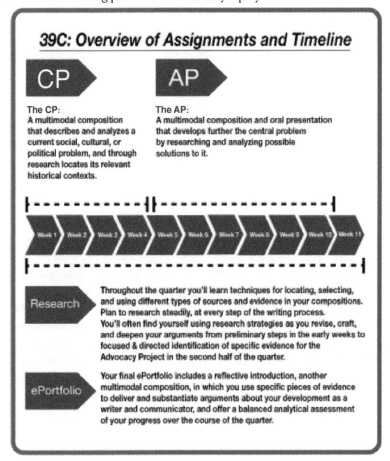

**39C: Overview of Assignments and Timeline**

**CP**

**The CP:**
A multimodal composition that describes and analyzes a current social, cultural, or political problem, and through research locates its relevant historical contexts.

**AP**

**The AP:**
A multimodal composition and oral presentation that develops further the central problem by researching and analyzing possible solutions to it.

Week 1 Week 2 Week 3 Week 4 Week 5 Week 6 Week 7 Week 8 Week 9 Week 10 Week 11

**Research**
Throughout the quarter you'll learn techniques for locating, selecting, and using different types of sources and evidence in your compositions. Plan to research steadily, at every step of the writing process. You'll often find yourself using research strategies as you revise, craft, and deepen your arguments from preliminary steps in the early weeks to focused & directed identification of specific evidence for the Advocacy Project in the second half of the quarter.

**ePortfolio**
Your final ePortfolio includes a reflective introduction, another multimodal composition, in which you use specific pieces of evidence to deliver and substantiate arguments about your development as a writer and communicator, and offer a balanced analytical assessment of your progress over the course of the quarter.

## Research Tips

### Tip #1: Read Widely, with an Open Mind

As you read and explore, write down your questions and your reactions to the things you read. Be mindful of ideas and arguments that make you wonder, or perhaps make you mad. Such reactions and the questions they generate are the first steps toward discovering your arguments.

When you begin your research, you will probably have some ideas about what you want to argue. You will probably be tempted to establish a claim and then go and find some research to support it.

This approach, however, predetermines what you might argue *before* you've engaged with the sources. Remember: There's a difference between a good idea and an idea that is arguable, and the difference comes from the sources. Without sources and evidence, there is no argument. You'll need to push yourself to discover evidence and arguments by finding, reading, and selecting different types of sources—popular and scholarly, for example—that both describe your central problem and give you a sense for what the experts are saying about it.

> **PRO TIP: LOCATE THE RESEARCH GUIDE FOR YOUR COURSE THEME**
>
> Did you know that each course theme in 39C has its own library guide that will help you with your research? Check it out and explore! https://guides.lib.uci.edu/w39c.

Approaching your argument with preconceived ideas means you go on a scavenger hunt, picking sources that support your viewpoint and discarding those that challenge or contradict it. You could be wrong. You might have to change your opinions based on knowledge you'll acquire as you research and read.

Picking only those sources that support your point of view is called "cherry picking," and it will probably produce an argument that a reader could dismiss easily because of its inability to acknowledge counterarguments. It would be easy, for example, to find articles supporting my (as yet unproven) hypothesis that Colony Collapse Disorder is caused by pesticides. You could name an obvious culprit: profiteering multinational pharmaceutical corporations that make billions as they poison our ecosystems, land, and food supply. You can see from the rhetoric of the previous sentence that a particular kind of villain is easy to imagine—but such an approach may not be very helpful. Although further research may show that such an assumption is justified, the first task is to get an overview, see where the disagreements are, evaluate sources, and keep an open mind. Conclusive statements come later, after knowledge has been acquired.

## Try This: Discovering Researchable Questions

*Write down three questions that occurred to you as you did the first readings in your class.*

*How do you know if your questions are researchable?*

### Tip #2: Keep Good Notes and Records

To become a good academic researcher you will need to cultivate strategies for keeping track of all your good information and sources. You'll probably need to spend time developing file systems on your computer. You may even want to keep a research journal that helps you document the pathways you've explored. Consult with your teacher and a reference librarian when you're researching tips and guidance.

### GUIDING QUESTIONS FOR ORGANIZING YOUR NOTES

1. *What strategies do you use to organize your thoughts, your notes, and your research?*

2. *Which strategies have worked for you? Why?*

3. *Which have not? Why?*

### Tip #3: Look for Academic Sources Early in the Process

Google and Google Scholar will help you to find credible sources in both mainstream media and scholarly journals. Such sources can be very useful in helping you show readers that your problem is both current and pressing, and they can help you document people's stories that remind you and your readers of painful and distressing situations. But for an academic essay, the genre you'll be writing in 39C, you'll need to find academic sources that take on the problem with analytical rigor and with scholarly research. These specialized sources are available through Google Scholar and the library's website, both of which give you access to an extensive collection of databases. Your class library orientation will help you become more familiar with these databases and resources available to you.

**Remember Chapter 4, "Discovering Sources"?** Chapter 4 gives you very good advice for discovering and evaluating key sources, entering scholarly conversations, and framing questions to guide your research.

Academic sources are written by scholars in a particular field for other scholars in that field. This means that these sources are held to a high standard by people who know what they're talking about, and you can trust authors of academic sources to have done their homework. Further, using academic sources lends your own writing credibility. The smooth integration of authoritative, trustworthy, and expert support for your own points is a distinguishing characteristic of strong writing inside and outside the academy.

Finally, academic sources almost always feature arguments. Scholars develop opinions about their research, and they write academic articles and books to contribute to or change the research in their fields. These academic sources provide not only information, but also models for academic argument. As you read them, seek both information and ideas about how to structure and refine your own writing and thinking.

Of course, you should read academic sources critically. You don't have to agree with an author, and you can certainly challenge his or her credibility—especially if you find opposing evidence and arguments in other academic sources.

### ADVICE FROM FORMER WR 39C STUDENTS

"Take your time."

"Don't pick the first source you see. Read it, analyze it, do some background research, then make an educated evaluation of the credibility of the source and how it relates to your topic."

"Try to do some research every day."

"Don't expect to find an excellent source in a matter of minutes. Research takes time! Also, I don't just throw out 'bad' sources because even the weakest ones can give you keywords or hints that will lead you to better ones."

"Use sources that would prove both sides in order to strengthen your argument."

*Tip #4: Remember that Research & Discovery Take Time*

All researchers gather some information they end up discarding. It's actually a sign that you're doing a good job exploring if you find yourself pursuing a hypothesis and then you conclude later that the evidence you found and the arguments you generated led you to focus on more important and telling pieces of evidence. Remember that even if you don't end up using some of the sources you've found, or using them as support for main arguments, the process of finding and reading them has contributed to your journey to becoming an expert on the topic, which then forms a key part of your academic *ethos*. Be brave and explore when you research and when you write. You never know when that "light-bulb moment" will happen!

## Research Project Part One: Contexts

The Contexts Project (CP) asks you to do two things: **(1) research and deploy various types of sources to describe, contextualize, and analyze a significant contemporary political/social/cultural problem; and (2) summarize and evaluate conversations and debates happening between credible scholars, thinkers, and organizations about your topic.**

The CP asks you to engage with various types of sources that will help you to answer your guiding questions and to describe the problem that sits at the center of your focus. Another purpose of the CP is to begin the process of teaching you how to locate, evaluate, select, arrange, and integrate sources into a multimodal composition. As a genre of communication—and in the case of this assignment, one that frames a problem, delivers arguments, uses evidence, and speaks to a broad audience—a multimodal composition can be a synthesis of various rhetorical positions—visual and written for example—that work together to deepen argumentative positions and claims.

To start, you will want to generate a list of key research terms. Good keywords are specific: they involve names of key figures, communities, organizations, local, state, and federal laws, policies, organization and government reports, major protests, and political movements. While you will no doubt rely initially on Wikipedia or other encyclopedic information to give yourself a basic understanding of your topic, your ultimate goal is to find information that will help you to develop the researcher's more narrow and trained focus.

For example, if you Google "housing" you will get a billion and a half results. Some of them may be useful, but how do you decide? You might spend hours trying to narrow your focus only to realize you've clicked, skimmed, and collected your way to sources that are only related in the broadest of strokes to "housing." If, on the other hand, you have found a peer-reviewed journal article on housing in Los Angeles that mentions the Los Angeles Tenants Union, a tenants' rights organization, you can use that term to Google "Los Angeles Tenants Union." You might use the organization website to learn about the housing experiences of specific communities in Los Angeles County, local events, and important housing related laws, such as the Ellis and Costa-Hawkins Act.

## Try This: Generating Key Research Terms

1. *Use one or two of the sources you are currently reading to create a list of key research terms that will help you do further research on the context associated with that source's topic.*

2. *After you've searched by using at least 3 different specific terms, try to answer the following questions in a short reflective analysis:*

   • *What did your keyword searches help you to discover about the historical and/or rhetorical context of the topic?*

   • *What did your keyword searches reveal to you about the limitations of using broad terms? What about the benefits of using specific terms?*

### A Note on Confirmation Bias

Real researchers don't start with an argument and then find evidence to "back it up." As you learned above, such an approach to evidence is called "cherry-picking." We cherry-pick information when we have confirmation bias: the tendency to interpret the evidence we find as confirmation of our preexisting beliefs or hypotheses. We think, in other words, we have "found" information when, in fact, we haven't engaged any information that might challenge our preexisting beliefs or hypotheses. Because you will need sources that reflect a variety of perspectives and arguments from within various disciplines and professions, the "contextualizing" part of your research project helps to avoid confirmation bias.

### Historical Context and the CP

In order to write a successful CP, we need to move away from the idea that history is a collection of facts about things that happened in the past. Rather, history can be an indispensable tool for advocates who care passionately about pressing current issues. Looking at primary-source evidence—documents like court cases, political speeches, and journalism from the time period you're investigating—can help you articulate a deeply-informed description of a contemporary problem by understanding how it developed and what communities and institutions are stakeholders in it.

### Finding and Describing Arguments for the CP

In order to write a successful Contexts Project, we need to consider how various disciplines make arguments. Historians, for example, often look at primary-source evidence—documents like court cases, political speeches, and journalism from the time period they are investigating. Journalists might rely on the historian's grasp of these materials to articulate a deeply informed description of a contemporary problem. Judges might also rely on historians' expertise to make decisions that will impact the rest of society. Journalists and judges might also rely on the empirical evidence of social science researchers to better understand and make arguments about the problems that afflict communities and institutions.

### *An Example: Various Arguments for Same-Sex Marriage in Obergefell v. Hodges*

In *Obergefell v. Hodges* in 2015, the Supreme Court held in a 5–4 decision that the right to marry is guaranteed to same-sex couples under the Fourteenth Amendment, marking a decisive victory for gay-rights advocates everywhere. During this case, many organizations and experts acted in the capacity of amici curiae (friends of the court). They submitted amicus briefs in which they sought to influence the outcome of the court case by presenting their expert knowledge to the court.

## *Try This: What's an Amicus Brief?*

*Google this term. Look at an amicus curiae brief or two.*

*What does amicus curiae mean?*

*Where did you find your example? Is it credible?*

*How would you categorize an amicus brief as a source? In other words, what type of source is it and what can you do with it?*

### How Historians Argued About Gay Marriage Rights

In their amicus brief, the most prominent historians of marriage in the US as well as the American Historical Association argued that the court should decide in favor of gay marriage rights. Their opinion was based on decades of historical research carried out by them and their colleagues in the field. Historians used their historical research to advocate for marriage equality for same-sex couples. Some of their arguments are broken down as follows:

**1. "Marriage has served multiple purposes beyond procreation through-out American history."**

To people who say that gay marriage should not be allowed because a same-sex couple cannot conceive a child, historians responded that marriage has historically served many purposes that go beyond having children. Marriage is complex, and it has historically served political, social, economic, legal, and personal purposes. Moreover, many couples adopt: "non-biological children," they argue, "have long been integral to the American family."

**2. "Marriage has changed to reject discriminatory rules and restrictions."**

Over the course of the history of the US, marriage laws have discriminated against different people in many ways. Marriage laws have changed over the course of history to reflect changing social norms and values. These changes include changes in eligibility, roles, duties, and obligations. For instance, in early American law, women were treated differently from men. A marriage was treated as a single unit which was represented legally, economically, and politically by the husband. This early doctrine of marriage required that a husband support his wife and family and that a wife obey her husband. Married women could not own property, earn money, have debt, make a valid contract, or sue or be sued. Changing this view of marriage was difficult and very controversial. Opponents of making changes to the law in favor of greater equality argued that change would be blasphemous and unnatural, much like opponents of gay marriage argue today. Marriage was governed by "Divine Origin," opponents to change argued, and subordination was "the price which female wants and weakness must pay for their protection." What historians argued in this case was that marriage laws have been changed before in the face of great controversy and that they can be changed again.

### 3. "Race-based restrictions on marriage eligibility have been eliminated."

One example of these restrictions that the historians point to in their brief is the case of *Loving v. Virginia* decided by the Supreme Court in 1967. The case, which struck down Virginia's law against cross-racial marriages, invalidated all remaining state anti-miscegenation laws, and with them were "such restrictions on the basic freedom to choose one's spouse finally laid to rest."

## How Psychologists Argued About Gay Marriage Rights

Another amicus brief for *Obergefell v. Hodges*, written by the American Psychological Association, also argued that the court should decide in favor of same sex marriage. Their opinion was based, not on decades of historical research, but on empirical research and evidence drawn from the study of human behaviors. Some of their arguments, broken down as follows, were supported with multiple studies from within the field conducted over time:

### 1. "Homosexuality is a normal expression of human sexuality, is generally not chosen, and is highly resistant to change"

Writers for the APA note that in 1973 the Diagnostic and Statistical Manual of Mental Disorders (DSM) has determined that "homosexuality per se implies no impairment in judgment, stability, reliability, or general social or vocational capabilities." They also note that, shortly after the change in this official language, the "APA adopted a policy reflecting the same conclusion" that "homosexuality and bisexuality are normal expressions of human sexuality . . . ". They further cite studies that show gay and lesbian people overwhelmingly do not identify their sexuality as a choice. Evidence shows, moreover, that any efforts to change sexuality from homosexual to heterosexual are harmful and major national mental health organizations have adopted policy statements warning against such efforts.

**2. "Gay men and lesbians form stable, committed relationships that are equivalent to heterosexual relationships in essential respects."**

Pointing to multiple studies, writers for the APA conclude that "[e]mpirical research demonstrates that the psychological and social dimensions of committed relationships between same-sex partners largely resemble those of heterosexual partnerships. Same-sex couples form deep emotional attachments and commitments, with levels of relationship satisfaction similar to or higher than those of heterosexual couples. They also go through similar processes to address concerns about intimacy, love, equity, and other relationship issues."

**3. "There is no scientific basis for concluding that same-sex couples are any less fit or capable parents than heterosexual couples, or that their children are any less psychologically healthy and well adjusted."**

After a review of multiple studies and the evolving nature of scientific research among mental health professionals, the authors conclude that "the parenting abilities of gay men and lesbians—and the positive outcomes for their children—are not areas where credible scientific researchers disagree." They also point to the conclusions brought by The American Academy of Pediatrics (AAP), that "Many studies attest to the normal development of children of same-gender couples when the child is wanted, the parents have a commitment to shared parenting, and the parents have strong social and economic supports."

## GUIDING QUESTIONS FOR THINKING ABOUT HISTORICAL AND RHETORICAL CONTEXTS

1. *What other communities were invested in the debate about gay marriage that led to* Obergefell v. Hodges? *Can you find other sources making arguments about the case?*

2. *How do the arguments in other sources differ from the ones presented above? Who were those other arguments addressing, and what goals did they seek to achieve?*

3. *The* Obergefell *decision was handed down in 2015. How can arguments from and about* Obergefell *help us gain an informed perspective on to-day's issues (pertaining to, for example, LGBTQ rights)?*

### Conclusion

There are well over one hundred briefs from individuals and organizations that were submitted in this case—those in favor and those against. Including the two we just reviewed, there are a wide range of other perspectives that include religious organizations, LGBTQ organizations, think tanks, legal organizations and more. What we can learn when we engage some or all of them is not only the wide range of perspectives engaged in this topic, but also that those perspectives often draw upon conventions unique to the disciplines, political viewpoints, or religious communities they represent. To view a full list of the amicus briefs, go to: https://www.supremecourt.gov/ObergefellHodges/AmicusBriefs/

## GUIDING QUESTIONS FOR THE CP

*As you move through the CP's writing and research process, here are few questions for you to keep in mind. (You might even write reflectively in response to them.)*

1.  *What are your guiding research questions? How did you formulate them? How have they changed as you've researched and drafted your CP?*

2.  *What key concepts, people, institutions, and events do you need to identify and contextualize to clearly present your problem? Where in your research did you first hear about these key terms, and how will you learn more about them?*

3.  *What sources are you using to provide historical context for your problem? How do they function in your composition to support your description of the problem and your attempt to persuade readers that the problem you're addressing is current, important, and pressing?*

4.  *Which of your primary sources help you historically contextualize your problem, and how? Do they register significant and meaningful historical changes that contributed to the development of your problem?*

5.  *How are you using secondary sources, such as scholarly arguments, to deepen your understanding of your primary sources?*

6.  *Which scholarly disciplines are most invested in trying to understand and explain the impact of your problem? What is the specific investment of each relevant discipline, and what are the different questions they're asking about the problem?*

7.  *Which of your sources, both primary and secondary, contain arguments about your problem? How are those arguments shaped by their rhetorical contexts—whom the author is addressing, and how they are attempting to impact their audience?*

8.  Do you offer a rich and descriptive summary of your CP's central problem, one that justifies its contemporary importance? Where in your composition is this description most concisely and directly stated?

9.  How many different types of evidence do you use in your CP? Can you list these types and describe how they function differently in your composition?

10. Explain how the arrangement of your evidence works. Why have you chosen to arrange your evidence in the way you have, and how does this arrangement contribute to the narrative cohesion and analytical depth of your composition?

## An Interlude on Multimodality

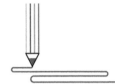

Multimodality sits at the center of all the assignments in 39C. Multimodality will help you define your research topics and your guiding questions. It will help you arrange your evidence, develop your arguments, and alter the course of your research. It will deepen and enrich your argumentative style and your rhetorical strategies, both when you write and when you deliver your ideas orally and visually in a presentation to your class.

Multimodality is defined in detail at the end of Chapter 3, "Citing and Integrating Sources."

### GUIDING QUESTIONS FOR UNDERSTANDING MULTIMODALITY

1.  What modes have authors used in the various texts you've read for your class, and how did different modes work to create rhetorical effects?

2.  What modes are at work in your compositions and what function does each serve?

3.  What modes are at work so far in your ePortfolio? Is multimodality in your ePortfolio different from that of your CP and AP? How so?

Don't wait until the last minute to find multimodal evidence to experiment with in your drafts. As you make a case for a problem or a solution use your evidence in multimodal ways to articulate claims and arguments that words alone can't convey. Think about how striking inequalities can be when represented visually in graphs, diagrams, or photographs; consider how a footnote's supplementary information can help a reader to better understand context; and notice the way an annotated summary helps a reader gain a more comprehensive understanding of a source that has only been partially engaged in the essay.

When it comes to writing about your own writing, consider how an ePortfolio is, by definition, multimodal: it requires readers to "navigate" through various pages and hyperlinks. How carefully you have attended to the spatial dimensions of communication in your ePortfolio can be the difference between a discombobulated reader and an orientated reader. Besides spatial and linguistic, there are other modalities at work in the ePortfolio. When, for example, you use a screenshot of your drafts and the comments you've received from your teacher or your peers, digital photographs of your notes, outlines, and books, you are using a visual mode of communication. Your visual elements should be in conversation with your prose elements, not just through effective captions, but through textual analysis. You might also include video or audio of yourself! Use whatever it takes to communicate your message most effectively to your reader.

The old cliché says that picture is worth a thousand words. There's a valuable point there—that not all media are created equal for every communicative task. Depending on the rhetorical situation, you will find various media to be the most useful, offering you the most effective, efficient, or impactful way of communicating a message to your readers. This fact results from the different affordances—or possibilities for use—that different media offer. It would be difficult to use only a photograph to define a key term in your essay, just as it would be tough going to grab your reader's attention *in an instant* with a long descriptive paragraph where a powerful photograph would work perfectly.

Take a look at the following example from a student's composition (Figure 9.1).

The challenge facing universities nationwide today is finding a way to respond to violence and hate speech on campus. In the past and even today, many colleges have attempted to solve this issue by creating free speech zones on campuses, areas in public spaces that are set apart for protest and other controversial speech. Writing for the Heritage Foundation, a popular conservative think tank, Senior Policy Analyst Jonathan Butcher noted the pitifully small sizes of some campus speech zones saying, "Los Angeles' Pierce College has a zone no larger than three parking spaces…and at California State Polytechnic University in Pomona, the zone amounted to 0.01 percent of the campus" (Heritage Foundation). These free speech zones by definition limit the scope of free speech and do very little to nothing to help foster campuses that encourage free expression.

Many colleges and universities establish free speech zones, but the free speech zones by definition, limit the scope of free speech and expression. This figure shows a clash of ideologies regarding free speech zones

Other colleges like DePaul University, which requires "students to get an administrator's permission to use a particular slogan" for clubs and activities, resort to all forms of censorship and speech codes to protect their campuses from mob riots and violent protest (The 10 Worst Colleges for Free Speech). The reactive stance that so many colleges like DePaul and Cal Poly have against violence and protest caused by free expression have proved more or less futile in getting to the root of the issue.

Figure 9.1

Here you'll see a student drawing on a variety of sources to describe the extent to which some college campuses attempt to control or limit free speech. To support the claims and introduce the audience to the debate at the heart of this controversy, the student uses an image to contextualize the impact of free speech zones on campuses. The photo also lends itself to critical interpretation, as the handwritten rebuttal, in an act of free speech, has been placed beside the official sign. Finally, the student includes an informative caption that helps frame the problem and propel the argument forward, which adds depth and complexity to the overall usage of multimodality.

When you write multimodally, you should ask yourself what different media can do better than uniformly text-based writing. What can images, sounds, the spatial arrangement of the page, embedded videos, and other multimodal sources of evidence do, both on their own and in conjunction with your words?

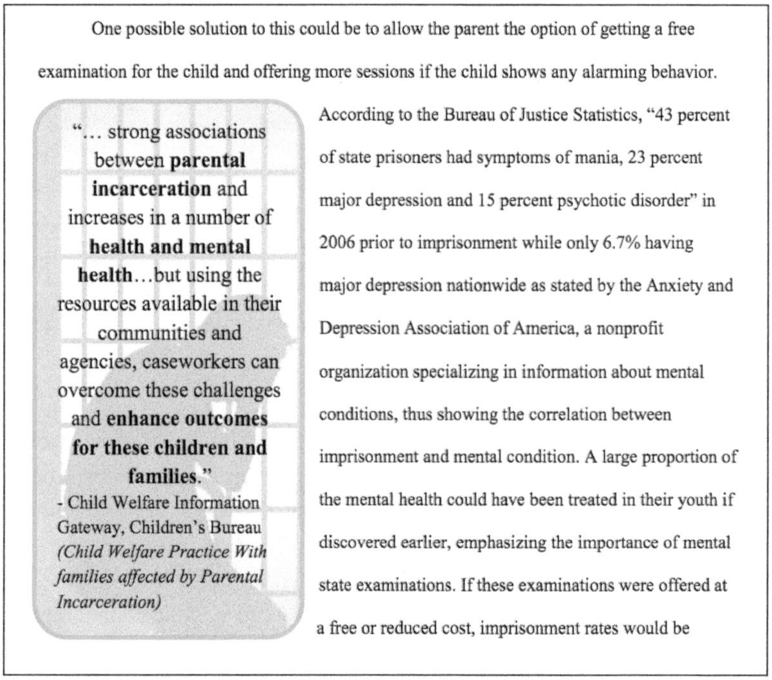

One possible solution to this could be to allow the parent the option of getting a free

examination for the child and offering more sessions if the child shows any alarming behavior.

"… strong associations between **parental incarceration** and increases in a number of **health and mental health**…but using the resources available in their communities and agencies, caseworkers can overcome these challenges and **enhance outcomes for these children and families.**"
- Child Welfare Information Gateway, Children's Bureau *(Child Welfare Practice With families affected by Parental Incarceration)*

According to the Bureau of Justice Statistics, "43 percent of state prisoners had symptoms of mania, 23 percent major depression and 15 percent psychotic disorder" in 2006 prior to imprisonment while only 6.7% having major depression nationwide as stated by the Anxiety and Depression Association of America, a nonprofit organization specializing in information about mental conditions, thus showing the correlation between imprisonment and mental condition. A large proportion of the mental health could have been treated in their youth if discovered earlier, emphasizing the importance of mental state examinations. If these examinations were offered at a free or reduced cost, imprisonment rates would be

Figure 9.2

This example raises a couple of important points (Figure 9.2). First, how do the different elements on the page interact with one another? Did the primary text shape or enhance a reader's understanding of the pull quote and background image? How will that image, in turn, affect the way the reader receives the essay?

In the following example, how does the student's simple breakdown of two potential laws help the audience quickly and easily grasp the salient details (Figure 9.3)?

Even though Texas yet failed to decriminalize marijuana and pass laws to legalize medical marijuana, it does not mean there is no possibility of legalizing recreational marijuana in Texas. Texas can take small steps slowly toward legalization. Delightfully, there were two big progress this year that increased future possibility of decriminalization and legalization. House Bill 81 and House Bill 2107 managed to pass through the House committee, but failed to be scheduled for a vote (See figure 5).

| Medical Cannabis HB 2107 | | Decriminalization HB 81 | |
|---|---|---|---|
| ✓ | Introduced in House and Senate | ✓ | Introduced in House and Senate |
| ✓ | Bipartisan support with 77 co-authors | ✓ | Bipartisan support with 41 co-authors |
| ✓ | Public Hearing (outstanding testimony!) | ✓ | Public Hearing (outstanding testimony!) |
| ✓ | Passed House committee with 7-2 vote! | ✓ | Passed House committee with 4-2 vote! |
| ✗ | Scheduled for a vote in the House. | ✓ | Scheduled for a vote in the House. |
| | | ✗ | Vote on by the House. (Beat by the clock.) |

Fig 5. Texas House Bill 2107 and House Bill 81. Table. Texasmarijuanapolicy.org. June 2, 2017

Texas House Bill 2017, Representative Eddie Lucio III's bill was aimed to legalize medical marijuana for patients in need of marijuana treatment. With passionate work of Eddie Lucio and Jason Isaac, the Bill became the first medical marijuana bill in Texas to be voted by the House committee. Even though the bill passed the House Committee with 7-2 vote, it failed to be scheduled for a vote because of limitation of time (Fazio, 2017). However, this is an

Figure 9.3

Composing multimodally should open your eyes to the fact that your own writing process is fundamentally interactive—you cannot create every photograph, sound clip, table, graph, GIF, and map that might end up in your completed essay. Just as a multimodal piece of writing forces readers to interact with it by appealing to a variety of senses (look, listen, think!), it also makes us aware of our own interactions as writers with a community of composers whose material we draw upon to produce a new text.

Here the visual element is a "textual" example that accompanies and deepens the central narrative presentation but does not interrupt it. Notice that the main text interprets the material set aside in the bracketed box by using short and selected elements from it, and that the aside presents contextual information around the selected elements that the reader can choose to pause and read thoroughly.

## Sample: Multimodal Evidence

*In 1996, the Rehnquist Court dealt with the question of whether the Communications Decency Act violated the First and Fifth Amendments as the Act was broad and vague in defining "indecent" material. The Court ruled unanimously in favor of the ACLU and the First Amendment; in other words, the Court ruled that the First Amendment was violated because the Decency Act enacted "content-based blanket restrictions"—the Act did not define "indecent" material, show that adults would not be impacted, or demonstrate that the "offensive" material had no inherent social value (Reno v. ACLU). More important to the matter at hand, net neutrality, is that Reno represents the Court's first direct involvement with Internet regulation (Bagwell 137).*

"From the publisher's point of view, the Internet constitutes a vast platform from which to address and hear from a worldwide audience of millions of readers, viewers, researchers, and buyers. Any person or organization with a computer connected to the Internet can 'publish' information. Publishers include government agencies, educational institutions, commercial entities, advocacy groups, and individuals... No single organization controls any membership in the Web, nor is there any single centralized point from which individual Web sites or services can be blocked from the Web."

— Justice John Paul Stevens, Majority Opinion, *Reno v. ACLU*

*Justice Stevens delivers the Court opinion, emphasizing its belief that the Internet is "a unique and wholly new medium of worldwide communication" and is "located in no particular geographical location but available to anyone, anywhere in the world, with access to the Internet" (Reno v. ACLU). Additionally, Stevens illustrates how no single organization can control membership and how no "single central" point from a Website or service may be blocked. Thus, it can now be argued that network neutrality's aim— to prevent any single ISP from controlling the Internet's membership and discriminately "censor" websites or services at their discretion, through blocking or throttling outgoing bandwidth—rings synonymously with Justice Steven's thoughts.*

### GUIDING QUESTIONS FOR USING MULTIMODAL EVIDENCE

1. *What other forms of evidence can be used like the quote in the example?*

2. *How is this use of a quote different in its rhetorical effect from quoted material integrated into the flow of the argument on the sentence level?*

3. *How is this use of a quote different in its rhetorical effect from a quote used as a block quote?*

## Metacognitive Checkpoint: An ePortfolio Moment

*You can use your responses to the guiding questions for using multimodal evidence as material for your ePortfolio by capturing screenshots of your use of multimodality and then by comparing your use to the examples, both textually and visually.*

▶ *A number of other chapters in the Anteater's Guide relate directly to 39C. What have you read so far? How have the strategies helped you? Are you repurposing strategies in 39C that you used in 39B?*

▶ *What have you read so far that has helped you with your researching and writing processes for the CP?*

▶ *What have you learned about locating, evaluating, and selecting sources?*

▶ *How many different types of sources are you using in your CP? Can you explain how and why different types of sources can support argument and give the author (you) credibility?*

▶ *Have you entered into a discussion among scholars and experts?*

▶ *Have you used counterarguments? Give examples and analyze them.*

### An Example from a Student's ePortfolio

Now look at the following example from a final ePortfolio. Here we see a student documenting the evolution of his or her outlining strategies. We can see clearly how the act of outlining evolved for this student from a simple method of listing ideas to provide very general guidance when writing a first draft, to a robust method for inventing arguments, rhetorical positions, and for organizing ideas, sources, and arguments. Without the visual comparison here, we would wonder whether this student really did become "more selective and conscious" of his or her sources, and whether outlining really did help this student to discover "transition sentences."

This method proved to be beneficial in my Advocacy Project because I was more selective and conscious of what sources I should incorporate. Whereas in my HCP, I felt that I was talking about too many ideas at the same time – I went from talking about the achievement gap to dropout rates, to oppositional behavior theories, to acting white, to the school-to-prison pipeline. In this aspect, I felt I lacked cohesion throughout my whole essay. That is why pre writing, such as organizing my ideas in an outline (see below), helped me to take a step back and truly see if all my ideas linked to a main argument.

"HCP OUTLINE" on sticky note

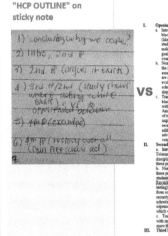

**VS**

"AP OUTLINE" from Prospectus

Outlines are a great way to plan ahead and guide me as I am writing my first drafts. As you can see, my HCP outline and AP outline greatly juxtapose each other. First outline bares little to no details. The numbers indicate what sources I have and where I should integrate them. For instance, the fourth source was intended to be incorporated into my third and second paragraphs of the HCP. On the other hand, my second outline has better quality and quantity of ideas, which serves to link each paragraph – it helped to dedicate a subsection to transition sentences. I kept referring back to my thesis when completing the outline, that way I reminded myself of the main argument.

## Information Literacy and Working with Sources

Throughout the quarter in WR39C, you'll find, evaluate, select, and use various types of sources to help you understand the issue you are researching and to build informative, credible, and persuasive multimodal arguments. In so doing, you'll put into practice the information literacy skills discussed in the "Discovering Sources" and "Citing and Integrating Sources" chapters of this guide.

As you research, always be on the lookout for a range of sources, as different types of sources will serve different purposes. For example, news sources will give you information about the most recent developments on your research topic. Such sources often poignantly capture the stories of the people most affected by the problems you'll study, and such human interest rhetoric can help you to meaningfully frame the issue and its relevance for your reader. However, a news article is not a scholarly source, and oftentimes it is not analytical. Such sources offer reports, and the academic expectations of the genres in which you are writing demand rigorous analysis and the use of scholarly sources.

You will encounter many different types of sources in your research process, and good use of these sources in your writing begins with a thorough evaluation of each source. One of the first questions to ask about a new source that you discover is what **kind** of source is this? What is the genre, and how does that shape the content of the source? Is it popular or scholarly, and if scholarly, what discipline does it come from?

### Evaluate Your Sources

Before you use the sources you've found, you need to read them carefully and make sure you understand the information being conveyed. Ask yourself the following questions as you decide which sources to include in your paper.

Go back and review Chapter 3, "Citing and Integrating Sources," and Chapter 4, "Discovering Sources," as needed, for more detailed information on managing and evaluating your sources.

- Is the source RELEVANT to my topic, and does it help to illustrate the importance and current urgency of my topic or my central problem?

- What is the GENRE of the source? Determine the genre, the audience, and think through how different genres can bolster your authority. For example, a credible news source can help you establish the background to your problem, and academic sources can guide you into the critical scholarly discussions about it.

- What AUTHORITY and CREDIBLITY does the author or authors bring to the topic at hand? What education, training, or experience does the author have that qualifies him or her to write on this subject and serve as an authoritative voice?

- What is the PURPOSE of the information? Is it to educate, to persuade, to convey factual information, to share opinions, to entertain?

- What EVIDENCE does the source include? Does the article include references and citations? If so, what are the genres of these sources, and how do they enhance or take away from the author's credibility?

- How TIMELY is the source in question? When was it written? Depending on the topic and the use you are making of it, some information becomes outdated when new information is available, but other sources that are fifty or one hundred years old can be relevant.

- Is the information BALANCED? Does the author or does the organization acknowledge alternative perspectives or do they include alternative viewpoints?

## Try This: Evaluating Sources

*Write a source evaluation following the format listed above for a source you locate in the publications listed below.*

- Wikipedia
- A recent article from *The Washington Post*
- A book review in *The Journal of Popular Culture*
- A *Time* magazine article published fifty years ago

- A study published by a governmental organization, such as the EPA or NIH

- A graph from the study you found that was published by a governmental organization

- An article from *The Journal of American Culture*

*Now answer the following questions:*

1. *When you evaluated the Wikipedia source, did you use a different technique to assess the credibility of a webpage than you did a popular or scholarly article located online?*

2. *How would you classify these sources in terms of their genres?*

3. *Explain the relationship between the genre of a specific source and the ways it might be used in an academic composition like the CP or the AP.*

4. *Evaluate the Works Cited page of a sample paper, a peer's paper, or even your own Works Cited.*

   - *How many different genres of sources can you locate?*

   - *Does the bibliography contain more of certain genres than others?*

   - *What expectations do you have about the composition and its arguments just from looking at the genres of the sources?*

   - *Now go and read the composition itself and see if you are correct in your prediction.*

---

*Annotate Your Sources and Create an Annotated Bibliography*

After you've evaluated a source and determined that you will find it useful for your project, write an annotation of the source. An annotation refines the information you put together in the source evaluation and reframes it by both summarizing the source and articulating how you are using it for your own argumentative purposes.

## GUIDING QUESTIONS FOR WRITING ANNOTATIONS

*An annotation is the basic entry in an annotated bibliography.*

1. *Who are the author and publisher? What authority does the author have on this topic, and what is the publisher's purpose in publishing this information?*

2. *What is the genre of the source? How does the genre influence how you will use the source and the information it gives you?*

3. *What kinds of evidence does the source draw on? What genres of sources does it use?*

4.  *When was the source published? Is this information current, a useful historical artifact, or simply out-of-date?*

5.  *How is the source relevant to your project, and does it help to illustrate the importance and current urgency of your topic or your central problem?*

### PRO TIP: BENEFITS OF WRITING EVALUATIONS AND ANNOTATIONS

- Make it a practice to write about sources that seem potentially useful, starting with writing out your evaluation of the source as well as an annotation that summarizes the main ideas or arguments and makes note of key pieces of evidence.

- While writing about your sources before you need to use them in a draft may seem like extra work, and you may be tempted to skimp on or even skip this writing—don't. Preliminary writing about your sources prepares you to use them in some important ways.

- Summarizing a source helps you understand and synthesize the information in that source, which is especially important when working with complex scholarly arguments. After all, successfully paraphrasing a source or introducing and analyzing a quotation requires a solid understanding of the original source.

- Writing down your evaluations helps you achieve new insights about the credibility and relevance of the source that will help you use it more thoughtfully and purposefully in your composition.

- Well-crafted annotations and evaluations create a record of what each source argued, key evidence used, and your initial assessment of the source's level of credibility and relevance to your project. Tracking this kind of information so that you can refer back to it days or weeks after you have read a source helps you remember the defining characteristics of sources and the differences between them, and will save you time in the long run.

- Some of the sentences you draft for your annotations and evaluations will end up in your compositions as part of your analysis.

- Revisit and revise your annotations and evaluations throughout the quarter to keep them up to date as your understanding of your sources and their role in *your* research and writing evolves. You will find that writing about your sources before you use them is actually one of the most important steps in your research process.

# Techniques to Help You Bridge the CP and AP

As you develop your AP and its arguments, keep in mind that you are seeking your audience's cooperation. Your audience may be composed of groups or individuals with a range of values and concerns related to the problem and the various and possible solutions. If you take on multiple perspectives when explaining the problem and analyzing various solutions, you will likely succeed in persuading your audience to follow you through your argument, to keep reading, and to consider your arguments seriously. You will probably need to employ a number of argumentative strategies to become a convincing advocate. Your CP should provide you with a steady foundation on which to stand as you repurpose the knowledge you've gained for the different argumentative purposes of the AP. Here are a few techniques you might use to bridge the CP and the AP.

## Causation

What are the root causes of the problem? Some problems will lend themselves to this type of argument, some will not. Nevertheless, a robust discussion of possible solutions to most of the problems you will be able to address will have to involve analysis of causes and effects of possible solutions.

**Research Direction:** If while researching for contexts, you found persuasive evidence of particular causes of your problem, research to find further evidence that directly addresses that cause.

## Coverage

Do the potential solutions discussed by scholars and experts satisfactorily address the problem for a significant number of those most affected by the problem? How comprehensive are the proposed solutions in addressing the scope of the problem?

**Research Direction:** To support a coverage analysis, you will need to show how many people, or what groups of people, will be affected or have been affected historically; for example, you might present demographic data or studies that quantify the effects of the problem and solution on different groups of people.

## Cost/Benefit

Do the solutions debated by scholars and experts exceed the costs?

**Research Direction:** To support a cost/benefit analysis, you will need to detail how much a potential solution or solutions may cost to implement, what benefits will result, and how long it will take for benefits to be seen. You will also need to consider what other solutions have been tried in the past and then document and analyze the results. Although this will often take the form of an analysis of financial costs and benefits, other factors—like human well-being—can also be used. For federal policy proposals, the Congressional Budget Office, for example, may have budget estimates available; some think tanks may also have this information.

### Feasibility

Are the solutions being debated feasible? Is one or another easy enough to implement without significant negative consequences for other social interests? Does a particular solution have enough support from significant parties to make it likely to be accepted by stakeholders, interested parties, and others in positions to take real action?

**Research Direction:** To support a feasibility analysis, you will need to present evidence to show that implementation of a particular solution or solutions is feasible in terms of money, time, and support. You will want to offer historical comparisons that tie such feasibility claims to past failures or partial successes. You may also need to show that there is enough political or popular will to support a given solution and/or demonstrate that implementation would not be overly difficult or expensive. You might present budget data, public opinion polls, or politicians' statements and voting records on similar proposals.

### Comparison

Comparison is usually a type of feasibility argument. To make a comparative argument, you ask, Have similar solutions worked well, not so well, or failed in another comparable context? Such a comparable context can also draw from the past, as you may have done already in your CP.

**Research Direction:** To support a comparative analysis, you present evidence to show, for example, that a similar policy has worked before in a similar context (i.e., in another city, state, or country, or at some time in the past). In addition, you must show that the other context is comparable to the current circumstances. You may want to look at historical data or policy reviews, for example.

Metacognitive Checkpoint:  Moving from the CP to the AP

▷ *How do you think you will repurpose the knowledge you gained in your CP?*

▷ *In what ways do you think your AP has or will evolve beyond your CP? How have your evidence and your body of sources evolved?*

▷ *How many different types of sources are you now using? Why are you using different types of sources for the AP?*

## Research Project Part Two: Advocacy

Like the CP, the main assignment of the Advocacy Project is a multimodal composition that uses various rhetorical positions and different types of evidence to make arguments. This one, however, is a bit different from the first in that over the course of these next few weeks, as you research and evaluate various sources, and as you draft, craft, and organize your thoughts and evidence, you will at some point have to make a decision to advocate solutions to your central problem according to the following framework: **1) describe, analyze and evaluate one or more existing efforts to address the significant and current political/social/cultural problem that sits at the center of your project.** From there, **2) argue, along with scholars/advocates, for or against the effort (or a combination of efforts or solutions) that you presented in part one, and try to offer possible next steps.** Be sure you give careful consideration to the obstacles at work in implementing all efforts—those you support and those you do not. By the end of this project, your advocacy positions and arguments will become, after weeks and weeks of diligent engagement, a richly textured thesis statement, one that deepens your articulation of the problem at hand and argues convincingly for ways to move forward.

## *Try This: Comparing Arguments in the CP and AP*

*Explain the differences between a CP argument and an AP argument.*

*How does your own AP argument differ from that of your CP?*

When we think of the act of advocating and when we imagine a person or an organization who advocates a cause, we think of strongly held opinions delivered with intensity from a rhetorical position that appears unshakable, deeply confident in the ethical rightness of its arguments and the accuracy of its knowledge. If we look at advocacy in such ways, we can understand why it takes time to become a convincing advocate and for an AP thesis to develop and mature.

245

Academic writers in many disciplines often write with the purpose of advocating solutions to political/social/cultural/environmental problems. When they do so, they are expected to consider and present positions that run against theirs in various ways—call them counterarguments—in order to meet the expectations of their academic audience. They must demonstrate their mastery of established arguments and knowledge in areas of discourse and recognize the legitimacy of other perspectives, even if the author (you, in this case!) seeks ultimately to dismiss them.

Effective advocates deliver strong and impassioned arguments, in part, by considering and responding to various perspectives and pieces of evidence that potentially undermine their case. When putting forth arguments in academic or public settings, in other words, the most convincing advocates do not simply deliver solutions without first comprehending the informed debates in which these solutions are situated. Rather, successful advocates draw from a deep well of knowledge when carefully selecting the evidence and rhetorical appeals that will make their case about how to address the profound social problems they put before their audiences.

**This assignment challenges you to become that strong advocate,** one who articulates the depth and complexity of a current and pressing problem and then analyzes various solutions to it. You cannot, in all likelihood, be this advocate at the beginning of the project. You will need to spend time researching and evaluating sources and you will need to explore various arguments and perspectives as you write proposals and drafts. But you will choose an advocacy position at some point, after deepening your knowledge and probably after writing a full draft or two.

As you move through the writing and researching process for the AP, your teacher may ask you to prepare and deliver an oral and visual presentation. Your presentation may include a short question-and-answer period. The presentation gives you an opportunity to try out your arguments and attempt to convince your peers of the legitimacy of your positions and the credibility of your solutions. It also gives you a forum to ask for and receive feedback on your work in progress.

The oral and visual elements of your presentation should work together but not like they do in a conventional presentation in which the visual elements simply restate what you are delivering orally. You can deliver much more information with a couple good visuals than you can possibly talk about in five minutes. So you should make good use of your visual presentation; select important pieces of information and data and create visuals that argue for you without your having to describe all of the details they make visible.

The ability to perform an argument, in this age of multimodality, using whatever technological means are most ideally available is a critical skill.

Your job with the presentation is to convince your audience that you are not only pursuing important questions about a pressing social problem, but that they should care about it, and perhaps even feel compelled to do something about it once you've delivered your arguments, your research, and your guiding questions.

## *Try This: Understanding Counterarguments*

Did you know that using counterarguments can actually strengthen your argument and enhance your credibility?

1. *Locate two or three examples of counterarguments in sources of various types: one of your course texts, an academic article, an article in a popular journal, your own work.*

2. *Explain the purposes of these counterarguments in each example.*

3. *Evaluate the rhetorical effectiveness of the counterarguments in each example.*

4. *Imitate in your own work these argumentative moves.*

Remember, there's an opportunity here to create material for your ePortfolio!

---

## HOW TO PREPARE YOUR ADVOCACY PRESENTATION

When you give your oral/visual presentation, you'll be hard at work on your AP project.

At this moment, you'll be working on your arguments in three modalities at the same time:

1. *Written (in your drafts)*

2. *Oral (presentation)*

3. *Visual (presentation)*

**Reflective prompts:**

What did you discover about your arguments while you prepared for and delivered the presentation?

Did your advocacy arguments evolve as a result of the presentation? Explain.

- **Deliver** your presentation with authority, and pace yourself.

- **Present** your arguments, thesis statement, or guiding questions clearly and in interesting ways.

- **Describe** and summarize the significant political/social/cultural problem you're addressing.

- **Frame** this problem with motives, which are current examples or incidents that show your audience that the problem you're addressing and the solutions you're analyzing are alive and relevant right now.

- **Document** for your audience the deep foundation of research on which your positions stand.

- **Demonstrate** how your oral arguments work together with the visual arguments to articulate your arguments or thesis statement.

At the end of your talk, the audience should be able to respond affirmatively to all of the questions below:

- Was the problem, context, and solution clearly expressed?
- Was there a balanced and effective employment of *ethos/pathos/logos*?
- Did the presentation flow well?
- Did the presenter seem prepared?
- Was the graphical evidence argumentative and persuasive?
- Were you informed?
- Were you persuaded?

## The Final ePortfolio

Your final ePortfolio is assigned on the first day of class and due at the end of the quarter. Think of your portfolio as a growing archive that will become full of interesting pieces of evidence as the quarter progresses. You will quickly accumulate artifacts that you can use to document your learning: things like drafts, instructor or peer comments, organizational notes, before-and-after versions of sentences and paragraphs, and final versions of your compositions, for example. Use these pieces of evidence **to document the work you have done, demonstrate your role in your learning, and articulate your intellectual strategies as they pertain to college-level rhetoric, composition, and communication.**

You'll write a reflective introduction to your portfolio. This introduction introduces you as a writer, thinker, and communicator to a community of your peers, and it makes good use of the evidence you've accumulated. You take responsibility for the quality of your work in this document (and in your ePortfolio) by assessing your performance. *The reflective introduction is an analytically incisive, multimodal composition that delivers balanced arguments about your learning and supports them with carefully selected pieces of evidence. The reflective introduction should be characterized by a clear narrative that can be organized like an essay; but it can also use cross-referencing strategies, such as hyperlinking, to direct the reader to other sections of the portfolio and other pieces of evidence and their captions.*

Your reflective introduction should be a rigorous multimodal composition that documents the rich textures of your learning this quarter and perhaps throughout the WR39 sequence of courses (39A, 39B, and 39C). The introduction should analyze your learning in four areas, which are listed below and followed by prompts that you may use to organize your thoughts.

## HOW TO PLAN YOUR REFLECTIVE INTRODUCTION

Be prepared to write about:

1. *Knowledge transfer*

2. *Your composing process*

3. *Rhetoric, argumentation, and multimodal communication*

4. *Your revision process*

### Knowledge Transfer

Now that you are at the end of 39C (and the Lower-Division Writing Requirement), take a look back to where you were at the beginning of the quarter, or even at the beginning of your college writing experience, and analyze how your practices and habits of researching, writing, and organizing have changed and evolved. You might consult your Week 1 Self-Assessment to get you started.

- How have your experiences in your writing classes at UCI influenced your personal history as a writer in academic contexts? Has the WR39 series of courses and 39C in particular influenced your ability to make effective choices about how to approach writing assignments in other classes? Assignments such as lab reports, business memos, blue book exams, short response papers, and any other examples of writing you have been assigned here at UCI? In other words, have you applied what you learned in the WR39 series to writing assignments in other classes? Have other classes and assignments influenced your writing process; if so, which ones? Please explain using specific examples.

- Are you using a variety of different strategies to approach your writing assignments in all of your classes? Are you using the same strategies in different contexts as you consider the demands of different situations and assignments? If so, please explain such situations and assignments, and give examples.

## *An Example from a Student's ePortfolio*

Here the student connects the process of researching and writing not only to the development of her confidence and academic interests, but also her vision of how she can succeed in her chosen discipline.

*Through the close reading of various sources, I was able to enhance my understanding of my major's future content. I was previously aware of what data mining and machine learning were, but I'd gained a new perspective on its application to fake news detection.*

*In fact, I'm interested in recreating another iteration of the University of Arizona's data mining program for my future senior capstone project. It's only my first year, but the capstone project frightened me because of how large-scale it could potentially be. I knew I had four years to build up my repertoire and start on smaller projects, but just thinking about the capstone project made me feel lost. The data science major at UCI is very young (less than four years now), but some of the projects my upperclassmen are working on seemed very daunting in comparison to everything else I'd even imagined of creating. More so than anything else, the process of researching and composing the CP/AP has given me a sense of comfort.*

*As I develop my programming/coding skills these next three years, I might find another project I want to work on instead. But knowing that I have something that has the potential to contribute productively to my field gives me more confidence for my future projects. So funny enough after a long ten weeks of stress, I leave Writing 39C having gained confidence in both my writing and likelihood of academic success.*

### Your Composing Process

Explain what you have learned about the process of generating a research-based composition.

- What have you learned about arranging the elements of your composition? Have you become more skillful and able to control your presentation of evidence and integrate various pieces of evidence into a coherent and meaningful argument?

- How did conducting research all throughout the drafting process help you to make decisions about the organizational logic of your compositions? In what ways, specifically, did you formulate and reformulate research strategies, framing questions, and guiding claims/arguments by using research?

- Explain how your process of writing drafts, source evaluations, and annotations evolved over the course of the quarter. Did you become more effective at prewriting tasks?

- Have you experienced moments when the light bulb suddenly illuminated? Can you explain why and how this happened?

## Sample: Using Google Doc Method to Keep Track of Sources

One student uses a "Google Doc" method of keeping track of sources by copying and pasting links. The first screenshot shows the student's list of sources and the second shows an annotated source.

Annotated Bibliography

Alkiviadou, Natalie (2019) Hate speech on social media networks: towards a regulatory

framework?, Information & Communications Technology Law, 28:1, 19-35, DOI:

10.1080/13600834.2018.1494417

Alkiviadou discusses the causes and effects of hate speech on social media in her essay. Her

main argument is that hate speech is becoming quite common on these websites and there needs

to be some sort of regulation of this type of speech. This is because these social media companies

lack the motivation to regulate hate speech even though they have set guidelines "defining" what

hate speech should be. She proposes that social media and hate speech should be regulated in a

similar manner to Germany's NetzDG where social media companies are required to hire

government agents who make sure these companies censor speech that the government deems as

inappropriate. If these companies do not, they will be fined. What is particularly interesting is

how Alkiviadou favors how European government deals with social media regulation. The thing

is that American ideologies do not match European ideologies, so we would not know if

Alkiviadou's proposal would actually work in the U.S. Her proposal seems to favor total

government regulation of these social media websites.

This student expressed that he found the annotation method of keeping track of sources helps him identify arguments and other important information specific to a source.

### Rhetoric, Argumentation, and Multimodal Communication

- What have you learned about argumentation and persuasion through the process of generating two multimodal compositions?

- Explain how creating a multimodal composition helped you to articulate your arguments and understand your *ethos* as the author.

- Can you explain how you arrived at the solutions you chose to advocate? Did you experiment with other solutions before deciding on the one(s) you chose to advocate?

- Was there a specific moment when your thesis became clear to you, and can you explain what you did to arrive at such a moment of clear insight?

- Explain and demonstrate why and how you used various arguments and counterarguments and numerous and different sources to strengthen your claims.

## *Sample: Reflecting on Footnotes*

*The first research paper gave me a chance to experiment with multimodality, and my biggest use of it came in the form of footnotes. I had never utilized footnotes, and I had no idea what their purpose was. It wasn't until my first conference about the CP that I finally realized the importance of them. It was easy as a click of a button and helped to improve the prose of my writing! This is because their primary usage is to explain things without interrupting the flow of the sentence. This could be done by referring the reader to other readings, giving background on a topic, or defining terms. This image captures one page of my research paper where I utilized footnotes. I utilized these footnotes to define key terms, as seen in footnote 1,2, and 4, while also using them to explain terms as seen in footnotes 3 and 5. As I practiced with the concept of footnotes in the first research essay, I felt that the footnotes in the next phase of the research project benefited as I had received feedback and guidance on how to integrate them into my essay.*

---

[1] A nonprofit corporation that receives funds from both individuals and for-profit corporations for the purpose of electing or defeating a candidate.

[2] A documentary that sought to slander Hillary Clinton, a presidential candidate at the time

[3] The movie was an example of electioneering communications due to its reference to a candidate for a federal office, and its attempt to be publicly distributed

[4] Any public communication made by a political committee that does not expressly advocate the election or defeat of a federal candidate or solicit a contribution

[5] PACs are required to reveal who donated to them, and how much capital they contributed on a regular basis

## Revision

- Explain your process of revision. How big of a role does revision play in the process of generating and discovering arguments?

- Explain how you used feedback from your teacher and from your peers both in workshops and in conferences or office hours.

- How do you respond to criticism and what sort of critic are you becoming? Use examples of feedback you received on your works-in-progress, your final versions, and in workshops, as well as advice you gave to your peers to address these questions.

- Analyze how you benefit from writing multiple drafts in terms of argumentative presentation, evidentiary support, and narrative development.

- Explain and analyze the types of revisions that benefit you. Do you make broad, conceptual revisions? Do you make structural revisions and reorganize paragraphs? Do you rewrite sentences? Do you make fine word choices? Do you alter your body of evidence through research or omission?

## *Sample: Reflecting on Revision Strategies*

> limitations upon their students. The DFSCA and GFSA informed zero-tolerance policy as it grew
>
> into its modern-day identity, and influenced the manner in which the definition of zero-tolerance
>
> came to encompass drug use, possession of weaponry, and personal misconduct by students on
>
> school campuses. Both acts weren't initially signed into law for the purpose of regulating the
>
> manner in which student disciplinary measures are enacted and carried out; zero-tolerance policy
>
> was not invented to be applied inside the classroom, but instead was meant to deal with heavy-
>
> duty issues such as those which are managed by the DFSCA and GFSA. This is the exact reason
>
> why zero-tolerance policy fails to manage student behavior in the same way that it controlled and
>
> restricted drug use and firearm possession in public schools nationwide.

The above statement highlighted in yellow would have been a much stronger statement had I incorporated a piece of evidence that supported the highlighted claim. While the claim itself is not incorrect, my failure to present a solidified source (e.g. quoting the Congressional definition/statement of the purpose of both acts in their respective legislative documents) that supports my claim makes the statement appear to be assumption-based rather than fact-based. I failed to incorporate a piece of supportive evidence into this section of my argument because I was short on time, and finding a piece of evidence for information that could have been easily found with some research was not a priority of mine at the time. Being able to critique my work in this manner allowed me to begin writing the AP with more understanding of what is required to create a compelling and strong written argument.

The examples from student portfolio work in these pages showcase the idiosyncratic nature of the ePortfolio assignment. Students reference excerpts from their own experience and writing to illustrate the various ways in which research has transformed their composing processes and how reflecting on that transformation will remain a valuable tool in the future. How has your overall writing process developed? What skills will you transfer?

### Advice on Reflective Writing

The Reflective Introduction to the final ePortfolio, the ePortfolio itself, and a variety of exercises along the way will require you to write about your writing process, reflecting on the rhetorical decisions you made throughout the quarter. Keep a writing journal, and save multimodal evidence of your writing and research progress. Self-reflection helps us develop techniques that can improve the rhetorical persuasiveness of our work while increasing our awareness of intellectual strategies and how we as individuals learn from and communicate with the world around us. Reflecting on learning strategies can also build self-confidence.

In 39C, reflective writing is not limited to an after-the-fact review of what we have done. Rather, it is a dynamic method we use throughout the quarter to better understand our work, our rhetorical strategies, our revision techniques, research methods, work habits, and the list could go on. If we are serious about tracking the progress of our research projects in a weekly self-reflective journal, as well as in a few mid-assignment, mini self-reflections, and a brief self-reflective paragraph or two after every major assignment, we will start to become increasingly aware of individualistic learning habits as they pertain, for example, to grammar, syntax, tone, citation format, paragraph construction, topic sentences, transitions, thesis derivation and development, scholarly and multimodal source analysis, historical and contemporary articulation of a problem, and analyses of solutions.

Frequent and brief self-reflection will lead us to come up with our own ways of analyzing our writing, thinking, and communicating strategies, ways that don't just come down to value judgments like "good" or "bad" or even "strength" or "weakness." We can use self-reflection as a way to challenge our ideas and improve our work, by starting to think about things like the difference between summary and analysis of sources, by asking whether we got at the heart of a scholarly debate or just skimmed the surface of our sources and by moving from the high school model of writing a report, or even a thesis/example/explanation/proof model of writing, toward a model of research-driven analytical synthesis realized as we progress through the 39C assignments.

Ultimately, everything you write about your composing process can and should end up in your final ePortfolio in some form, whether in the final reflective introduction to the ePortfolio; in the captions and commentary that introduce, contextualize, and analyze artifacts of your writing; or in the creativity with which you name, organize, and design the various sections of your final ePortfolio.

## STRATEGIES FOR REFLECTIVE WRITING IN WR39C

### 1. Ask productive questions.

Ask yourself a series of questions about what you are trying to achieve when you write self-reflectively. Here are some examples: How and where am I defining and analyzing a problem, and how can I refine the description of the problem I'm studying in order to set up a clearer connection between the CP and the AP? Where in my draft do I simply restate the main points of my scholarly sources and how can I shift toward situating and analyzing debates between groups of scholars? Where are the spots in my writing that define, address, and attempt to persuade a given audience or reach a broader audience?

### 2. Reflect before, during, and after the assignments.

Experiment with the timing of self-reflection. Write a weekly self-reflective journal, but don't forget to keep a running "sideline" commentary open while writing, so you can jot down your plans or impressions. It's important to write a brief, 1-2 paragraph reflection after you finish each major stage of research and each major assignment. Ask your teacher for advice about the timing of such writing and for examples of prompts you might use to get you going.

### 3. Mix it up.

Reflect on a variety of aspects and stages of your research, from topic formulation, through search engine information literacy and search term refinement, all the way to the assessment and analysis of sources.

### 4. The personal can become the analytical and the political.

Use self-reflection as a way to articulate the personal, intellectual motivations behind your research. How are you personally invested in the problems you've studied? Use this occasion to speak out to the world and expand on the larger social, cultural, and political importance of your 39C research projects.

### 5. Use multimodal evidence.

You're making and collecting a series of multimodal artifacts that will serve as evidence for claims you make about your learning in the final reflective introduction to your ePortfolio. Take screenshots of your writing process. Take photos of your notes. Take pictures of places where you write and things that inspire you. What else? It's up to you!

*Hayden Sugg won the 2016–17 Upper-Division Social Sciences Writing Award for his paper "Legal Financial Obligations in the United States Criminal Justice System: A Mechanism of Social Control." I interviewed him in May of 2017 in my office, and we later revised our conversation to present it in writing here. Hayden was never a student in 39C, having fulfilled his lower-division writing requirements at a community college. However, his writing process for this award-winning paper showed patience, open-mindedness, care, and passion—the same qualities I've seen in other successful 39C student-researchers. I hope you will learn from Hayden, as I did. — Lance Langdon*

Lance Langdon (LL): Can you start by telling our readers about your research project?

Hayden Sugg (HS): I study legal financial obligations. That's criminal debt that is accumulated through fines, fees, restitution, surcharges. The majority of people in society know criminal justice through incarceration; there are a lot of movies about that, for example. But I don't think there is enough attention to the fines and fees, and how those are tied to the reproduction of social disadvantage in society.

LL: How does the research process begin for you?

HS: I try not to confine myself to a template too early. I just start out with literature first. Go out there, if you have an idea, and review what's going on, maybe even do some observations that don't count toward your research.

LL: For 39C that might mean looking at popular sources, like the news.

HS: Sure. For me, I start with a very broad idea of what I want to research. When I'm out at dinner, when I run, or exercise, I have another part of my head that's thinking about ideas all the time. What could I research? Maybe I can look into this idea or that one.

One practice I've found to be extremely helpful is when those ideas emerge, write them down. When I first started researching, I thought, "I'll remember that," but then a week later I'd try and realize, "That was a really cool sentence I had. Oh well, that's gone." So yes, write your ideas down.

I'm a gamer, I play video games. Some days I'll be playing a video game and I'll just turn it off, and go straight to Google Scholar; some idea will pop up and I'll just instantly research it.

LL: Can you talk more about doing your literature review?

HS: When I conduct my basic review, go through Google Scholar or whatever database I'm using, let's say I find an article. How do I get to my next source? How do I keep building? I look for keywords, using the keywords section in the abstract.

Say you've got a starting idea you're working on, and you have keywords you're searching with. In my case those might be "criminal justice" or "restitution." If you go into these sources, and you're working through them and you're interested, you're going to read what another author has said, and you're going to pick up on it.

I've read certain sources and I find a keyword and I go, well that's a different way of framing this issue. So let's take that, plug it in a new search, and see what happens. And sometimes the new search spits out a whole bunch of stuff.

Other times, I'm on YouTube and I'm listening to a video on the justice system. Or I listen to stuff that's verbal, oral communication, like an interview with Ta-Nehisi Coates. I'll take that phrase, what he said, and try it out as a new search.

Also, if I find an article that's extremely well written, other articles are going to be citing it in the literature review. So this is another strategy that's taken over my bibliography building: going to the reference section in my source, and just going through it.

**LL:** In 39C we first consider the causes of a social problem and write a paper. Then we select a policy that addresses the problem and write an essay advocating for that policy. I'm interested in what advice you'd give to students about that first paper. Do you have any tips, when doing a literature review, for instance, for how to understand the causes of a problem and how to think historically when dealing with contemporary issues?

**HS:** It's about looking at the structure. Some people are visual learners and some people are auditory, but I do think for this part that visual mapping might help some people think through the process of understanding the causes of a problem. Write out the structure. Even if you have to draw, draw the issue and kind of map it out.

For incarceration, when I'm identifying that marginalized communities are the predominant composition going to prison, you start evaluating, how are these individuals part of the socially marginalized class? How did they get there? I took that critical lens that I learned from writing, and I said, look, these people don't have the same opportunities. Look at the geography that they're based in. Look at the quality of schools those individuals have, what type of jobs they have.

Sometimes the history part might be the most important part of the problem. Because you can understand urbanization, industrialization—people migrating away and urban ghettos that got stuck right in the middle, and how that creates an isolating effect, and I know this sounds like I'm going way out there, all of this ties into why these individuals have a disproportionately high contact rate with the criminal justice system.

LL: So what I hear you saying is you start mapping out the structure of the problem. And as you do, you might focus in on the different aspects of the problem, in this case the individuals who are being incarcerated due to marginalization, and then marginalization in itself becomes its sub-research topic, and then you map out the factors leading to that.

HS: Yes, break the issue down, so you don't have a web of ideas just floating around. Create subsections in your notebook if you need to.

Go through all the notes that you've compiled. For my research into legal financial obligations, my desk at home was just a clutter, and I was going through it. I looked for themes that were reappearing in the literature and from what I'd seen through my interviews and observations. I started combing through everything, and marking things up on the paper, putting a bubble, basically categorizing stuff. Then from there I started to sit down and go, what theme encompasses all these ideas? And that's how I developed my subsections.

If a legislator is going to listen, they're going to want to know the different pieces of the problem. I bring that hypothetical situation into my advocacy, because it brings a holistic approach to the analysis and conclusion: What can I say to a legislator that might change their mind?

LL: I noticed your paper dives deep into a wide range of sources and arranges them all methodically. There's a logic to your development, almost a story you're creating. How do you give your ideas that shape?

HS: I feel that when I'm writing analysis, I can convey my points a lot better than when I'm having a conversation. And it's just because you're watching it get typed out and you're typing it, and you can backspace, you can switch words. Obviously when you're talking, it's kind of impromptu, versus when you can think in your own peaceful environment.

I was talking to my dad the other day about jobs. He said, "After you got into college, you matured and you developed. When we're at dinner and we're having a conversation, you think before you speak now, and you really articulate what you want to get across." And he attributed it to writing.

LL: Any last tips for our 39C students?

HS: You've got to have patience with research, and you have to be able to work with what's going to come. Otherwise, when you begin to guide the data, and you begin to mold what's going to come out of it, it takes the fun out of the process.

Writing is mental exercise, and it should be, because we're thinking critically about how these complex issues evolve, but I try to enjoy it as much as possible.

LL: Thanks, Hayden, for taking the time to share what you've learned.

HS: Thank you.

# Index